W9-CPB-646

Sunday School for a New Century

Bill L. Taylor
and Louis B. Hanks

© Copyright 1999 • LifeWay Press
All Rights Reserved

No part of this work may be reproduced or transmitted in any form or by any means,
electronic or mechanical, including photocopying and recording, or by any information or
storage or retrieval system, except as may be expressly permitted in writing by the
publisher. Requests for permission should be addressed in writing to:
LifeWay Press, 127 Ninth Avenue North, Nashville, TN 37234-0173.

Permission is granted to reproduce for use in a local church the pages designated
in the table of contents with this symbol (◆). Some of these items as well as additional
reproducible material are included on the diskette in the *Sunday School for a New Century
Planning and Training Pack*. See the ordering information on page 177 in this book for
ways to place an order for this item.

ISBN 0-7673-9372-4

This book is a resource in the Leadership and Skill Development category
of the Christian Growth Study Plan for course numbers LS-0048, LS-0066, and LS-0107.

Dewey Decimal Classification: 268.434
Subject Heading: SUNDAY SCHOOL

Printed in the United States of America

Sunday School Group
LifeWay Christian Resources of the Southern Baptist Convention
127 Ninth Avenue North
Nashville, Tennessee 37234

Cover design: Keith Tyrrell
Cover photography: Tony Stone Images, Peter Weber and Olney Vasan

Acknowledgements:
Unless otherwise designated all Scripture quotations are from the *Holy Bible New
International Version*. Copyright ©1973, 1978, 1984 by International Bible Society.

CONTENTS

FOREWORD

It was time. The world He had created had chosen its own way and was hopelessly lost. God had a strategy that would transform the world—one that would replace fear with faith, despair with hope, hatred with love, spiritual darkness with light.

God chose to enter the kingdom of this world personally, in Jesus Christ, transforming forever anyone who would receive Him. The kingdom of this world was intersected, once and for all, by the kingdom of God. Through Jesus, God overcame sin and death with His righteousness and eternal life.

Jesus demonstrated God's love for all people. His life and ministry were a living portrait of perfect love. Jesus loved God with His entire heart, soul, mind, and strength; and He loved His neighbor as He did Himself. Jesus demonstrated this love by obediently fulfilling God's strategy to reconcile a lost world to Himself. Jesus willingly submitted His life as a sacrifice, through death on a cross, to free each of us from the ultimate penalty for our sin. Jesus made a way for us to receive abundant, eternal life. Everything about Jesus revealed God's strategy to act.

Jesus' mission extends to all of His disciples throughout time. He has called us to continue His work, and He has equipped us for that work (Matt. 28:18-20). We are to be transformed people. We are to be agents of transformation.

God has given us a powerful and underutilized tool in that transforming task. Sunday School is the strategy that can engage people in Great Commission ministry, leading them to faith in the Lord Jesus Christ and building Great Commission Christians. When people gather to encounter God through the study of His Word in the company of His people, the Lord is with them in a special way. Sunday School must stay firmly grounded in God's living and written Word. However, there is more to Sunday School for a new century than gathering for Bible study, as important as that is.

In the 21st century, Sunday School must provide opportunities for people to come to know Christ and to engage Christians in leading others to faith in Him. Sunday School for a new century must provide seven-day-a-week opportunities to grow in understanding of and in obedience to God's Word. Sunday School must provide opportunities for people to express their love for God and for people by engaging them in ministry and missions. It must build unity and fellowship in the church, and help people find ways to express their love for God in all that they do.

It is time. It is time because of the opportunities. Today churches have a wonderful opportunity to fulfill the Lord's command. The new world of the 21st century and the third millennium is not unlike the world God entered when He divided time forever with Jesus' birth. Our world, continuing to choose its own way, remains hopelessly lost without Christ. It is time because of the overwhelming need.

Each section of this book opens with some personal insights—and also highlights someone from my experience in the Sunday School Group who represents an important aspect of strategic Christian leadership in the 21st century. You will find space to record your thoughts and personal reflections. As the book more fully describes the implications of Sunday School as strategy, "Your Time Is Now" activities can further help you apply personally what you have read.

The mission and ministry of Christ was God's strategy from the beginning. His strategy is ours. Your time is now.

Bill Taylor

THE KINGDOM PERSPECTIVE
for the Ministry of Sunday School

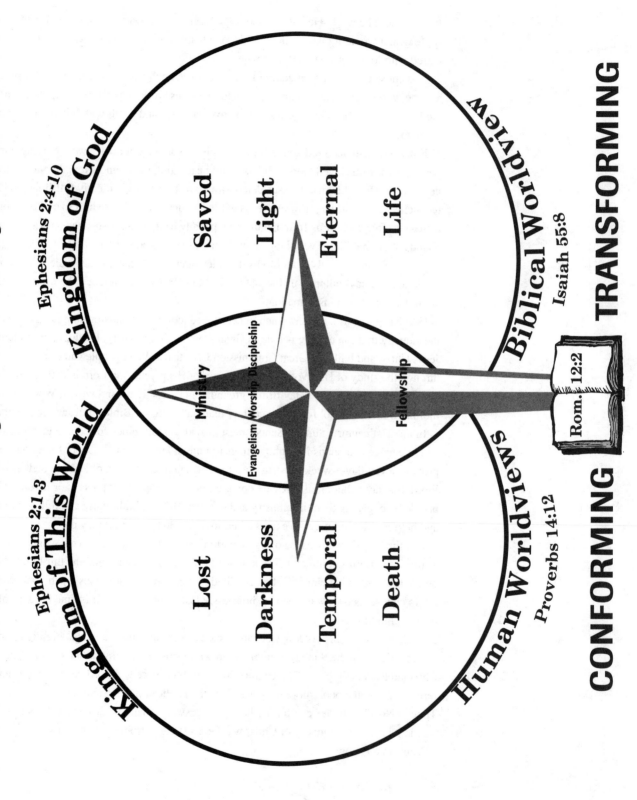

Kingdom of God
Ephesians 2:4-10

Kingdom of This World
Ephesians 2:1-3

Saved
Light
Eternal
Life

Lost
Darkness
Temporal
Death

Ministry
Evangelism Worship Discipleship
Fellowship

Biblical Worldview
Isaiah 55:8

Human Worldviews
Proverbs 14:12

Rom. 12:2

TRANSFORMING

CONFORMING

Section 1
Laying the Foundation

Louis Hanks, associate director, Sunday School Group, is a leader who points others to the Cornerstone of all we do, Jesus Christ.

In 1994 Harry Piland, then director of the Bible Teaching-Reaching Division, invited a group of educators to Nashville to update them on some improvements to be made to a Bible study curriculum series. I was seated in the back of the room, but could not help but notice a tall gentleman standing next to Dr. Piland.

Within moments, Dr. Piland introduced Louis Hanks, who for 15 years had been an editor and later manager in the youth curriculum section. Recently Louis had been promoted to director of the Youth-Adult Department. In his new role Louis would help lay the foundation for sweeping changes in one of the major curriculum lines produced by the Division.

Little did I realize when I left that meeting to return to my home in Phoenix, just how much in the providence of God Louis would become entwined in my life. Within a few months Louis Hanks would become anything but a stranger to Bill Taylor.

Later that same year, after Dr. Piland's retirement, I became director of the Bible Teaching-Reaching Division. In my new role, I soon discovered firsthand how important it would be to lay a proper foundation if we were to take actions that enhanced the effectiveness of Sunday School ministry in the churches.

Even then, pastors and Sunday School leaders were facing challenges that threatened how they were doing Sunday School. Some leaders were beginning to question the value of Sunday School and to wonder whether something new was needed to help churches reach people for Christ and grow believers who would invest themselves in kingdom ministry.

Several things happened that would sharpen the focus of our assignment. And who would be a major influence in those changes? I could see then that Louis Hanks was going to be a significant part of shaping the future of Sunday School ministry. His quiet but thorough approach to his work would help lay the foundation.

First, Louis brought to me data about the current state of Vacation Bible School. This significant activity had been a mainstay in Southern Baptist churches for Bible study and for reaching people. However, signs indicated that if we wanted to remain on the forefront in promoting and using VBS, some positive changes would need to be made to help recapture the spirit of excitement so critical to the success of VBS. After reviewing data and consulting with other department directors, I authorized some immediate changes. The effect can be seen in the excellent response by churches to a renewed emphasis on VBS and to a new wave of VBS resources. Louis had laid the foundation upon which decisions could be made and upon which other people could build.

Then, under Louis' influence, a proposal was developed for a nationwide meeting to discuss the possibilities of a new curriculum series for Southern Baptists. This event ultimately became known as The Summit, a significant gathering that met in Nashville in March 1997. Southern Baptists educators dialogued with leaders of the Bible Teaching-Reaching Division about the role of Sunday School in the churches and the kind of Bible study resources that would be needed. The outcome of that gathering influenced the new Sunday School ministry and Bible study curriculum plan for the 21st century. Again, a foundation had been laid upon which other people could build.

Think about some individuals in your life who have influenced you, your work, or some decisions you have made. What kind of foundation did they lay upon which you were able to build?

Identify the people in your church who do foundational kinds of work upon which your church can build. Are you one of those people?

What type of foundations need to be laid as you make preparation for Sunday School ministry in your church in 1999-2000?

A third action Louis initiated was the creation of a task force of managers to review and evaluate principles and practices that were influencing Sunday School ministry and resource development. The group spent two years in study, dialogue, and prayer. They involved educators and leaders at every level, from seminary presidents to LifeWay Christian Resources executive management; from pastors and age-group ministers to teachers, preschool through adult. Excitement abounded, for everyone sensed a fresh moving of God.

God was already at work. We knew that. We just needed to recognize where He was at work and *join Him.*

The structure for doing that work looked familiar. It was Sunday School—not Sunday School as an organization or a program but as the *foundational strategy* for effective ministry in a local church. Sunday School as strategy was built upon the foundation of the Great Commission. We had been looking for a fresh approach, and it was there all the time. We just needed to reaffirm its effectiveness.

Even so, as we moved from theory to reality, some concerns arose. Change is not easy, especially when the change affects something as critical to our history and tradition as Sunday School. Would church leaders accept a focus on Sunday School as *strategy?* How could the message of Sunday School as strategy be communicated to the vast audience of Southern Baptists?

Throughout all these moments of uncertainty, discomfort, and debate, one voice stayed steady. Louis Hanks was convinced change was needed, that it would be good, and that we were building on a solid foundation. He stressed the value of leading believers to be transformed by the power of the Truth and to acquire and live according to a biblical worldview. How exciting it would be to plan Sunday School ministry and Bible study resources with that end in mind.

Louis prepares and challenges us in our work by being a foundational leader, one who lays good foundations upon which we can build. He does so by pointing us toward the One who is the cornerstone for all we do, Jesus Christ.

My oldest son is an architect. We have shared many conversations about how essential the foundation of a building is, how it exists prior to anything visible coming out of the ground. A builder must start with a strong, true foundation, which most people will never see.

> The bricklayer laid a brick on the bed of cement
> > Then, with a precise stroke of his trowel, spread another layer
> And, without a by-your-leave, laid on another brick.
> > The foundation grew visibly,
> The building rose, tall and strong, to shelter men.
>
> I thought, Lord, of that poor brick buried in the darkness
> > at the base of the big building.
> No one sees it, but it accomplishes its task,
> > and the other bricks need it.
> Lord, what difference whether I am on the rooftop or in the foundations
> > of your building, as long as I stand faithfully at the right place? [1]

Michael Quoist, *The Brick*

[1]Michael Quoist, *Prayers* (New York: Sheep and Ward, 1963), 23.

Louis Hanks is the kind of person who is more concerned about being used by God than about being seen on the rooftops of fame and notoriety.

1·5·4 Principle of Growth

1

driving force for church growth:

The Great Commission

5

essential church functions for church growth:

Evangelism
Discipleship
Fellowship
Ministry
Worship

4

results:

Numerical Growth
Spiritual Growth
Ministries Expansion
Missions Advance

Christ's Commission to His Church: "Make Disciples"

At its core, the Great Commission (Matt. 28:18-20) is a command to join Christ in His mission. It represents the overriding mandate to any New Testament church. That mandate is "to make disciples."

Sometimes we have thought of "disciple-making" as the process of leading believers toward maturity in Christ. While that is true, the necessity of first leading people to be believers cannot be overlooked. Therefore, the first step in making disciples is intentional evangelistic effort in which the gospel is presented and hearers respond in faith to the convicting power of the Holy Spirit.

When Jesus gave His disciples the Great Commission, He knew they would be "going." After all, they would not be staying on the mountain (v. 16). Jesus wanted them to go with purpose so He gave them one—to "make disciples."

The Great Commission is not just biblical history. Nor was it a mandate given only to a few. The commission is contemporary to followers of Jesus in any era of time. *Churches who realize the Great Commission gives them their purpose and reason for existence look for an effective way to mobilize their members to intentional gospel presentation—the "going" aspect of the Great Commission.*

Making disciples also includes assimilating new believers into the life and ministry of the church. The salvation available in Jesus brings a person into the kingdom, not for rest but for service. Believers who are on mission for Christ through His church, more often than not, are "joy-filled" Christians. *Churches who take seriously the mandate to "make disciples" look for an effective way to assimilate new believers into the fellowship—the "baptizing" dimension of the Great Commission.*

Making disciples does include leading believers toward maturity in Christ. The goal of teaching is obedience to the commandments of Christ. And at least one command of Jesus is to "make disciples." *Churches who take seriously the mandate to make disciples look for an effective way to disciple new believers—the "teaching" dimension of the Great Commission.*

Is there an effective strategy to help a church mobilize, assimilate, and teach believers—to help a church make disciples? This book offers Sunday School as a strategy that helps the church do all three aspects of the Great Commission.

God's blessings can be realized in at least four ways as you lead your church to make Sunday School your strategy for focusing more intentionally on the Great Commission.

- Spiritually lost people will come to faith in the Lord Jesus Christ and be baptized into the fellowship of the church.
- Christians will grow in their understanding of and obedience to Christ as they study the Bible individually and with others.
- The ministries of the church will expand as God's people discover their gifts and abilities, identify opportunities to minister to others, and respond to the call to serve people in Jesus' name.
- The mission of the Lord will advance as God's people go into their world in His power with His good news.

Sunday School: The Foundational Strategy

In most churches Sunday School classes and departments continue to involve more people than any other church ministry. Even so, we may have lost perspective on what Sunday School is. Too often, Sunday School has been reduced to the sum of the parts of its name—a teaching-learning institution that meets one particular day a week. In some cases, Sunday School has been reduced further to being a loose collection of homogeneous social groups that meet weekly for fellowship.

While teaching-learning and caring fellowship both are essential, they often are focused toward people who already have been reached. Sunday School that focuses only on those who have been reached has lost sight of the church's primary purpose—fulfilling the Great Commission.

If Sunday School is to become more helpful to a church, classes and departments—the Bible study groups where the work is actually done—must break free from the tendency to focus inwardly. Members of the Bible study groups must be challenged to serve Christ and follow His example. They must be organized for service, equipped for every good work, and mobilized for ministry.

For these things to happen, we need to rethink our understanding of Sunday School. It is not an educational entity. It is not a program or an organization. *Sunday School is a strategy, a plan for doing the work of the church.* It becomes foundational to everything we do.

Definition of Sunday School for a New Century	*Sunday School is the foundational strategy in a local church for leading people to faith in the Lord Jesus Christ and for building Great Commission Christians through Bible study groups that engage people in evangelism, discipleship, fellowship, ministry, and worship.*

The church that recognizes and chooses Sunday School as its foundational strategy for accomplishing the Great Commission will come to see Sunday School as

- a seven-day-a-week plan for involving people in seeking the kingdom of God and fulfilling the Great Commission, not a one-day-a-week study period;
- a way of engaging learners in the biblical model of instruction that leads to spiritual transformation; and
- an intentional effort to build ongoing, open Bible study groups that are committed to reproducing themselves. These new groups become the best long-term approach for building a ministry environment that—

    guides preschoolers and children toward conversion through foundational teaching;

    encourages unsaved people to come to faith in Christ;

    assimilates new believers into the life of the church; and

    supports believers in their efforts to lead others to Christ.

Biblical Assertions for
Sunday School as Strategy

As a strategy, Sunday School is founded upon certain biblical assertions. Sunday School as strategy—

• *Affirms the Bible as God's Word and as the textbook for understanding truth and for fully integrating truth into life.*—God provided the Bible as the authoritative written revelation of Himself to humanity. He assigned to the Bible's message the power to bring people to faith in Christ and guide them to follow Him in obedience (2 Tim. 3:15-17).

• *Accepts the Great Commission as the mission mandate to God's people and becomes a way of fulfilling that mission as people are lead to obey Christ's commandments.*—Jesus commands His followers to acknowledge His authority over all things, to evangelize the world, to bring people into fellowship with God and one another, and to lead them to become His disciples (Matt. 28:16-20). The Lord also commands His followers to love Him completely and to love others as they love themselves (Matt. 22:37-40).

• *Recognizes God's active purpose of reconciling a spiritually lost world to Himself and provides a way for people to join Him in the work of intentional evangelism.*—God loves all people and desires that they hear the gospel and receive salvation through His Son, Jesus Christ (John 3:16; Rom. 1:16-17; 2 Pet. 3:9).

• *Affirms the Christian family as the primary institution for biblical instruction.*—God desires for parents to teach His Word to their children as an integral and natural part of daily living (Deut. 6:4-9).

• *Engages people in spiritually transforming ministry opportunities through Bible study groups that lead people to love, trust, and obey God.*—God urges His followers to worship Him by submitting their lives to His leadership, allowing Him to transform their lives (Rom. 12:1-2).

• *Enables believers to be servant-leaders and offers them opportunities to discover, develop, and use their spiritual gifts and abilities in service to Christ and His people.*—Through the Holy Spirit, God gives Christians spiritual gifts and empowers Christians to use those gifts in His service (1 Cor. 12—13; Rom. 12:1-8; Eph. 4:12).

• *Provides a structure that enables the largest number of God's people to do the work assigned the church.*—God urges the church as the body of Christ to be unified and to work in harmony to accomplish His purpose (Eph. 4:1-6; 1 Cor. 12:12-27).

• *Requires leaders who are willing to be held accountable for calling forth and equipping new leaders. It is a way in which all believers can be actively involved in leading spiritually lost people toward faith in the Lord Jesus Christ.*—God intends for Christians to be accountable individually and collectively to develop new disciples (Matt. 25:14-30; 2 Tim. 2:1-2).

• *Leads people to be involved in Bible study that facilitates the transforming work of the Holy Spirit in a person's life.*—God intends for people to engage in Bible study that leads to transformational living (2 Cor. 3:18; 2 Tim. 3:16-17).

Sunday School: On Kingdom Mission

The Great Commission is the driving force for the growth of God's kingdom and the health of His church. The objective is spiritual transformation or conversion. Sunday School is a way to lead people to be on kingdom mission, not an institution's mission.

Sunday School addresses transcultural life issues common to individuals, churches, families, tribes, and nations regardless of geographic, ethnic, or language identity. The kingdom ministry carried out by the Sunday School strategy is a ministry worthy of investment of time, energy, and resources.

Jesus clearly intends for His people to invest their lives in others in such a way that they are transformed in their mind, emotions, and will—in how they think, feel, and act (Rom. 12:1-2).

People are searching for such an opportunity. They may never get excited about preserving the status quo, helping out the pastor, or otherwise going through the motions of "church work"; but they will respond to the powerful call of God to join Him and His people in kingdom ministry.

Sunday School: A Ministry of Prophetic Leadership

Sunday School strategy demands leaders who will respond to the call to a prophetic ministry—that of listening to God's voice, discerning His message, and declaring His truth to all people through His church. Sunday School classes and departments—Bible study groups—are more effective when the leader is the lesson, meaning the leader not only talks about the lesson, he or she models the lesson in everyday life.

Every leader is accountable for being an authentic example of Christianity in personal living and by producing new leaders for service through the ministries of the church. Leaders must give time to their own discipleship, to learning about the people they teach and allowing those people to know them, and to prayer for the people they teach and desire to reach.

That investment is in addition to the time needed for involvement in evangelism, ministering to needs, and developing teaching-learning experiences that challenge learners to grow in Christlikeness. Effective use of Sunday School's organizational components—classes, departments, or Bible study groups—and teamwork are essential to enabling leaders to fulfill their roles.

Sunday School and Church Functions

The church in the New Testament is characterized by five essential functions that grow out of the Great Commission: evangelism, discipleship, fellowship, ministry, and worship. These functions are evident in the practices described in Acts 2:42-47.

As believers, we need to be characterized corporately and individually by these same five functions if we are to fulfill the calling of Christ. Because Sunday School provides the primary framework for involving families and individuals in the comprehensive work of the church, it is an appropriate strategy for doing the Great Commission work described by these functions. Sunday School strategy recognizes missions as a desired result of all that we do through Sunday School.

Sunday School and Evangelism

We are not saved from our sin and separation from God merely for our own benefit. Because God desires that every person hear the gospel and receive salvation through His Son, Jesus Christ, we are to join Him in His work of reconciling the lost world to Himself. The key to accomplishing this work is obedience to Jesus in telling others about the good news of salvation in Christ.

When we share the good news, everyone is changed. The lost person becomes accountable for hearing the good news and for responding to the opportunity to receive salvation and new life through personal belief. The Christian becomes more like Christ through faithfulness to the Lord's command.

Sunday School as strategy focuses on obedience to Christ in the work of evangelism.

Leaders and members are constantly to be reaching people for Bible study. They must be dedicated to seeking, discovering, and inviting spiritually lost people to participate in open Bible study groups. Leaders and members work one-on-one to reach the unreached and to teach them the good news in settings away from church.

Classes and departments that are not leading people to faith in the Lord Jesus Christ are stale and stagnant. One great threat to the effectiveness of the strategy is the tendency of Bible study groups (classes and departments) to become closed groups, focused on the needs and interests of existing members to the exclusion of those who do not know Christ or the fellowship of His people.

Some Bible study classes become so focused on "deeper Bible study" that they assume a common level of foundational Bible knowledge, often unintentionally excluding those who are new to the study of God's Word. Or a Bible study class may become so focused on the fellowship within the existing group that members erect social barriers to "outsiders" who need to be reached.

Sunday School as strategy is marked by evangelistic Bible teaching through ongoing Bible study classes and other Bible study groups that are always open for anyone to participate.

This statement means providing foundational Bible study for preschoolers and younger children from which they will be encouraged to respond positively to the message of salvation as soon as they are able to do so. It means providing an environment in older children's, youth, and adult Bible study groups that encourages unsaved people to come to faith in Christ and encourages believers to lead others to Christ. It means seizing every opportunity the Holy Spirit provides to present the gospel through Bible teaching.

Sunday School as strategy provides a churchwide evangelism training network to equip members to become passionate soul-winners.

Sunday School is a systematic way of organizing, equipping, and mobilizing individuals to reach, teach, and witness to others in their networks of relationships. Participants are encouraged to pray for spiritually lost people throughout the world, and especially for people they know. Sunday School takes seriously the responsibility of witnessing to others through ongoing evangelistic visitation, both as a group activity and as an individual mandate.

Sunday School as strategy uses organizational expansion to encourage evangelism.

Starting new Sunday School classes and departments and other Bible study groups, is a priority because new units consistently seek, discover, and involve more lost people than do existing units. Special events such as Vacation Bible School support the evangelistic work of the church.

Sunday School and Discipleship

Discipleship is a process that begins after conversion and continues throughout a believer's life. Evangelism initiates this process, fellowship contributes to it, and ministry grows out of it.

Discipleship is not an option for the believer. Every Christian needs to grow in his or her understanding of and obedience to God (Eph. 4:11-16). Bible study is essential to the church's function of discipleship.

God has provided the Bible as the authoritative written revelation of Himself to humanity. He has assigned to the Bible's message the power to bring people to faith in Christ and to guide them to follow Him in obedience. The apostle Paul reminded believers through his words to Timothy that the Scriptures "are able to make you wise for salvation through faith in Jesus Christ. All Scripture is God-breathed and is useful for teaching, rebuking, correcting and training in righteousness, so that the man of God may be thoroughly equipped for every good work" (2 Tim. 3b:15-17).

Sunday School as strategy provides for foundational discipleship that places people in Bible study groups where they can grow in their understanding of God's Word and obedience to His commands.

Growth in a person's understanding of the Bible is a necessary goal of Bible study and Bible teaching. Knowledge, however, cannot be the end of Bible study and Bible teaching if we are to make disciples. Neither is it enough simply to understand a biblical truth and be able to apply it to an area of life.

The need is for Bible teaching that facilitates the Holy Spirit's work of spiritual transformation in the lives of learners. Believers are urged to integrate a biblical worldview into their minds, hearts, and lives through participation in ongoing systematic Bible study.

Sunday School as strategy encourages members to strengthen their Christian walk by participating in other discipleship opportunities.

Genuine discipleship involves guiding people to integrate biblical truth into the total fabric of their hearts, minds, will, and actions. Participation in a church's discipleship ministry greatly enhances a believer's spiritual growth. Involvement in missions ministries, music ministry, and other church ministries provide focused opportunities to grow in Christlikeness. Sunday School leaders are responsible to keep other church leaders aware of the discipleship needs of individuals in their Bible study groups.

Sunday School as strategy recognizes that Bible study is most effective when it occurs in the context of the learner's total life, especially family relationships, and when it considers the generational perspective, age and life-stage characteristics, and preferred learning styles of the learner.

Personal and family Bible study are a responsibility for every believer. Not only does the individual benefit from extended Bible study opportunities, but also that person's family is strengthened. God did not give us His Word to study as an addendum to our lives. Rather, His Word is to be upon our hearts.

Sunday School as strategy affirms the home as the center of biblical guidance. As such, it helps equip Christian parents to fulfill their responsibility as the primary Bible teachers and disciplers of their children.

For too long, churches have focused on Sunday morning Bible study as sufficient while neglecting the equipping of Christian parents to fulfill their role as the spiritual instructors of their children. God desires for godly parents to teach His commands to their children as an integral and natural part of daily living (Deut. 4:9b).

Sunday School as strategy encourages Bible study in ongoing groups, short-term groups, and through special Bible teaching events as effective ways to address specific life concerns, spiritual issues, church functions, doctrinal issues, and to promote outreach and evangelism.

Special Bible study events such as January Bible Study can strengthen discipleship. Additional short-term Bible studies that focus on specific topics or issues can address particular discipleship needs in a person's life. Participation in training toward leadership, evangelism, or another area of ministry or missions enhances a believer's recognition and use of his or her spiritual gifts for Christ's purpose.

Sunday School and Fellowship

Christians share a common belief in Christ and a unity of purpose that is rooted in God's love for us and our love for Him and one another. Jesus prayed that He, His disciples, and all those who would believe in Him through their message might be one (John 17:1-26). God intends for His people to join with other believers and to share their common life in Christ. The baptism Jesus commanded His disciples to perform as a part of the Great Commission is a symbol of being sealed in belief and in belonging.

Sunday School as strategy recognizes that genuine fellowship uses diversity to build unity rather than to separate.

People are different and believers have diverse gifts; but "in Christ, we who are many form one body, and each member belongs to all the others" (Rom. 12:5). Paul recognized that Christ gave believers a variety of gifts to "prepare God's people for works of service, so that the body of Christ may be built up until we all reach unity in the faith and in the knowledge of the Son of God and become mature, attaining to the whole measure of the fullness of Christ" (Eph. 4:12-13). The church as the body of Christ must be unified and harmonious in order to accomplish Christ's purpose.

Sunday School as strategy seeks to build relationships through the ongoing work of classes, departments, and other Bible study groups.

It places people in groups and calls for Bible teaching that facilitates the building of relationships in a ministry environment of grace, acceptance, support, and encouragement. The small group provides opportunities for participants to interact with God's Word, the study leader, and one another.

Sunday School as strategy includes classes, departments, and other Bible study groups that provide additional opportunities for people to build fellowship beyond the time the group is gathered for Bible study.

Some of these additional gatherings may be social functions that allow members to become better acquainted with each other. Nonmembers may be invited to these gatherings as a way to cultivate relationships with them. Individuals who are serving in leadership positions in an age group other than their own always should be included in the fellowship activities for their age group as well.

Perhaps the most effective efforts at building fellowship are those offering times for members to pray or to work together. For example, ongoing visitation for the purposes of outreach, evangelism, and ministry provides opportunities to bring unreached people into fellowship with Christ and His people. It also strengthens the unity of believers as they serve Christ together.

Special events and emphases offer opportunities for helping people find the place where they best fit in the life and work of a church. New member assimilation events help new Christians and new church members take the next step toward meaningful church involvement. Leader appreciation events spotlight the contributions of those who have been instrumental in helping the church accomplish its purpose.

Sunday School and Ministry

Ministry is the discovery and use of spiritual gifts and abilities to meet the needs of others in Jesus' name. Ministry naturally follows discipleship in the process of Christian development. However, we perhaps need to be reminded that the functions of the church actually are in operation simultaneously. Even so, Christian ministry flows from the life of a person who has received Christ into his or her life and is following Christ's example.

Through the Holy Spirit, God gives Christians spiritual gifts and empowers Christians to use those gifts in His service. Paul made it clear that these gifts were given "for the common good" (1 Cor. 12:7). Paul explained to the church at Ephesus that they were to "prepare God's people for works of service" (Eph. 4:12). Ultimately, those works of service or ministry are for the purpose of leading others to faith in Jesus as Savior and Lord.

Sunday School as strategy is committed to ministry.

Acts of caring ministry are an essential part of building and maintaining unity and fellowship in any Bible study group. However, ministry must not be limited to those who already have been reached. It is important for Sunday School leaders to make Bible study participants aware of ministry needs.

God's people desire to serve Him and others. Sometimes acts of ministry go undone and people suffer needlessly simply because others are uninformed. Sunday School leaders must keep the ministry function of the church before its members in order to encourage them toward missionary service to their world.

Sunday School as strategy organizes people for effective ministry.

Sunday School equips people for service individually and collectively. The strategy's structure for doing ministry takes into consideration the gifts, abilities, and resources available to those performing the ministry, as well as the needs of those who will receive the ministry.

Sunday School as strategy supports all church ministries and intentionally encourages its members to be good stewards, fully involved in the church's overall mission.

This support is accomplished through Bible study that builds disciples, and through working with other church ministries to train and develop Christians to be faithful servants to Christ.

Sunday School as strategy equips people for ministry, mobilizes them, and sends them into service.

Leaders identify and magnify opportunities for member involvement in ongoing, caring ministry actions through their Sunday School classes, departments, or other Bible study groups. Direct assignments to members help to involve them in specific ministry actions in one-on-one or family-to-family ministry situations.

The needs of specific groups offer special opportunities for ministry. For example, new parents can benefit significantly from acts of service that help them establish relationships with a church. They can draw encouragement from other parents through involvement in a Bible study group, as well as begin to build a spiritual foundation in the life of their child.

Ministry to homebound individuals is a way to send members into service as ministering teachers. As servant leaders, they relate to folk who otherwise might be left without the opportunity to hear the good news of salvation, share in caring fellowship of God's people, study the Bible with others, or share in ministry with others.

Sunday School strategy can ensure that people with special physical or educational needs receive Great Commission ministry. Providing training and resources for every teacher that will enable them to address special-education needs results in better Bible teaching. Such support also builds a caring ministry environment for classes as they make their group a place for everyone. Bible study groups for people with severe mental retardation can be an effective way to minister to individuals and families who often have been ignored or have withdrawn from involvement with others.

Sunday School and Worship

Worship is the act of knowing and loving God in spirit and in truth (John 4:23). The apostle Paul urged believers to "offer your bodies as living sacrifices, holy and pleasing to God—this is your spiritual act of worship" (Rom. 12:1). He understood the essence of worship: recognition of Christ as the almighty God of heaven and earth and a response of adoration of Him with all one's being.

All Great Commission work grows out of love and devotion—worship—to God. Without the honoring of Christ through a genuine understanding of who He is and what He has done for us, we labor in our own power.

Sunday School as strategy involves people in worship by leading them to acknowledge who Jesus is and to express love for Him personally and corporately.

Participation in classes and departments or other Bible study groups provide opportunities for people to worship through prayer and praise; stewardship of time, abilities, and resources; and other forms of expressing devotion to Christ.

Sunday School as strategy emphasizes the need to seek God's power and presence by seeking Him.

Leaders must set aside time daily in their own lives to remember who God is and to seek Him through personal prayer and Bible study. Sunday School leaders also encourage participants in Bible study classes, departments, and other Bible study groups to do the same. They strive to establish an environment in study sessions that leads people to encounter and respond to the life-changing God through the study of His Word in the fellowship of His people. Such an environment encourages people to open their lives to God. When people do, amazing things happen: evangelism becomes a priority; fellowship grows; discipleship deepens; and ministry expands freely.

Sunday School Strategy and Other Church Ministries

The premise of this book is that Sunday School is the foundational strategy for helping a church do the work of the Great Commission. What does this mean about the place of the various ministries that can be found in the life of almost any church?

A key to understanding the relationship of Sunday School as strategy to other church ministries is to clarify the meaning of the word *foundational*. A foundation is an underlying base or support. It is the basis upon which something stands.

Perhaps the most common illustration is to think in terms of a building. Jesus used this imagery to emphasize the importance of building one's life on His teachings (Matt. 7:24-27). A solid foundation is critical to the stability of any structure. It comes first because the rest of the structure is supported by it. The framework for the rest of the building is attached to it. No wise builder begins with the walls. Obviously, the roof is not constructed first.

To say Sunday School is foundational strategy is not to make it exclusive or better than other ministries. It is to say that as foundational strategy, Sunday School can give stability and provide essential support to other ministries. A church that wants to develop a comprehensive approach for doing and being that which is unique to the church as the people of God can lay a solid foundation by giving attention to the growth and development of Sunday School.

Obviously the church will have additional ministries: missions ministry, music, discipleship, youth, deacon ministry, just to name a few. Sunday School does not take the place of any of these, but can provide support by encouraging members to be participants. As members become involved in various ways, they discover these ministries to be ways to grow in Christ, to use the spiritual gifts with which they have been endowed, and to move the church toward greater fulfillment of its mission and objectives.

Even when considered as an institution, the church is a body made up of many parts or ministries. The effectiveness of the church is dependent on each ministry doing what it has been called out to do, working with all other ministries for the common good. Some ministries may be more visible than others but visibility is not always the sign of importance. Church ministries are not to be competitive, for no ministry has value apart from what it does to contribute to the work of the church.

The effective use of Sunday School as foundational strategy can help a church avoid duplicating its efforts; hence, a church is able to use its resources—especially people ones—with greater effectiveness.

For example, we shall see later in this book that Sunday School provides the foundational structure for outreach and evangelism. A church using Sunday School as its outreach and evangelism strategy will focus attention on improving the effectiveness of visitation by members in classes and departments. Only when the foundational effort is firmly in place will additional structures be developed. The same can be said for care ministries and prayer ministries.

Sunday School becomes a way for taking the great assignment given to the church and breaking it down into manageable pieces. It is a way of involving people judiciously, of using resources wisely, and of multiplying efforts strategically.

Strategic Principles for Sunday School for a New Century

If Sunday School is to fulfill its objectives as strategy, church leaders must champion and communicate the objectives in a clear, compelling manner. The following five strategic principles represent priorities to be addressed through Sunday School as strategy. They will be valuable as primary messages that guide the effectiveness of Sunday School for a new century.

The Principle of Foundational Evangelism

Sunday School is the foundational evangelism strategy of the church.

1. Sunday School emphasizes ongoing, open Bible study groups that reproduce new groups as the best long-term approach for building a ministry environment that encourages unsaved people to come to faith in Christ, assimilates new believers into the life of the church, and encourages believers to lead others to Christ.

2. Sunday School provides the most efficient churchwide evangelism training network to equip members to become passionate soul-winners.

3. Sunday School encourages Bible study in short-term groups and through special Bible teaching events as effective ways to promote outreach and evangelism and to address specific life concerns, spiritual issues, church functions, and doctrinal issues.

4. Sunday School creates a great center for missionary power as people tell and live the wondrous story of Christ's redeeming love.

The Principle of Foundational Discipleship

Knowing God through Jesus is the first step of discipleship. Sunday School is a seven-day-a-week strategy, and Bible study is a foundational step of discipleship for involving people in seeking the kingdom of God and fulfilling the Great Commission.

1. Sunday School provides the primary organizational framework for involving families and individuals in the comprehensive work of the church including evangelism, discipleship, fellowship, ministry, and worship.

2. Sunday School provides foundational discipleship and encourages members to strengthen their Christian walk by participating in other discipleship opportunities.

3. Sunday School emphasizes that every member who is a believer must become accountable for the responsibility God has given him or her as a minister and missionary to the world.

4. Sunday School supports all church ministries and intentionally encourages its members to be good stewards, fully involved in the church's overall mission.

The Principle of Family Responsibility

Sunday School affirms the home as the center of biblical guidance.

1. Sunday School helps equip Christian parents, including single parents, to fulfill their responsibility as the primary Bible teachers and disciplers of their children.

2. The Sunday School encourages Christian parents who by word and deed guide their children to integrate the Scriptures into their lives influencing how they think and act.

3. Sunday School involves families in the comprehensive work of the church.

4. Sunday School works to nurture sound and healthy families and seeks to lead non-Christian parents to Christ.

The Principle of Spiritual Transformation

Sunday School engages learners in the biblical model of instruction that leads to spiritual transformation.

1. Sunday School affirms that spiritual transformation is God's work of changing a believer into the likeness of Jesus by creating a new identity in Christ and by empowering a lifelong relationship of love, trust, and obedience to glorify God.

2. Sunday School champions the absolute truth and authority of the Word of God and compels believers to integrate a biblical worldview into their minds, hearts, and lives through ongoing systematic Bible study.

3. Sunday School recognizes that Bible study is most effective when it occurs in the context of the learner's total life, especially family relationships, and when it considers the special needs, generational perspective, age and life-stage characteristics, and learning styles of the learner.

4. Sunday School addresses transcultural life issues common to individuals, churches, families, tribes, and nations regardless of geographic, ethnic, or language identity.

The Principle of Biblical Leadership

Sunday School calls leaders to follow the biblical standard of leadership.

1. Sunday School affirms the pastor as the primary leader in its ministry of building Great Commission Christians.

2. Sunday School calls leaders to a prophetic ministry, listening to God's voice, discovering His message, integrating the message into their lives, and proclaiming His truth through His church to the nations.

3. Sunday School recognizes that the leader is the lesson in that every leader is accountable for being an authentic example of Christianity in personal living and producing new leaders for service through the ministries of the church.

4. Sunday School recognizes that planning is essential in implementing its strategy.

It's Time to Change Our Thinking About Sunday School

Sunday School has a heritage of over 200 years. It has been an important part of Southern Baptist churches for more than 100 years. Because of this lengthy heritage, some people may consider Sunday School a relic of the past. They may question whether Sunday School has anything to offer churches of the third millennium. We are glad to say that it does.

However, we need to develop a new way of thinking about Sunday School if we are to tap its vitality for a new day. So, what is new about Sunday School for a new century?

Sunday School is strategy. That calls for a new way of thinking about Sunday School. It is not a program we are attaching to an already overcrowded church schedule. It is not an organization we are trying to grow or at least perpetuate. Sunday School is a strategy, a plan, a way for the church to do the work of the Great Commission.

Sunday School is the church doing its work. Sunday School does not have tasks or work to do apart from that which belongs to the church. The focus is on the five functions of the church: evangelism, discipleship, fellowship, ministry, and worship.

Sunday School is the church doing its work in the context of small groups. The church gathers weekly in large group for worship and praise. The church also gathers in small groups where the work of the church becomes more focused and personal.

Sunday School is a seven-day-a-week strategy, not a one-day-a-week meeting. The effectiveness of Sunday School as strategy is organizing, equipping, and mobilizing members to live obediently as believers in their situations in life.

Sunday School has two objectives: (1) to lead people to faith in the Lord Jesus Christ and (2) to build Great Commission Christians. These objectives are accomplished by leading people to be participants in small group Bible study. Through Sunday School classes and departments people can be brought into an encounter with God's Word, the Lord Jesus Christ, and the transforming power of the Holy Spirit.

Where Do We Go from Here?

These pages have laid the foundation for Sunday School as strategy. But strategy, to be effective, must move beyond the philosophical and theoretical to the practical. That is what the rest of this book is about. How can Sunday School as strategy be implemented in your church?

In essence, the rest of this book is about the "best practices" of Sunday School. Best practices are recommendations for implementing biblical and strategic Sunday School ministry in a local church. They are rooted in the knowledge of how people and churches work, but foremost they come from observing effective work in a broad base of churches over an extended period of time.

In the sections that follow, here are some best practices that will be addressed:

1. Identify the Strategy
   - We will develop the strategy that leads people toward faith in Christ and builds Great Commission Christians.
   - We will implement the strategy through monthly and weekly actions.
2. Organize with Purpose
   - We will design an organization as an agent of a purposeful Sunday School strategy.
3. Build the Leadership
   - We will build leaders who are committed to the strategy as an expression of faithfulness to Christ, His church, and the mission mandate He has given.
4. Train Effective Leaders
   - We will enhance quality leadership by providing training.
5. Provide Space and Equipment
   - We will provide the best possible space and equipment for small-group Bible study.
6. Value Record Keeping
   - We will implement a record system that helps identify people, tracks their participation, and gives some indication of their spiritual growth.
7. Develop Soul-Winners
   - We will equip leaders and members through FAITH Sunday School Evangelism Strategy to become soul-winners.
8. Teach to Transform
   - We will teach the Bible with the intent that people will be spiritually transformed.
9. Conduct Special Events
   - We will provide additional Bible study events that target the reached and the unreached.
10. Choose Sound Curriculum
    - We will provide Bible study resources that cause learners to explore the entire counsel of God during their life stages.

Your Time Is Now

How is the definition of Sunday School as foundational strategy different from how you have defined Sunday School in the past? How would *strategy* be a new way of thinking and serving for your leadership team? Is it time for a change?

Section 2
Knowing the People

Minister

I often have wondered what it must have been like to walk with Jesus through Galilee and Judea, as the Twelve did. What sights they saw; what words they heard! They witnessed amazing miracles and were challenged by profound teaching.

As wonderful as all of that must have been, I truly believe that what must have amazed them most was the way Jesus dealt with people. Sometimes He did the very opposite of what they expected Him to do.

- When they tried to keep children away from Him on a particularly busy day, he rebuked them.
- Rather than avoid a Samaritan woman of questionable reputation, Jesus initiated a conversation with her.
- Instead of lowering His expectations to attract a rich young ruler, Jesus challenged him in such a demanding way that the young man sadly turned and walked away.
- Rather than denounce an unscrupulous tax collector, Jesus invited Himself to dinner at Zacchaeus' home.
- Jesus told about a Samaritan who was a hero instead of a villain.

Matthew showed keen insight into the ministry priority of Jesus: "When he saw the crowds, he had compassion on them" (Matt. 9:36). Acquiring Jesus' attitude toward people becomes a challenge as we develop Sunday School ministry for a new century. An effective Sunday School must be characterized by Jesus' love and targeted to meet the needs of people.

For me, Tommy Sanders, director of the Preschool Sunday School Ministry Department, models these two traits as well as anyone. After only a few brief moments with him, you realize how intentional Tommy is when it comes to people.

He still is remembered by his classmates and professors at Southwestern Baptist Theological Seminary for his tenacity in examining educational issues, especially those pertaining to the preschool child. He carried this same drive into his ministries in the local church. While serving the historic Hyde Park Baptist Church in Austin, Texas, Tommy became known as one of the ablest leaders of Preschool Sunday School ministry in the Southern Baptist Convention.

A couple of years after leaving Hyde Park to join the staff of LifeWay Christian Resources, Tommy returned to Hyde Park to lead a conference sponsored by the Baptist General Convention of Texas. The people whom Tommy previously had served were delighted to see him again. He had made an investment in the lives of the people of Austin. He loved them, and they loved him in return. Tommy had learned how to see people through the eyes of Jesus.

Love and genuine concern draw people. People are much more willing to go where they feel cared about. Sunday School Bible study groups—classes and departments— are to be those kinds of places. Therefore, leaders need to have a better understanding of and appreciation for the people who are part of their Sunday School. As Sunday School leaders, we need to learn as much as possible about the people we lead, teach, or are trying to reach.

Tommy Sanders, director, Preschool Sunday School Ministry Department, is a leader who strives to see people through the eyes of Jesus.

Who are some people in your church who could be described as "people persons"? What kind of actions do they take that earns them that title?

Look around your church on Sunday and see how many different generations you can identify. For more information, look at the generational influences section that begins on page 36.

What can you do personally to give more encouragement to the people who serve with you as Sunday School leaders?

Just as it helps us to know about the needs and characteristics of the age groups we teach and attempt to reach, it would benefit most of us immensely to know more about generational influences. This topic hardly has been an issue in the past, but today's church leaders dare not overlook it. Some congregations are represented by as many as five generations.

I urge you to read carefully the information beginning on page 36 of this book. Use it to help other leaders become aware of the effects of generational influences on the people with whom they work and are trying to reach.

One generation we cannot overlook is the youngest segment of the latest generation—preschoolers. I believe that Preschool Sunday School ministry must be a priority if churches are to build a strong 21st-century Sunday School strategy. Neglect in this area can raise question about the church's genuine concern for people.

Critical questions to ask yourself are these: *How well is our church providing adequate resources, trained leaders, age-appropriate teaching, and nurturing care for preschool children? How effectively are we ministering to their parents?* Parents of preschoolers have high expectations of the kind of care that is provided for their children. Yet, in too many churches, the preschool area is understaffed and under-equipped.

Tommy Sanders is determined to do something about this situation. Although he is only in his 30s, he already speaks with an authority and a passion far beyond his age. He is thoroughly schooled in the basics of preschool ministry. He has paid his dues as a practitioner. His respect among his peers continues to grow. It is obvious to all who know Tommy that he intends to make a difference for the preschool child during the next 30 years of service, God willing.

Leadership is a key. While the parents of preschoolers have high expectations, they may not be as willing to assume leadership roles themselves. Even when they do, they may not stay in service for long periods of time. Other preschool leaders may rotate in and out of these departments on a frequent schedule.

The pressures of this society may contribute to such behavior, but do they justify it? Whatever your answer, the ones who are most penalized are the preschoolers. Therefore, we must take definitive action to respond to them and their families.

Tommy sets an example for other men by serving in the preschool department. The need for men to serve in preschool departments is great. The broken homes from which so many preschoolers come make even greater the need for men to be in teaching and caring roles and to be positive role models in the lives of these boys and girls.

As a professional in designing preschool curriculum resources, Tommy is raising the bar in providing the best teaching tools possible. He challenges the present while recalling the roots of the past. He beckons to the future while providing help for the present.

In building your Sunday School strategy, do not forget the people. They are what we are about. We are to reach people—all kinds, all sizes, all races and cultures, and all ages, from adults to preschoolers. What do you think about them? What do you know about them? What are you willing to learn and do?

"When Jesus saw the crowds, he had compassion on them" (Matt. 9:36).

Knowing the Preschoolers

Preschoolers are birth through five years of age. These are critical developmental years that must not be taken for granted. Understanding the needs and characteristics of preschoolers will enable Sunday School leaders to make a difference in the lives of preschoolers today and long into the 21st century. For additional help see *Preschool Sunday School for a New Century* (LifeWay Press, 1999).

Basic Needs of Preschoolers

Preschoolers come from many different backgrounds and situations, but they have the same basic needs: *love, trust, acceptance, independence, security, freedom, guidance,* and *a sense of accomplishment.*

• *To the preschooler, love is an action rather than an abstract feeling.* A preschooler must feel loved to have his need for love met. A child expresses love as a result of how he has experienced love. When a teacher smiles, listens, hugs, or spends time with a child, she communicates love to the child.

• *Trust is developed when needs are met regularly.* Consistency is the key to successful trust-building. The trust a child develops is the basis for faith and trust in Jesus when he is older. When a teacher feeds a baby or changes his diaper promptly, she communicates trust to the child.

• *Acceptance grows from the unconditional love of parents and teachers.* Because a child is made in God's image, she is worthy of acceptance and respect from the adults around her. When a teacher listens and gives a child his undivided attention, he communicates acceptance of and to the child.

• *Independence develops from being allowed to do things by himself.* A preschooler needs the opportunity to discover his unique gifts and abilities. When a teacher allows a child to complete a puzzle by himself, she fosters independence in the child.

• *Freedom is learning to make appropriate choices.* When parents and teachers guide a preschooler in making appropriate choices, they help the child develop independence or self-reliance. When a teacher provides several different learning centers/activities, she communicates freedom of choice to the preschooler.

• *Security is a worry-free environment where the child knows he is welcome, safe, and free from harm.* A preschooler feels secure when he sees the same teachers and children in the same room following a familiar routine. When a teacher is in the room to greet the child each Sunday, she helps a child feel secure.

• *Guidance is direction given by a teacher to help the child guide his thinking in making choices.* A teacher guides through words, actions, and room arrangement. A teacher needs to guide the child to know how to treat himself, others, and property. Through positive guidance, teachers give the child the opportunity to learn right from wrong and to make wise decisions. When a teacher corrects a child's misbehavior by offering two positive options, she is both redirecting the child and giving him an opportunity to make a wise choice.

• *Sense of accomplishment results from being given opportunities to succeed.* As a child develops and learns new skills, he gains a sense of accomplishment through completing an activity. Teachers need to provide activities that challenge yet do not frustrate. When a teacher provides both 7- and 12-piece puzzles in a class of 3-year-olds, she provides an opportunity for each child to succeed at his own level.

Common Characteristics of Preschoolers

Each child is a unique creation of God, created with a sense of awe and wonder about the world around him. Even though each child is unique, he exhibits some characteristics common to all preschoolers.

A preschooler is curious.

She learns by using all her senses to explore the world around her. She wonders how the world works and what objects do. She investigates the things that interest her. A four-year-old is constantly asking "Why?" in order to understand her world.

A preschooler is active.

Physical activity is part of the natural growth of a child. Provide a teaching environment that allows preschoolers to move around. If a teacher asks a preschooler to sit still too long, learning may stop because all of the child's energy is focused on not moving.

A preschooler is creative.

A child's imagination is enhanced when teachers provide an environment conducive to free expression. Giving a child a box of art supplies and blank paper rather than a coloring sheet allows the child to express her own ideas and feelings.

A preschooler is self-centered.

He can think about the world only from his own point of view. He is not necessarily selfish but relates to everything from his own personal experience. A two-year-old may have difficulty sharing the puzzles in the room.

A preschooler is sensitive.

Even though she cannot verbalize her feelings, a preschooler can read the emotions and feelings around her. She needs a consistent, positive environment to help her grow. Without this type of environment, she may feel insecure and uncertain.

• *A preschooler has a limited attention span.*

His attention span is approximately one minute for each year of life. A child can only remain involved in an activity as long as his attention allows. A teacher encourages a child to work at his own pace by providing a variety of activities. The teacher allows the preschooler to choose and move among those activities.

• *A preschooler is literal-minded.*

She thinks in terms of what she has seen and experienced. She understands words only in their concrete meanings. The use of symbolic language at home or church may confuse her. If a preschooler hears the phrase "You have grown another foot," she will look down to see where her new foot has grown.

A preschooler explores limits.

A young child explores limits for two reasons. First, he wants greater independence. Second, he wants to be reassured that his environment is safe. As the child questions limits in his learning experiences, the teacher has opportunity to provide firm but loving guidance to ensure safety and a secure environment.

Spiritual Development of Preschoolers

Spiritual growth in a preschooler is an increase in knowledge and understanding of God's love and care for her. From the first time a child comes to church, preschool teachers build foundations for spiritual growth. As teachers meet the child's physical and emotional needs, they communicate God's love to the child. As a child begins to trust her teachers, the spiritual foundation is laid. This simple foundation of trust in her physical surroundings will be the basis for later trust in Christ.

The child will begin to associate positive feelings toward God and Jesus as she hears "God" and "Jesus" in relation to positive experiences at church. As a baby she may not know who Jesus is, but she will know that He is someone very special from the feelings and attitudes of her teachers. When teachers say Bible verses and sing songs, the child begins to associate the Bible with her world. The child begins to sense that the Bible is an important book for her.

Adults must not miss an opportunity to build on the spiritual foundations in the life of a child every time he comes to church. Quality baby-sitting may occur at every child-care facility in the city, but laying spiritual foundations in the life of a child sets the church apart from child care.

As preschoolers grow, teachers continue to build spiritual foundations. Preschoolers need to be taught Bible-based concepts about God and Jesus on their level of understanding. Activities should be child-oriented to engage the child in learning biblical truths. Each child needs to feel satisfaction from having participated in an activity with the teacher. The relationship built between teacher and child helps to develop spiritual foundations.

Teachers communicate the love of Jesus to the child by saying: "I am glad you came to church today. We have happy times together as we learn about Jesus. Thank You, God, for my friend, Joey." A child who enjoys coming to church and enjoys learning in a Sunday School department will form positive attitudes toward church. He will see church as a place where people care about him and want to help him.

These attitudes will carry over into adulthood, forming a foundation that will impact how the child views and understands the role of church in his life. Biblical and spiritual foundations last a lifetime. A Sunday School teacher is extremely important in the lives of preschoolers in shaping attitudes about spiritual matters.

The greatest influences in a preschooler's emotional, mental, social and spiritual growth are his parents. Many parents take the task of raising their child seriously and often are overwhelmed by the task. Although some parents do not see the need of being a part of church for themselves, they are looking for a place to take their children for moral and spiritual education. Preschool leaders and teachers need to be willing to help educate parents about the spiritual development of their preschoolers and commit to partner with them in guiding and introducing the child to God.

Your Time Is Now

How much do you really know about the purposes, methods, and goals of preschool ministry? About *your* ministry's effectiveness and potential? Based on implications drawn from reading pages 25-29, who are you willing to contact to find out more? In the space provided write the date this important conversation took place. _____

What do you need to know about Preschool Sunday School ministry to more effectively lead others? Remember, you cannot take others where you have never been!

Knowing the Children

Children are ages 6-11 years or in grades 1 through 6. They are special and important to God. Just like Jesus, each child is growing and developing in many ways: physically, intellectually, socially, emotionally, and spiritually. They do not grow at the same rate, but they all go through the same stages. And while there are many ways in which children are alike, each child is unique because of individual, family, regional, and cultural differences. To be the best teachers and ministers possible, we need to get to know our children. For additional help see *Children's Sunday School for a New Century* (LifeWay Press, 1999).

How Do Children Grow?

"And Jesus grew in wisdom and stature, and in favor with God and men" (Luke 2:52). Children today grow as Jesus did. To understand and know a child we must look at all areas of his life. A child's physical development will impact him socially; his emotional state may impact him intellectually. We can minister and teach best as we look at all aspects of each child.

Behind everything a child does, there is a reason. Whether or not we know or understand those reasons, we can be sure there is an underlying cause. Why does Susan daydream? Why does Chad want to be the center of attention?

As they grow and learn, children pass through similar stages. A progression exists from the easy tasks to the more difficult, and each stage builds upon the previous one. A wide range of normal development exists among girls and boys. Some move through the stages rapidly, while others do so more slowly.

A child's growth is a product of his maturation (the unfolding of his God-given potentials) and of his learning (the growth that results from effort and exercise). Children experience five basic areas of growth—physical, intellectual, spiritual, social, and emotional. Growth spurts—periods of rapid change—tend to be followed by periods of slower change.

The importance of Children's Sunday School workers being aware of where a child is in his growth is underscored by the fact that a child cannot learn until he is ready to learn. Meet the child where he is in his growth.

Some Things Children Hold in Common

No matter where they live, what they wear, how much money they have, and whether they have one or both parents; all children share some things in common.

All children are gifts from God.

We must value children—all children—as the good gifts God intends them to be.

• *All children play.*

Playing is how children learn and explore. Playing is how children find out who they are. In their play you see them trying out different roles: discovering what they can do, seeing if they can do something better or higher or faster; seeing how things work, seeing what happens when they do something.

All children have the capacity to get on your nerves and then turn right around and capture your heart.

On one hand, a child can absolutely drive you crazy, and then love you back to sanity. She can make you feel like the most important person on earth. She can dissolve your pretense and demolish your smugness and self-importance. Her sadness makes you sad. Her smile can give you back life. She can bring sunshine to your day. She can make you feel important beyond your worth. She can make you want to be better than you are. And she can show you God, and His love, and His forgiveness.

All children have basic needs that must be met.

Each child needs and deserves healthy food and adequate clothing, shelter, health care, education, and safety.

All children have great potential.

The potential our children possess is almost unimaginable. Each child has something to give that will make his family, your church, and this world a better place—if adults just see to it that she gets the chance.

And, children are not just the future of our church and our country; they also contribute in the here and now. They bring questions, curiosity, and passion for discovery. They bring freshness, openness, energy, enthusiasm, joy, and happiness. They bring wonder, and awe, and the kind of faith that Jesus held up as our example.

All children need their families.

Whether that family is large or small—with many members or just the child and you—nothing on this earth is more important in a child's life than a loving family. And we understand that what is supremely best for a child is to be part of a Christian family who love and honor God.

All children need and deserve the nurturing and protection of their church family.

Families do not raise children in a vacuum. Children need the church and the love and support of the family of God. Children need to see what it means to be a Christian adult.

Christian adults must see and care for all children as family. This is expressed not just by writing checks to hire it done; not just with programs that say "take your child over here so we can get on with the important stuff of adults," but by involving themselves in the lives of girls and boys—looking, listening, laughing, loving, and appreciating God's children and His presence through their presence.

All children need good examples.

The most persuasive moral teaching we do as adults is by example. With children, as with all ages, the leader very much is the lesson.

All children need God.

Without question, we need to help children feel welcome in the family of faith, to feel they are a significant and important part of God's plan. Our job, in part, is to show them God in our lives, but it also is to be ready to answer their questions about becoming a Christian when God's Spirit begins to work in their lives. We need not push nor restrain, but to trust God in His timing.

Your Time Is Now

How much do you really understand about how children learn and why we engage them the way we do? About how children's workers build bridges to the entire family? How do any new understandings of Children's Sunday School ministry reshape your thinking about Sunday School as foundational strategy?

Knowing the Youth

Youth are ages 12-17 or in grades 7 through 12. If you are like most folks who relate to teenagers, you sometimes might say, "I don't need to be working with youth because I'm just not in touch with them." You are not alone. Those who work with teens, however, do need to make an effort to get in touch. For additional help see *Youth Sunday School for a New Century* (LifeWay Press, 1999).

Learn About Youth and Their World

Staying in touch may mean that you know where to find information about teens. Here are some important elements of youth culture about which to familiarize yourself.

- Learn about the "Top 40" songs. (But don't feel too proud of yourself for knowing the "Top 40" songs this week; they surely will change next week!)
- Learn about the top recording artists; but again, that changes frequently. Very few musicians enjoy longevity with students.
- Learn about movies. We may not want to encourage students to watch some current movies; but the reality is, they are watching them anyway.
- Learn about magazines. If the magazine targets itself to a certain age, then students two to three years younger probably are reading it.
- Learn about radio and television. Students still listen to around 28 to 30 hours a week of professionally recorded music on the radio or their stereos. And they watch around the same amount of TV programming each week.
- Learn how youth spend their money. In the United States, students between the ages of 12 and 20 spend an amount that is equal to half of the national defense budget.
- Learn about youth issues. Peer pressure, integrity, cheating, drugs/alcohol/tobacco, premarital sexual activity, family problems, violence, and many others issues are difficulties with which teens have to deal.
- Learn how youth feel, especially about themselves. If students feel good about themselves, they are less likely to participate in self-destructive behavior. However, even students who seem to have everything going for them sometimes have difficulty feeling good about themselves.

Characteristics of Youth

There is no such thing as a typical teenager. Each individual is a unique creation of God, influenced by heredity, environment, and personal experiences. Ours is a diverse nation, with a multitude of cultures, urban and rural settings, and backgrounds of wealth and poverty—with many levels in between. All of these factors influence an adolescent's development. By itself, chronological age does very little in helping us to understand teenagers, except to give us a general idea of where they are in school.

Physical Growth and Development

Physical growth and development is rapid in adolescence and plays a major role in all other areas of development. Natural physical development also varies greatly among teenagers of the same age. As much as a 6-year span in physical development can exist between a 13-year-old girl who matures quickly and a 13-year-old boy who is a late bloomer. While some adolescents may still be children physically, others already may be sexually mature adults.

The early teenage years bring growth and change at an alarming rate, second only to the rate of growth that takes place during infancy. Younger adolescents experience a physical growth spurt, including a doubling in weight, maturation of the reproductive organs, massive increases in production from the endocrine system, and development of secondary sex characteristics—such as breast development, facial and pubic hair growth, and voice changes.

These changes are known as puberty, and generally take place earlier for girls than for boys. Puberty in both sexes is taking place earlier than it did in the past. Today's teens also are growing taller and heavier than past generations.

Physical changes begin to slow during middle adolescence—usually around ages 14 to 16. Secondary sexual characteristics continue to develop; it is at this stage when teens begin to develop an intense sex drive. They also begin to regain some of the energy and excitement of childhood. Acne begins to trouble teens during middle adolescence, and this can be a factor in low self-esteem.

By late adolescence the physical changes are usually winding down. Girls have generally reached their maximum height and weight, with boys continuing to grow until they are approximately 21 years of age. Teens start to take more of an interest in their personal health at this time, and begin to take better care of their bodies.

Emotional Development

Adolescence is a time of great emotional upheaval, with many highs and lows along the way. In adolescence, teens begin to separate themselves from their parents and develop their own personal identity. This search for self is the primary psychological task of early adolescence. Teens begin to try on various roles in order to find one that fits. This is why a youth may act one way at home, a different way at school, and yet another at church. (In fact, the same youth may act totally different each time you see him at church!) A teen may be interested in drama one week and plumbing the next.

As a leader, you must be sensitive to this personal search and allow youth flexibility in their choices. Affirm their worth in Christ as they seek out their own self-worth.

The insecurity of early adolescence causes teens to be self-conscious. It is, however, generally a time of enthusiasm and friendliness and they have a strong desire to be involved. As they mature into middle adolescence, youth become more self-assured and independent. They do not shy away from the spotlight, but begin to seek recognition for their achievements as a means of affirmation.

Fear and love are two common emotions felt by teens in new ways. Childhood fears subside, but are replaced by fears of growing up, planning for the future, and facing new experiences. The reality and fear of death becomes a dominant theme in much of the writings and drawings of youth. With the increased incidence of suicide, violence, and death due to AIDS in the past decade, today's youth are perhaps more fearful of death than were previous generations.

While younger youth still are very self-centered, middle adolescents become more aware of those around them and are able to give of themselves and receive from others. A strong sense of security and self-confidence marks the period of late adolescence.

Intellectual Development

Adolescence brings with it a new way of thinking. Formal operational thinking allows youth to move from the concrete into the abstract. True scientific and abstract thought becomes possible during adolescence, allowing teens to solve complex problems related to past, present, and future situations. They can think through situations in a systematic fashion and arrive at realistic conclusions.

Adolescents want facts and proof, and they are unwilling to change their views unless they are given just cause to do so. Personal value systems influence these views. Early adolescents still tend to see situations in black and white, but they enjoy examining alternatives. They still hold idealistic views that influence their decisions, but they now are able to think through the consequences of their behaviors when asked.

Adolescents in the middle years begin asking deep questions and demanding logical answers. Older adolescents are capable of making mature decisions and are able to resolve conflicts based upon their own judgment and assessment of the facts. Teachers must be prepared to respond to questions consistently, intelligently, and truthfully. It is better to say to a teen, "I don't know, but I'll find out," than it is to try and make up a plausible response just to have an answer.

Younger adolescents still are very much self-centered. They often believe that everyone is looking at them and that everything they do, say, and wear has an impact on everyone else. They create and live a personal fable that leads them to deny the truth in many situations.

Social Development

Social life is highly important for youth and a key factor in their behavior. Going along with the crowd is extremely important for younger youth. They develop cliques of the same sex and are most comfortable in these small groups of trusted friends. This peer pressure peaks in middle adolescence and is less of a factor when youth have established their own identity and become comfortable with who they are.

Rebellious behavior begins as youth develop, often taking the form of rebellion against authority figures during middle adolescence. The need to separate from parents in order to become one's own person is a key factor in this rebellion.

Younger youth begin to identify their heroes and develop crushes on members of the opposite sex, with very little actual interaction. However, by middle adolescence the same-sex peer groups that characterize young teens begin to diminish in importance, with only a close circle of friends remaining. These teens begin joining groups or clubs, often reflecting values quite different from those of their parents.

A driver's license provides the necessary freedom to allow dating and greater social choices for the adolescent. Rebellion against authority lessens as teens are allowed to leave home more often on their own, and they become even more independent when they get a job and bring in their own income.

Spiritual Development

Spiritual life takes on an entirely new dimension during adolescence. Increased mental development has a tremendous impact on the spiritual lives of adolescents. As they begin to think for themselves, separate from parents, and question previously held beliefs and opinions, they begin to test their own faith and relationship to God.

The ability to think in abstract terms gives youth the opportunity to truly understand Christ's sacrifice. Terms such as *faith, love,* and *grace* are understood more fully. Youth are able to distinguish between right and wrong and they struggle to live up to those standards.

The emotional development taking place during adolescence often causes teens to judge themselves harshly when they know that they are not behaving in a Christlike manner. Adolescents have a hard time forgiving themselves, let alone accepting the forgiveness of God. Young adolescents are sure that their peers are aware of everything they have done and are judging them accordingly.

Middle adolescents begin searching the Bible for standards of behavior and begin praying for forgiveness when those standards are not met. The increased interest in members of the opposite sex at this point in life often causes youth to feel guilty or anxious. They become frustrated, as did the apostle Paul, by their inability to change undesirable behaviors.

Older adolescents are able to make and keep strong spiritual commitments. As their beliefs are constantly challenged they ask questions and express doubts about their own spiritual condition. This type of questioning leads to a mature faith, one that is tested and found true. Previously, faith has been largely based on feelings, which can change with the weather.

The spiritual struggle of adolescence is to develop a mature faith, based on the truth of God, accepted by faith.

Your Time Is Now

What do you need to learn about youth, youth culture, and youth ministry? How do you plan for your church's strategy to benefit from your new understandings?

Try this exercise: With each new insight or fact gained about youth/youth ministry, try to associate the information or insight with a specific youth in your church. This young person may represent any number of situations including a need, an opportunity, a threat, or a challenge. You may discover that one of the most important things you can do is become better acquainted and involved with your youth and youth leaders.

New Fact/Insight	Who Does This Represent in Our Church?
_____	_____
_____	
_____	_____
_____	
_____	_____
_____	

Knowing the Adults

People Are People

Young adults (ages 18-24) and adults (ages 25 and up) are the subject of "Knowing the Adults." Often the generic term *adult* will be used unless a specific reference to *young adults* is needed for clarity. For additional help, see *Adult Sunday School for a New Century* (Lifeway Press, 1999).

Adults share certain fundamental needs that bind them with all other adults. The Bible speaks to the most basic needs of adults. All adults seek to understand where they came from. All adults seek to understand where they fit into the world around them. All adults seek to understand where they are going in the future.

While adults share certain fundamental needs, each adult is unique. Despite the uniqueness of each person, adults do have many common characteristics, experiences, and interests. Adults can be grouped in many ways: baby boomers, retirees, parents with or without children, singles, gifted, and so forth. These common traits provide handles to give us a better idea of how to reach, minister to, and meet the needs of adults in a world that changes by the very minute.

The Generational Influence

Just as individuals develop particular traits and personalities as they grow through the stages of life, groups that move through time together develop traits and personalities that distinguish them from other groups. Church leaders need to look at the generational perspective and how life is influenced by the life experiences of each generation.

People who make up a generation share a common age location in history with common attitudes and common behavior patterns. They tend to react to life in similar ways and show distinctive differences from people who make up other generations.

Understanding generations is helpful for understanding how to teach and minister to young adults (ages 18-24) and adults (ages 25 and up) in Sunday School. Because a generation is anchored in time, adults who make up a generation often have similar life experiences. A generation gap, therefore, develops because each generation sees life differently from other generations.

Yet no adult will model every characteristic of one generation. Adults born close to the end of one generation or the beginning of another may exemplify characteristics of either generation—or both. Because sociologists do not agree across the board on the birth years of each generation, it is difficult to assign hard-and-fast anchors for each generation. Birth years used to begin and end an age cohort should be viewed as suggestive rather than specific and absolute.

Based on these qualifications, five adult generations live today. Each can be assigned a name to describe its personality, as well as characteristics and events related to that segment of people. Each generation redefines the stage of life it occupies. (The following descriptors are adapted from more comprehensive information found in *Vision, Variety, & Vitality: Teaching Today's Adult Generations*, by Louis B. Hanks.)[2]

The PowerBuilder Generation (born 1901-1925)

PowerBuilders comprise the firstborn generation of the 20th century. They grew up being seen as good, constructive, and deserving. Also called the "G.I. generation," as

[2] Louis B. Hanks, *Visition, Variety, & Vitality: Teaching Today's Adults* [Nashville: Convention Press, 1996].

adults they brought home victory in World War II. Community was valued over self. Teamwork was stressed, creating a powerful peer-directed generation.

With a positive future ready to build the best and the biggest, they made colossal achievements—propelled the United States into modern superpower status and brought economic growth, military triumph, and technological progress. The infusion of this generation's unusual collective energy has changed a negative perception of old age to a positive one.

PowerBuilders are the church's most loyal financial givers and tithers among today's generations. They prefer traditional approaches to Bible study and worship, respond well to teachers who use a lecture approach, enjoy activities that involve them with other PowerBuilders, and willingly make personal sacrifices to benefit their church or class. But they dislike change or breaking traditions.

The PeaceMaker Generation (born 1926-1944)

The PeaceMaker generation's boundaries are sandwiched between the patriotic, get-it-done PowerBuilder heroes of World War II and the fiery passions of the self-absorbed PathFinders who silenced the PeaceMakers' setting of much of the national agenda. This "silent generation" learned to adapt to the issues of those who immediately preceded and followed them, developed a keen sense of humanity and a tender social consciousness, and emerged with a strong sense of "other-directedness" and inclusion. Oppression—whether linked to governments, corporations, marriages, or the treatment of people—moved this generation. Their tendency toward other-directedness and their reaction to oppressive issues were expressed in pluralistic attitudes, public service, the civil rights movement, the women's movement, and the environmental movement.

Early marriages and families ultimately led to an epidemic in divorce. This generation's second wave spawned the highest rates of abortion, divorce, and broken families of all 20th-century generations. They called the materialism and secularism of the previous generation into question even though they greatly benefited from it. The second wave led the emerging PathFinder generation down the road to rebellion.

PeaceMakers bring strong relational skills to the learning setting, enjoy intergenerational Bible study classes, often prefer inductive logic or learning as a way to explore and apply knowledge, may accept secular humanism, and test truth by practical consequences. They are open to discussing new ideas, a trait that can be a liability when they tolerate too much diversity in beliefs.

PeaceMakers are excellent facilitators of the learning process. Creative and artistic, they also enjoy music. Their dominant learning style is auditory, often reflecting a preference for discussion and debate. They value structured learning experiences and tend to develop highly organized class structures and roles. Also, they may be intense pragmatists who value social action that leads to change in culture.

The PathFinder Generation (born 1945-1963)

With the rise of the PathFinders, also known as "baby boomers," culture shifted from the outer world of a secularized and institutionalized society to an inner world of ideas, values, and spiritual awakening. PathFinders see themselves as an authentic generation due to the analysis they have endured during five decades.

PathFinders grew up in a time when moms stayed home, gas station attendants pumped gas and cleaned windshields, and cars were chrome-laden machines.

Relatives lived nearby, drugstores had a soda fountain, Vacation Bible School ran for two weeks, and TV burst onto the scene. PathFinders turned into Beaver Cleavers, rebellious hippies, bran-eating dieters, corporate yuppies, and righteous puritans.

While much divides the generation, there is significant common ground. PathFinders, the first generation to grow up with TV, are one of the most self-absorbed generations in American history. Since the end of World War II, they have been the cultural and spiritual focal point of American society. Unlike their PowerBuilder parents' desire to build a society, their mission is to purify society.

They sampled religion from a foundation of prayer and Bible reading in the public schools to the Jesus movement to evangelical expressions of faith to New Age. This strong-willed generation has unyielding opinions about all issues and may see its best contributions to society come late in life as wisdom and vision.

PathFinders are changing churches in North America—music, drama, and preaching reflect personal involvement and idealism; worship is personal, visual. With little concern for denominations, they seek truth wherever they can.

Intense idealists, PathFinders value the world of ideas, vision, and principles. They desire to shape cultural and moral issues, demonstrate a compelling search for spiritual satisfaction, prefer deductive logic over inductive experimentation, and readily accept biblical truth but are slow in putting truth into action. Shaped by the visual medium of TV, they respond favorably to visual teaching approaches and require a high level of personal choices in learning methods and study topics and materials. They expect quality religious education for their children.

The PaceSetter Generation (born 1964-1981)

PaceSetters entered the world during a time of social revolution, bitter war, a divided nation, self-immersed parents, disintegrating homes, racial riots, schools with unclear missions, and unwanted pregnancies dismissed by abortion. They were teenagers during an extreme and harsh period for youth, a time marked by low test scores and high rates of suicide, crime, and substance abuse.

PaceSetters are an unjustly maligned generation. They have deviated from norms set by other generations. First impressions of PaceSetters by older generations have been both negative and unfair. Typical labels include "baby busters," "slackers," "whiners," "grunge kids," and "generation Xers." They entered young adulthood as bicycle messengers, speeding pizza delivery drivers, inner-city "crack" gang members, investment bankers, computer hackers, and young professionals with goatees. These survivors view themselves as self-reliant, realistic, quick, practical, nonconformist, streetwise, and able to understand the game of life. Email, voice mail, and VCRs are the toys of choice.

To be a Pacesetter is to be a leader. From Desert Storm heroes to online Internet surfers to friendship valuers to family protectors, PaceSetters do what they do best—set the pace of American life in the 21st century. Practical in their faith and willing to take a stand for what they believe, PaceSetters have led in movements such as CrossSeekers™ and True Love Waits®. They are adept at reaching people who feel alienated from the church and society.

The Young Adult Division in churches (ages 18-24) is made up primarily of PaceSetters. They look for church leaders who are not afraid of speaking the truth plainly. These young adults are limited in their foundation of Bible knowledge and their respect for Scriptures. They are intense realists who rely on fact, reject the

impractical and visionary, and learn best from looking at the lives of biblical characters rather than "abstract" theology. They may view the Bible study leader as a parent. They often desire love, attention, and direction from leaders. They are receptive to the corrective dimension of Bible study and are open to changing behaviors. They may question their need for God, but are interested in exploring the Bible for practical and relevant handles for life and action-oriented ministry.

They often prefer a structured, purposeful learning setting and a multimedia approach. Their learning style is a blend of auditory, visual, and kinesthetic.

The New PowerBuilders (born 1982-2000)

The new PowerBuilder generation, also called the "millennial generation," is the fifth and last generation of the 20th century. Their membership is still growing, and most of this generation could live past America's tricentennial in 2076. This generation represents the last high school graduating class of this century.

Parents of some new PowerBuilders have made a strong effort to raise children who are smart, powerful, dutiful and who have positive attitudes, rational minds, and selfless team virtues. Other parents have set out to produce children who will experience the love and care they never received, children who will not have to grow up with difficult experiences. In strikingly similar ways, this generation parallels the attributes associated with their grandparents and great-grandparents, the PowerBuilders of the first decades of this century.

Health care, family, and education are high priorities for this generation. New PowerBuilders will grow up in a world stressing more values, structure, and protection. One major sign of the new valuing of children is the decline of abortion. While abortions in the 1980s hovered over the 1.5 million mark each year, the abortion rate peaked in 1981. The 1992 abortion rate was the lowest since 1976. The number of abortions per year is expected to continue to decline.

Because the experiences that influence this generation are still formative, it is difficult to develop a picture of influences that shape this generation. Yet, what is happening in society today ultimately will influence churches and leaders as they develop educational ministries and choose appropriate teaching methods and approaches for enabling this generation to grow spiritually.

Because new PowerBuilders will dominate the Young Adult Division (ages 18-24) in a few years, church leaders must begin now to prepare for how they will reach and engage this generation in life-transforming Bible study.

Being an Adult

Most people pass through some common experiences in life. Events common to most adults often happen at different rather than at predictable points in life. For example, adults in the past moved from high school right into college or into chosen careers and professions. They spent the majority of their adult lives working in one job or career, retiring at a predictable age, and moving out of the mainstream of the working world.

Today many young adults postpone higher education for a few years and then enter academic settings, only to return a few years later to study for an entirely different career. In fact, with the changes in technology and the corresponding disappearance of types of jobs and careers each year, many young adults will face more than one return visit to an academic or vocational training setting to prepare for an entirely new career.

Many adult experiences are predictable ones that can be addressed systematically by leaders of young adults and adults in Sunday School. Each experience will be "filtered" through the generational portrait. How teachers and other leaders address the needs will be balanced by how each generation moves through life. Consider some common experiences most adults have today.

Leave Home.—At some point, adults must break psychological ties with parents and other family members, choose careers, enter work relationships, and adjust to independent living. Handling peer relationships takes on new meaning. They learn to manage a home and time while discovering how to solve problems and manage stress.

Stand Alone.—Most adults want to become independent. They are comfortable making decisions for themselves and do not want to return to dependency on parents or other family members. Many are in the process of selecting a mate and beginning a family. They begin to settle in work and possibly move up the career ladder. Becoming involved in community life is common at this stage too. These young adults learn to consume wisely and some even buy their own homes. Like adults in every stage, they learn how to solve new problems and deal with additional stress.

Move Forward.—By the time adults move past the 30-year-old point in life, most are searching for personal values. They probably have made progress in careers. Some postpone marriage until now while others are in the process of having children or adjusting to the fact that their children are growing up. They may have put down roots and achieved a "permanent" home.

Reflect.—Many adults who are approaching 40 struggle with their identities and may search for new meaning in life. They reassess marriage and reexamine work. Some learn to relate to teenage children and to aging parents at the same time. This may cause them to reassess personal priorities and values. Life changes cause some to face the adjustment to single life.

Get Settled Again.—Adults often have to make adjustments in life. They launch children from home and adjust to an empty nest at the same time. Many become more involved in community life through active participation in local concerns. Some face increased demands of older parents or of children who return home. Some who exit the work world early learn to manage leisuretime. They may face economic changes as they try to manage their budgets to support college-age children and ailing parents. Some may adjust to being single.

Approach Retirement.—Age brings adjustments to new health problems. Many learn to deepen personal relationships not only with family and friends but also with spouses. As they prepare for retirement, they may expand avocation interests and plan ways to finance new leisuretime activities. Many adjust to the loss of their mates as aging brings early death for some adults.

Retire.—Adults at this stage disengage from paid work, often reassessing their finances and future. They become more concerned with personal health care. Changes in health may prompt a search for new achievement outlets. Retirees must manage leisuretime. Some have to adjust to having a spouse around the house more often. Many older adults search for meaning, especially when they lose a spouse and face the adjustment of being single. Many come to grips with death in a personal way.

Recycle.—In recent years, research by many sociologists suggests that adults may retire more than once—possibly several times—depending on health, financial needs, even on the desire to do something different. In this stage, adults reevaluate life and how they will live out their remaining years. They may search for opportunities to continue investing themselves in the generations coming behind them. Some return to the workforce part-time or begin a new full-time career. Many seek new hobbies and interests or invest themselves in mentoring younger adults. They also adjust to physical limitations and to conditions and circumstances they may find unfamiliar.

Relating to Young Adults, Ages 18-24

Young adults have little time or interest in organizations and institutions, particularly those with little sense of purpose or mission. Some avoid "traditional" churches.

Today's young adults possess an intentionality in life. They want to invest themselves in missions activities and service opportunities that make a difference in the lives of those around them and to make the world a better place for themselves and their children. Their sense of who they are often is related to the actions they take to make their world better.

Many young adults, both collegians and those who enter the workforce after high school, feel that the core issue of adulthood is freedom—freedom to drink, to have premarital sex, to live a lifestyle without hindrances, particularly limitations established by parents and church. But the lifestyles of these young adults usually lead to physical, emotional, spiritual, and even psychological disaster. Dealing with issues and demands of life, including how to live out one's faith, is part of becoming an adult. They are open to mentoring relationships, which includes spiritual matters.

Most young adults do not want to be told how to live. Spiritual growth occurs best as they discover for themselves what the Bible says about living out their faith.

Many young adults, brought up by self-absorbed parents and day-care providers, lean strongly toward family values and concerns held by pre-boomer generations. Yet, they have received conflicting messages about marriage and family from their role models. They search for ways to reduce the threats of crime, drugs, and violence.

Young adults, disillusioned by the shallow Christian living of some church members who do not link their words on Sunday with how they live during the week, seek religious experiences that bring about change in a person and search for leaders of integrity whose lifestyles and values match their words. They search for opportunities to become leaders—they want to be a part of decision-making processes and desire significant roles in planning what happens in their Bible study groups.

Your Time Is Now

Paradigm shifts such as the following will be even more apparent as we move into the 21st century:

In some communities hospitals, reflecting a growing recognition of the importance of new mothers' receiving immediate support after a baby's birth, are enlisting senior adult women who also are mothers. The assignment for seniors? To be a role model and mentor to a new mom. What great potential exists not only to nurture a physically and emotionally healthy child and family, but also to build a uniquely satisfying relationship between women of different generations!

How do such ways of thinking about age groups challenge you as you anticipate Sunday School in the 21st century? What is your church doing to build mentoring relationships between the generations—relationships that support both the individual and the family?

Knowing About People from Other Cultures or Ethnic Backgrounds

The latter part of the 20th century has brought a significant shift in cultural issues. While Americans 30 years ago sought complete integration of culture groups, people over the past 10 years have moved more toward cultural uniqueness. Even in Canada, where 2 distinct culture groups—Anglocanadians and Francocanadians—dominate society, the tendency still is toward cultural distinction. The Multicultural Act of 1971 in Canada designated that nation as multicultural in a bilingual framework.

The perspective has not changed. American cultural patterns have moved more in the Canadian direction than toward a complete melting-pot identity. Despite anti-segregation laws and equal-housing opportunities, culture groups are establishing their identities. Diversity has not lessened the desire for celebrating heritage and roots.

How do we address the changing identity of America? We must see the people around us as they want to be seen and respond as Christ would respond. We must face the ethnic challenge with openness and intentionality, and an understanding of certain cultural perspectives—transcultural, multicultural, and cross-cultural—can help.

Providing facilities for language and culture groups is one step toward "Judea and Samaria" today; for example, one church in Nashville, Tennessee, has Korean and Egyptian congregations meeting in its facilities as separate church groups. Churches may design multicultural ministries that meet the needs of several culture groups within the larger context of the church; for example, a church in Miami could offer Hispanic classes and English-speaking classes within the same department for adults in a designated age range.

Transcultural ministries are those that are general in nature and can be applied effectively with adaptation by its leaders. The principles on which the ministry is built will apply broadly across people groups and can be fleshed out in target-specific ways based on how the culture groups think, act, feel, and respond.

Cross-cultural ministries are those that apply essentially as they are to all people, regardless of language or culture group. Although carrying out a ministry is easier when everyone speaks the same language, sometimes a ministry may involve a number of people from many backgrounds. Room in the Inn, a ministry to homeless people, is one example. Room in the Inn may have several culture groups represented, but not everyone in the group speaks English or another common language. Thus, the common "language" becomes the ministry itself.

Cultural sensitivity to methods should not result in culture-altered values. The Bible is clear that the truths of God's Word cannot be altered or changed to meet the whims of changing society. In fact, the Bible is a cross-cultural book that provides absolute standards for life. Love for one another and forgiveness, for example, know no bounds.

As people continue to move from one part of the world to another, the call for cultural sensitivity must be heard by the 21st-century church. How will churches adapt to changes in the cultural portrait?

Does your church see the fields? They are white unto harvest—and have been for a long time.

Knowing About People Who Are HIV Positive

AIDS, or Acquired Immune Deficiency Syndrome, is a growing concern for many Americans, and rightfully so. Not only is AIDS a serious medical concern, this illness also has critical ethical and moral connotations as well. Although many people have died from tainted blood transfusions that contained the HIV virus (human immune deficiency virus) or were born with the virus because the mother was infected, AIDS generally is associated with homosexual lifestyles or contaminated syringes used with illegal drugs.

While we do not and should not affirm deviant or immoral lifestyles, each person and church is challenged to learn how to reach out in love to people with AIDS. While the example of Jesus indicates that the sin should be addressed, so should the sinner, but in such a way that the person is told the good news of transformation by the power of Christ.

Sunday School leaders must wrestle with how to minister to all people for whom Christ died, including those who have AIDS and their families. This is a life issue to which the gospel speaks. Jesus ministered to people with deviant lifestyles or incurable illnesses: the lepers, the woman at the well, and even Zacchaeus who was a social outcast by virtue of his politics, profession, and lifestyle. How will we respond to this contemporary plague and to those who suffer from it ?

Transmission of the Virus

According to the National Center for Disease Control, transmission of the HIV virus takes place in one of four ways:

- sexual activity (heterosexual as well as homosexual)
- intravenous drug use, as drug needles and syringes are shared with an infected person
- blood transfusion
- blood transmission during pregnancy, labor, or delivery.

Some Precautions to Take

Considering the means of transmission, HIV-infected persons may be participants in regular group. Nevertheless, here are some precautions that need to be taken.

- Consider everyone's blood as potentially contagious. Cover cuts and scrapes where bleeding occurs.
- When giving medical attention, no matter how minor it may seem, use disposable latex gloves.
- Use disposable towels and a bleach solution to clean up blood spills
- Disposable items in contact with blood need to be placed in a plastic bag, tied closed, and placed in a trash container.
- Clothing in contact with blood should be properly laundered or dry cleaned.
- After performing any of the above procedures, wash hands thoroughly with soap and water.

With preschoolers and younger children, additional precautions may be needed.

- Keep an infected child's toys and bottles away from others.
- Do thorough cleanup of any infected items and areas.

Knowing About People with Special Needs

Special Education covers a broad field, including mental retardation, visual impairment, learning disability, gifted, physical disability, multiple disabilities, and other areas like deaf/hearing impairments, behavior disorders, speech impairments, autism, and brain injuries.

An estimated 54 million Americans have disabilities. An estimated 10 to 20 percent of a community's population will included exceptional people. For any 1 person with disabilities, 2 to 4 other family members are affected in some way. Many of these people are unchurched and do not know Christ. Yet more than 90 percent of all churches do not have any type of purposeful ministry in special education.

Steps to Beginning a Special Education Ministry

Beginning a special education ministry requires preparation and planning. Here are the steps to take.

1. *Pray.*—This is the Lord's work. It is important to consult Him about it.

2. *Talk to the church ministry staff.*—Share your vision of special education ministry. Secure their support.

3. *Establish a planning group.*—Don't try to work alone. A group of coworkers can provide you support and strengthen the effort.

4. *Survey the building.*—Determine whether the building is accessible to persons with physical disabilities. Assess what modifications will be required.

5. *Survey the membership and the community.*—Church members can help identify prospects Some special-needs persons are in your community waiting for someone to express interest in them.

6. *Contact local agencies.*—Learn what local services are provided for special-needs persons. As your ministry expands beyond Sunday morning Bible study, your church may be able to provide ministry that supplements or complements what is available elsewhere.

7. *Recruit and train leaders.*—Some people in your church will have the interest but lack the skills. Help to alleviate their fears and develop their sifts by providing training.

8. *Remove barriers.*—Possible barriers to be addressed may be physical, psychological, stereotypical, or theological ones.

9. *Promote the ministry.*—No one will know what you have available until you tell them.

10. *Visit prospects.*—You discovered prospects. Nothing can make an impression like a personal visit to the person and his family.

11. *Begin the ministry.*—All the preparation and planning will lose its value if you do not have a beginning time for the ministry.

12. *Evaluate.*—Determine what is working and what is not. Make adjustments as needed.

For more information about beginning and maintaining a ministry to special needs persons see *A Place for Everyone: A Guide for Special Education Bible Teaching-Reaching Ministry* by Athalene McNay (Convention Press, 1997).

A Philosophy for Special Education Bible Study Groups

Churches beginning to reach out to persons with special needs may struggle with what approach to take for most effective response. Two basic approaches are mainstreaming and separation.

Mainstream the person with an extra worker, if necessary to meet particular needs, into existing groups of persons without a handicapping condition. A separate, specialized department should be provided only for those who are mentally retarded with disruptive behavior or extremely low comprehension. Other mentally retarded persons, up through 18 years of age, can be mainstreamed with these prerequisites: a receptive leader who is willing to learn how to work with mentally retarded persons; a sensitized class of peers; and competent coworkers.

More often than not preschoolers with mental retardation are more like their regular peers than unlike. It is easiest with this age group to adapt regular preschool curriculum resources to lower functioning levels. More one-on-one attention may be required.

Mainstreaming preschoolers where appropriate is an excellent method for both providing modeling for those who have disabilities and for sensitizing the other class members to persons who have disabilities. A helper may be required until there is an adjustment by the other class members to those who have disabilities. In the same way, the special-needs person will need some time to adjust to other members of the class.

Working with children is much like working with preschoolers. In teaching-learning settings, adapting activities to lower functioning levels will help ensure that these children learn biblical truths and apply relevant truths to everyday living. Knowing the individual and his or her interests, strengths, weaknesses, and family will add to the spiritual nurture provided.

Mainstreaming youth with mental retardation can be difficult without a positive, receptive leader, sensitized peers, and an additional helper for the period of adjustment. Youth can appreciate being "different" and can more easily accept differences of abilities in other youth if there is appropriate sensitizing.

Organization Guidelines for Special Education Departments and Classes

- In most cases, the person who is higher functioning should be mainstreamed in the regular department of his or her own age.
- Special departments or classes—versus mainstreaming—are needed for mentally retarded persons in these circumstances: (1) the mentally retarded person has disruptive behavior and needs to have it brought under control; (2) the person's intellectual comprehension is so low that the teaching of biblical truths in his or her regular age-group class would not be appropriate. These departments and classes require qualified leaders and suitable space.
- Special departments may be comprised of a variety of groupings, made up of all functioning levels, ages, and causes. Subgroupings should be developed within the department for certain activities.
- Departments for those who are extremely low functioning or who have multiple disabilities should have no more than two members per teacher.

Enlisting Leaders for Special Education Classes and Departments

Qualifications for special education leaders with mentally retarded persons are the same as those required for leaders in other age-group classes and departments, including a deep concern for the spiritual needs of the mentally retarded persons, and a basic understanding of mental retardation, its causes, and its effects upon the individual and the family.

- A department with a limited enrollment requires only two leaders: a director and a teacher, both a male and a female, who serve as role models and are available for emergency situations.
- In departments comprised of persons of varying levels and ability and wide differences in chronological ages, special groupings may be desirable within the department for part of the session. Special groupings should be based on functioning levels rather than age. Such departments still require at least one man and one woman on the leadership team.

Your Time Is Now

1. What knowledge do you have of other cultures and ethnic groups in your area? Are you making effective user of demographic surveys and other profile and statistical information? *Assignment:* Check with your director of missions for up-to-date data and for help in understanding the implications for your church and for strategic ministry.

2. Church and Sunday School leaders, including the pastor, have agreed that Sunday School is their foundational strategy for accomplishing the work of the Great Commission. What implications does this decision have for—

• ministering to persons who are HIV positive and their families? Offering training and/or developing written guidelines for all leaders?

• providing for individuals with special needs? Reaching out to members of their families?

• knowing the people we teach and reach?

• discovering new people?

Planning and Organizing the Strategy

servant

The first time I remember hearing the word *strategic* was in the movie "Strategic Air Command," starring Jimmy Stewart. The story line was built around the important work of the United States Air Force SAC unit to maintain the safety of the nation.

Strategic. I like the word. Even the sound carries a certain swagger. It gives me a feeling of confidence and assurance. When someone says, "That was a strategic move," I sense that something important has taken place. On the other hand, when someone says about another person, "He is not a strategic thinker," that causes me concern.

Soon after coming to lead the Sunday School Group in 1994, I discovered that much of my time and energy would be devoted to strategic planning. In fact, the first move toward strengthening evangelism in the Sunday School grew out of one of the key initiatives in the 1995 strategic planning process, which focused on "reclaiming the birthright of Sunday School." We have seen this strategic initiative come to life in the FAITH Sunday School Evangelism Strategy, which is being implemented in hundreds of churches around the world.

The Sunday School Group is blessed with many strategic thinkers. One of the best is Rick Edwards, director of the Adult Sunday School Ministry Department. The department's assignment encompasses curriculum development as well as field service training events for adults. As department director, Rick has been instrumental in implementing the improvements in the curriculum series published for adults in recent years and will provide important leadership in future curriculum developments.

I have particularly enjoyed my association with Rick. He is a most affable person; it is obvious that he genuinely cares for people. He is what I consider a "strategic thinker." He is neither quick to speak nor to demand his own way. I have noticed in the myriad of meetings during these four years of ministry together, that, when Rick speaks, he does so with keen insight.

Recently he sent me an email message in which he shared some ideas about a paradigm shift he saw for the new century. The following principles that he offered were intended to foster dialogue and move us toward a new way of thinking about how to develop leaders in the future:

Principle 1: Leadership development should be the core emphasis of the Sunday School Group in the 21st-century design. Sunday School in the new century will continue to be a strategy that depends upon the leader in the local church—the end-leader. We have assumed that, if we provide great Bible study content through our resources, a Sunday School will grow. While we have known intuitively that this is not true, we have focused our resources increasingly on delivering Bible study content rather than on providing leadership assistance. The future will require us to find ways to address the unique needs of the end-leader.

Principle 2: Listening is part of our work. Listening to the needs of the end-leader is not

Rick Edwards, director, Adult Sunday School Ministry Department, is a leader who is willing to think strategically and to stretch the parameters.

Think about some of the
strategic thinkers in your
church. How can you take
advantage of their skill and
insight in planning your
Sunday School ministry?

a peripheral aspect of our work; it is the core. Training should be provided to our staff that will equip them to be better listeners. The end-leader has to be heard.

Principle 3: Leadership is part of our work. In order to provide solutions and meet needs, we must be leaders ourselves. We must understand the work in which we are engaged and be able to speak to the needs of end-leaders with credibility. We've got to be able to say, "Here's how we're doing it." This may mean limiting the number of events in a year that require our consultants to be out of town so they can be actively and consistently engaged in leadership roles in their local church.

Principle 4: The end-leader is our primary network. Other networks are important and useful but are secondary to the need to work directly with the end-leader. Resources should be allocated that develop and enhance the end-leader network.

Principle 5: Communication does not always require travel. The end-leader pool is too large to visit in person through travel. Other forms of communication must be better utilized. The leader guide should become a stronger communication tool that provides more than Bible study content. Leadership resources in print format should be given to end-leaders as an added value to using our resources. Emerging technologies will make video-conferencing and distance learning strong options to travel. The Internet offers unlimited opportunities. The phone is still a great way to communicate.

I was moved as I read Rick's email message—not just because the ideas he espoused were different; but I had a sense that what he was sharing was for him much more than rhetoric. Although his major assignment is the production of Bible study curriculum, Rick could see that effective Sunday School ministry was dependent on leadership development. The best materials without well-equipped leaders to use them would not achieve our mission.

Rick used a word that I had not heard before: *end-leader.* I knew what an end-user was but this was a fresh, new way of referring to those people who could make a difference in everything related to Sunday School.

Who are the "end-leaders" in
your Sunday School ministry?
What actions can you plan
that will help them develop
into even more effective
leaders?

And I liked his thoughts on listening. We need to move from a "telling stance" to one that gives attention to what others are saying. Is that really significant? I think it is. Our ability to listen to each other is imperative for doing quality Sunday School ministry in the 21st century.

Regarding communication, Rick's ideas are revolutionary. LifeWay Christian Resources has operated from a stance of placing consultants across the nations to provide leadership training. This needs to continue. However, the work has grown so large, it is impossible to meet the gigantic needs that exist in all the churches. We need to continue our search to find the best ways to communicate simply and clearly.

Strategy. Strategic thinking. Problem-solvers. Innovative leaders. Effective end-leaders. I like all that!

Years ago, early Sunday School ministry leader P. E. Burroughs wrote about Sunday School as strategy. He stated, "This school constitutes a wing of the conquering army, which is to bring this world under the sway of Jesus Christ. This school is not only to be missionary; it is to be evangelistic. It is an institution conducted in His name who gathered unprecedented multitudes to His teaching ministry. Socrates, Plato and others devoted their teaching ministry to the select few; Jesus of Nazareth assembled and taught the multitudes."[3]

That is what we need—a strategy that will help us do what Jesus has called us to do. Develop plans with that in mind.

[3] P.E. Burroughs, *Building a Successful Sunday School* (Fleming and Revell Co., 1921), 18.

The Clock Is Ticking

A new world is coming. We are on the verge of an experience in time that only a small percentage of people ever witness. We stand on the threshold of a new millennium. Such an event is cause for reflection and anticipation. What will the next chapter of human history contain?

Consider these factors that likely will influence what takes place in the 21st century. The list is not all inclusive. You will know of other factors. And who knows what new factors are over the horizon?

Tension between certainty and uncertainty.—Like the birth of the 20th century, the beginning of the 21st century will be a world moving from certainty to uncertainty. To some degree we know what is; we don't know what will be. So we enter this new era with confidence tempered by uncertainty of the unknown.

Technological innovations.—The new world will be a world of high-velocity technological changes that will move human life to a new level of existence.

Continued new ideas.—During the first half of the 20th century we saw our world changed through countless new ideas, institutions, movements, themes, and worldviews. The new world of the 21st century will continue to produce new ideas that challenge us both for good and bad.

Generational changes.—A new way of thinking about people has emerged to identify and describe people: a generational point of view. The vast winds of generational change will continue to create broad, structural changes in American society.

Cultural diversity.—The new world will be a world of rich diversity in people groups. For example, projections are that by the year 2005, nonwhite races will comprise more than 30 percent of the United States population.

A shift in age and gender.—Our new world will be an "older" world as life-expectancy rates increase. Women will be a vital force in politics, business, and other professions.

Family life renewal.—The new world will be one in which the positive nurturing and protection of the family must take center stage again. Christians in the 21st century have an obligation to trumpet the call for sound and healthy families.

Focus on young adults.—The new world we face will be one in which the well-being of our young adults (born 1964 to 1981) must be valued as never before. This generation, often unjustly maligned, will emerge as tomorrow's leaders.

Protection of the youngest.—The new world will face the challenge of providing for the well-being of the young as never before. The challenge will be to avoid the rise of individualism and self-centeredness that almost decimated the generation of children born during the 1960s and 1970s.

A war of the world of ideas.—This new world will be celebrated by those who win the battle between biblical faith and secular thinking. The critical wars of the future will be fought not with machines but with compelling ideas.

Indeed, a new world is coming. In this new world, how will Sunday School as strategy respond to the opportunities that come with challenges? Sunday School remains strong and stands prepared to assist the church as it seeks to meet the challenges and embrace the opportunities.

This will not happen haphazardly. Sunday School is a strategy—a plan. Like any other carefully chosen strategy Sunday School must be worked annually, monthly, and weekly.

Benefits of Annual Planning

Resolutions, good intentions, visions, and dreams often have gone unfulfilled because plans were never made to bring them to fruition. We know we need to plan and we say we will plan. But when all is said and done, more has been said than done. We often just do not get around to planning.

Annual planning is hard work. It takes time and energy. But the results will save you time later and bring more positive results. Planning ways to implement the strategy turns out to be worth the time and effort. Consider these benefits of developing an annual plan.

Annual planning is an intentional design to close the gap between where your church is and where it wants to be.—To do that, two essential questions need to be answered: Where are we now? Where do we want to be when this year is over?

Annual planning gives you the opportunity to solve potential problems.—Some leaders are so absorbed in "putting out fires" that they cannot give attention to preventing them. During annual planning you have the opportunity to prevent "fires" by directing your energies toward a desired outcome.

Annual planning allows you to learn from the past, better understand the present, and move purposefully toward the future.—The present may be better understood if it is viewed in the context of the past. Current actions, based on lessons learned in the past and carried out in the context of the present reality, can successfully move the church toward a desired outcome in the future.

Annual planning helps leaders to be more productive.—Results that are planned for are more likely to occur. Energies and resources can be channeled to accomplish mission, vision, and goals.

Annual planning allows you to celebrate accomplishments.—An annual planning event becomes an opportunity to celebrate the accomplishments of the past year. You may want to determine ways you can share the successes with the congregation so they too can enjoy the celebration.

Annual planning helps you to anticipate future leadership and space needs.—In planning for future growth, you can anticipate expanded leadership needs, including replacing leaders lost through attrition. Space needs and space adjustments also can be anticipated, avoiding having to react to a crisis situation later.

Annual planning helps bring about balanced work.—Leaders need to determine whether they are doing balanced work or are giving too much attention to one area to the detriment of another. Unbalanced work will eventually deplete the strength of your strategy and the church.

Annual planning helps plans become "ours" rather than "theirs."—People likely will have more ownership for plans they have helped develop than for plans that have been developed by someone else, which they are expected to implement.

Annual planning helps you make the best use of resources.—God's resources are unlimited. We can call on Him for power, strength, wisdom, and leadership. However, human resources are limited, and we need to use them in the best way possible. Planning helps you be a good steward of resources.

Annual planning makes happier leaders.—Annual planning brings a sense of purpose and direction to the work. When leaders feel part of something purposeful and can see direction and results in their work, they are happier.

Conducting an Annual Planning Event

Who Does Annual Planning?

Annual planning is done best by a team. In many churches the team that develops the annual detail of the strategy may be called the Sunday School Planning Team. If Sunday School has age-group divisions, the team may consist of the pastor, educational staff, general officers, and division directors.

If Sunday Schools only has age-group departments, the planning team may consist of the pastor, educational staff, general officers, and department directors. In smaller churches, the team may include the pastor, Sunday School director, and a worker from each class or department. Some churches include the Discipleship director on the team.

Whatever the composition, this team leads out in the planning process and formulates details of the strategy at an annual planning retreat. Because these leaders are in close touch with people in the classes or departments or Bible study groups where the work of is to be implemented, the plans have greater potential for broader acceptance. It becomes more than the preacher's plan or even the group's plan.

Get Ready for the Event

Take these steps to get ready for your annual planning event.

Set the date.—How early should annual planning be done? Many churches do their annual planning in the spring for the church year that begins in the fall. Two factors will influence the time. First, do annual planning far enough in advance of the new year to affect organizational, space, and leadership needs. Second, prior to the annual planning event, complete the enlistment of the people who will be leaders during the new year so that the appropriate leaders can be involved in plans.

Determine the schedule.—Several schedules are possible for an annual planning event. Consider these options; choose the one most suitable for your situation.

- **Friday**

6:00 p.m.	Supper
7:00	Welcome
	What We Hope to Accomplish
	Agenda Review
7:15	Devotional on the Great Commission
	Prayer for God's Leadership
	Sharing the Vision for Our Sunday School Strategy
8:00	A Look At Where We Are—Evaluation
9:30	Dismiss

- **Saturday**

8:00 a.m.	Breakfast
8:45	Devotional
9:00	A Look at What Our Evaluation Shows Us—Needs
10:30	Break
10:45	Setting Priorities and Determining Goals
12:00 p.m.	Lunch
12:45	Building Action Plans
3:00	Committing Our Plans to God
3:30	Dismiss and Head Home

- **Saturday morning—afternoon**

8:30 a.m.	Continental Breakfast
9:00	Welcome
	What We Hope to Accomplish
	Agenda Review
9:20	Devotional on the Great Commission
	Prayer for God's Leadership
	Sharing the Vision for Our Sunday School Strategy
10:00	A Look At Where We Are—Evaluation
11:00	A Look at What Our Evaluation Shows Us—Needs
12:00 p.m.	Lunch
12:45	Setting Priorities and Determining Goals
1:30	Building Action Plans
3:30	Committing Our Plans to God
3:45	Dismiss and Head Home

- **Several weeknights**

Spread the agenda items over a series of sessions meeting several evenings.

Secure the location.—Select a location that allows participants to avoid distractions, helps them focus their thinking, and stimulates creativity. Many times annual planning is done best at a location other than the church. Some possibilities are
- associational assembly or encampment,
- local hotel or motel conference room,
- state park accommodations,
- vacation/recreation cabin,
- neighboring church, or
- home of a member of the planning group.

If none of these options are possible, your church still can be a good planning location. There are some benefits of meeting at the church, such as easy access to records and other materials and the opportunity to view space and equipment. If you use your church, find ways to add to the spirit and anticipation of the meeting as being something out of the ordinary.

Wherever you meet, provide an atmosphere that is conducive to good planning. Meeting around tables makes it easier to look at materials and take notes. Participants will be sitting for a long time, so arrange for comfortable chairs. Also, arrive early to check the temperature and finalize room arrangements.

Gather the resources.—For your annual planning to be beneficial, you need to have the necessary resources on hand.

1. Annual Planning Guide (for 1999-2000, *Sunday School for a New Century*)
2. Records

Reviewing what your Bible study groups have accomplished during the past year specifically and the past several years generally is a valuable part of planning. Provide a summary of the enrollment and attendance records for each class and department in your Sunday School. Gather other information that helps leaders answer questions. such as the following

- What was the total enrollment at the beginning of the year? The end of the year?
- How many people were enrolled? How many were dropped?
- What was the net gain?
- What was the total average attendance for the prior year? What was the total average attendance for this year?
- What were the number of contacts reported for each class and department for the year?
- How many visitors were reported for each class and department?
- Were there any deficiencies in record keeping by any classes and departments that may have affected the accuracy of the statistics?

Additionally, prepare a breakdown of the total enrollment, new people enrolled, people dropped from enrollment, and average attendance for the past 5 to 10 years. This kind of information helps leaders see any trends that have developed.

Bring training records to the annual planning event. A review of the church's Christian Growth Study Plan summary can provide helpful information in planning for training. Secure that information online at http://www.lifeway.com/cgsp.

3. Calendars

Obtain copies of the church calendar (dates committed to this point), associational calendar, state calendar, Southern Baptist Convention calendar, Glorieta® Conference Center or Ridgecrest® Conference Center schedules. Pull dates from these calendars that relate to your plans. Compile the dates on a sheet to be distributed during annual planning.

4. Budget information

During annual planning you will begin formulating your annual Sunday School strategy budget. Budget and expenditure information for the previous and current year can be helpful in budget development. Of course, the new budget needs to reflect the plans that are being made for the year.

5. Goals

Review goals that were set for the current year. If churchwide planning has been completed by the pastor, staff, and Church Council, secure information about goals that have been set for the coming year. Determine how the Sunday School strategy can help the church achieve these goals. Use information growing out of work done with Sunday School Strategy Plan Sheets (pp. 62-67).

6. Organizational information

A major subject of discussion during annual planning will be the structure of the organization for the coming year. Use the list of current classes and departments along with the enrollment and average attendance figures and prospect information for each to help leaders determine where new departments and/or classes might be needed.

7. Prospect information

The number of prospects and their status will be useful in projecting goals and making plans related to evangelism, enrollments, leader enlistment, new units, budget preparation, and so forth.

8. Evaluation instruments

Lead other members of the planning team to complete Sunday School Checkups (pp. 57-61) before the planning event.

Your Time Is Now

Do you know why you're doing what you are doing—in Sunday School strategy as well as in the planning process? If not, you may be perpetuating the situation described by this statement: *The more you do of what you've got, the more you get of what you've got.* If with your team you have set this strategy and direction, the following six-step process can help you plan something very "different than what you've got."

A 6-Step Process for Doing Annual Planning

Step 1.— Make Spiritual Preparation

• *Read the Bible and pray for God's direction.*

Consider what the Bible says related to planning. Acknowledge that planning is a faith process. It is seeking to know where God is at work and how your Sunday School can be the strategy for helping your church join Him and fulfill the Great Commission.

To do that, seek God in prayer. Specifically ask God to reveal Himself to the planning team and to give them insight and guidance as they plan. Let prayer be a major part of the annual planning meeting.

• *Review the Great Commission.*

The Great Commission, Matthew 28:18-20, is the foundation on which the work of the church is to be built. These words from Jesus form a blueprint for the mission and ministry of the church. Discuss what it has to say to your church about its work and mission.

• *Ask God for a vision for your church's Sunday School.*

Do not put limitations, barriers, or boundaries on the vision. Spend time as a planning team sharing the vision and asking God to reveal His direction for your church's Sunday School.

Step 2.— Evaluate Present Work

Evaluation answers the question "Where are we now?" Work to keep the evaluation positive, but honest. Evaluation will reveal strengths and weaknesses. The discovery of strengths and weaknesses can help to clarify the direction the church needs to take in the new year.

• *Evaluate the work of your church in light of the Great Commission and the purpose of Sunday School.*

Sunday School is the foundational strategy in a local church for leading people to faith in the Lord Jesus Christ and for building Great Commission Christians through Bible study groups that engage people in evangelism, discipleship, fellowship, ministry, and worship.

• *Examine records for the past year.*

Review the records of enrollment, new members, losses, new units, baptisms, other changes in church membership, and leadership training. Compare that data to the same information for several years to identify any patterns or trends. Look beyond the numbers to the meanings and people the numbers represent.

• *Evaluate the effectiveness of your Sunday School strategy in relationship to the functions of the church.*

• Review the discussion on Sunday School and church functions. The Sunday School Checkups and Strategy Plan Sheets also can reveal areas of effectiveness and of need.

• *Evaluate the organization components of your strategy in light of enrollment and number of workers.*

Providing an effective organization is a major aspect of the strategy. Proper size of organizational units and the appropriate ratio of workers to pupils are major factors that influence how the work is done.

Step 3 —Identify Needs on Which to Focus Next Year

Build on the spiritual preparation made in Step 1 and the data gathered in Step 2. Identify the major needs of Sunday School strategy implementation in relationship to

- the Great Commission,
- definition of Sunday School as strategy,
- church functions,
- leader enlistment and training,
- outreach and evangelism,
- organization.

You and your group also may think of other areas of your Sunday School strategy in which needs exist. List each need revealed. Be as specific and inclusive as possible.

Step 4 —Determine Priorities

A thorough evaluation ordinarily will reveal more needs than leaders can address during a year. This may be true in your case. Do not be overwhelmed.

For this reason, the appropriate next step is prayerfully and carefully to review the list to determine priorities. Identify the needs that are most important and specify what must be accomplished first.

Put the priorities in writing. Some examples are identified in the "Objective" statements in each Sunday School Strategy Plan Sheet (pp. 62-67).

Step 5 —Set Goals That Will Fulfill the Priorities

Now that you have determined priorities to be addressed by your strategy for the coming year, you are ready to set goals. Goals should state specific outcomes you want to accomplish by the end of the year (or during the year if a goal can and should be accomplished sooner).

In some cases the goals will be numerical. Set specific numerical goals in enrollment, average attendance, baptisms, leader enlistment and training, and organizational units.

However, not all goals will be numerical. For example, a goal based on a priority need related to leader enlistment might be to equip all leaders to personally enlist their workers. Actions to accomplish this goal might include conducting a leader enlistment campaign, providing training during Sunday School leadership team meetings, and working with key leaders one-on-one.

To lead individuals and families to establish a daily encounter with God through Bible reading and prayer (an objective designed to accomplish the Worship function), this goal might be set: Enlist 75 percent of all Sunday School leaders and members to commit to reading the Bible through by December 31, 2000. Such a goal is measurable and specific. Actions can be planned to accomplish it.

Goal statements are not intended to be action statements. Goal statements should indicate the desired outcome at the end of the year. Goal statements take priorities from the level of need to a desired outcome.

Step 6.—Plan Actions to Achieve Goals

The planning process is incomplete and will be ineffective unless it results in determining specific actions to be taken to achieve the goals. An action plan should be built for each goal. Such a plan identifies the action, the person responsible, and the date the action is to be completed. Action plans may include multi-detailed projects and emphases, but they also may be a specific, single action; for example, "Order the appropriate size chairs for the older preschool department."

Of course, planning does not end with simply developing action plans. The person responsible for the action must understand his or her responsibility for completing the action. The actions need to be monitored throughout the year. The Sunday School Planning Team in its monthly meeting assumes responsibility for monitoring action plans and making modifications as needed.

Give annual planning your best work. However, recognize that planning is a spiritual task, and commit each phase to God for His guidance, empowering, and wisdom.

Sunday School Strategy
and Evangelism Checkup

On a scale of 1 to 5 (1 being low; 5 being high), how would you rate your Sunday School in leading people to faith in the Lord Jesus Christ? How would you rate yourself?

SS	Me	
___	___	Making a commitment to personal evangelism
___	___	Praying for spiritually lost people to come to know Jesus Christ as personal Savior and Lord
___	___	Seeking, discovering, and inviting spiritually lost people to become involved in a Bible study group
___	___	Enrolling unreached people
___	___	Seeking, discovering, and enlisting members to serve in leadership positions related to outreach and evangelism
___	___	Appropriately teaching the Bible for evangelistic results
___	___	Making an investment in teaching others about Christ in one-on-one settings away from church
___	___	Organizing and training individuals in personal evangelism.
___	___	Viewing ongoing evangelistic visitation as a group activity.
___	___	Viewing evangelistic visitation as a personal responsibility
___	___	Starting new Bible study units
___	___	Conducting special evangelistic Bible study events.

Sunday School as foundational strategy focuses on leading people to faith in the Lord Jesus Christ.

Sunday School Strategy and Discipleship Checkup

On a scale of 1 to 5 (1 being low; 5 being high), how would you rate your Sunday School in discipling others through Bible study? How would you rate yourself?

SS	Me	
___	___	Lifting up the Bible as the absolute truth and authority of God's Word, and using it as the textbook of the Sunday School
___	___	Regularly attending ongoing Sunday School classes, departments, or other Bible study groups
___	___	Providing training for all Sunday School leaders
___	___	Providing Bible study curriculum materials appropriate for preschoolers, children, youth, and adults
___	___	Providing space, equipment, and furnishings appropriate for Bible study with preschoolers, children, youth, and adults
___	___	Working to provide a ministry environment in Bible study that facilitates spiritual transformation
___	___	Encouraging involvement in the church's Discipleship ministry
___	___	Providing opportunities to be involved in special Bible study events beyond Sunday morning
___	___	Providing tools to help parents fulfill their role as the primary Bible teachers and disciplers of their children.

Sunday School as foundational strategy guides people to integrate biblical truth into the fabric of their hearts, minds, will, and actions.

Sunday School Strategy and Fellowship Checkup

On a scale of 1 to 5 (1 being low; 5 being high), how would you rate your Sunday School in establishing and building relationships with God and His people? How would you rate yourself?

SS	Me	
___	___	Establishing a ministry environment that encourages a sense of belonging
___	___	Encouraging new believers to unite with the church through baptism
___	___	Providing Bible study groups for preschoolers, children, youth, and adults
___	___	Creating an environment of grace, acceptance, support, and encouragement in ongoing Bible study groups
___	___	Providing opportunities for Bible study participants to interact with God's Word, the teacher, and one another during Bible study sessions
___	___	Providing opportunities to build relationships through social activities beyond Sunday morning
___	___	Providing opportunities to build relationships through ongoing outreach, evangelism, and ministry visitation
___	___	Providing opportunities to build fellowship through special emphases, such as Single Adult Day, Student Sunday School, and Senior Adult Day
___	___	Maintaining contact with members and prospects who are away from home and those who are serving in leadership positions in age groups other than their own
___	___	Praying together.

Sunday School as foundational strategy guides people to establish and build enduring relationships with God and with His people.

Sunday School Strategy and Ministry Checkup

On a scale of 1 to 5 (1 being low; 5 being high), how do you rate your Sunday School in ministry? How do you rate yourself?

SS	Me	
___	___	Calling people into the ministry of caring service
___	___	Identifying ministry needs and informing people about ministry opportunities
___	___	Assisting individual Christians in identifying their gifts and abilities for ministry
___	___	Organizing for effective ministry to members, prospects, and family members
___	___	Equipping people for ministry through ongoing Bible study and special training opportunities
___	___	Developing, maintaining, and using information systems to identify and address individual ministry needs
___	___	Involving individuals and groups in ongoing ministry actions through their Sunday School classes, departments, or other Bible study groups
___	___	Involving individuals and groups in ongoing visitation for the purpose of ministry
___	___	Involving individuals in specific one-on-one ministry opportunities through specific assignments
___	___	Involving individuals and groups in the ministry of intercessory prayer
___	___	Involving individuals and groups in ministry to specific groups in the church and/or community.

Sunday School as foundational strategy organizes, equips, and mobilizes its people for ministry.

Sunday School Strategy and Worship Checkup

On a scale of 1 to 5 (1 being low; 5 being high), how would you rate your Sunday School in involving people in worship? How would you rate yourself?

SS	Me	
___	___	Acknowledging Jesus as Lord of all and responding by expressing love for Him
___	___	Joining regularly with other Christians to encounter God and encouraging one another through the churchís corporate experiences of worship
___	___	Seeking God's power and presence by seeking Him personally through daily prayer and Bible study
___	___	Establishing an environment in classes, departments, other Bible study groups that leads people to encounter the life-changing God during and beyond Bible study sessions
___	___	Growing in commitment to evangelism as a priority
___	___	Growing in commitment to building fellowship through involvement in Bible study with others
___	___	Growing in commitment to discipleship through studying and obeying God's Word
___	___	Expanding in commitment to ministry and to missions.

Sunday School as foundational strategy emphasizes the need to seek God's power and presence by seeking Him.

Strategic Annual Planning

Your Time Is Now

As a planning team begin to personalize information about annual planning. Using the definition of Sunday School as strategy and the six-step process for annual planning, write objectives, goals, and actions.

Definition of Sunday School for a New Century	*Sunday School is the foundational strategy in a local church for leading people to faith in the Lord Jesus Christ and for building Great Commission Christians through Bible study groups that engage people in evangelism, discipleship, fellowship, ministry, and worship.*

While the Strategy Plan Sheets on pages 63-67 provide examples, they are not intended to be comprehensive. You will want to develop your own plans on a separate sheet of paper or by customizing the Strategy Plan Sheet in the *Sunday School for 21st Century Planning and Training Pack.*

Once the planning team has come to agreement on specific objectives and goals, consider asking your age-group leaders to follow a similar process. It is at this point that all workers can buy into plans for the new year. As a planning team, leaders can resolve areas of overlap or repetition.

Remember,

• *objectives* are broad statements that declare the long-term intent of the Sunday School related to a particular church function—the priority needs identified in Step 3 of annual planning;

• *goals* are focused short-term statements that can be used to track progress toward an objective;

• *actions* are specific, intentional steps toward accomplishing a goal.

Sunday School Strategy Plan Sheet:
Evangelism

Objective

To provide and promote weekly evangelistic visitation as a group activity

Goal

By August 31, 2000 have a minimum of _____ people in each age group.participating in weekly evangelistic visitation.

Actions

Discuss with the pastor the potential of the FAITH Sunday School Evangelism Strategy
- *Person Responsible*
- *Date to Be Completed*

(If appropriate), enlist a minimum of one representative from each age group to attend a FAITH Training Clinic with the pastor.
- *Person Responsible*
- *Date to Be Completed*

Work with appropriate leaders to choose a date and time for visitation that can involve the largest number of people.
- *Person Responsible*
- *Date to Be Completed*

Set up/strengthen the prospect file and prospect assignment process.
- *Person Responsible*
- *Date to Be Completed*

Plan at least one quarterly prospect-discovery activity.
- *Person Responsible*
- *Date to Be Completed*

Enlist new workers with the expectation to participate in weekly evangelistic visitation.
- *Person Responsible*
- *Date to Be Completed*

Sunday School Strategy Plan Sheet:
Discipleship

Objective

To equip parents as the primary disciplers of their children

Goal

By August 31, 2000, plan and conduct four parent training events and enlist the parents of 75 percent of all preschoolers and children enrolled in Sunday School departments to participate in at least one of the events.

Actions

Enlist a planning team to give general direction to planning and implementing the events, including budget development for the events.
- *Person Responsible*
- *Date to Be Completed*

Select resource materials and determine need for and extend invitations to outside resource persons to lead the events.
- *Person Responsible*
- *Date to Be Completed*

Work through church processes to secure calendar dates and meeting spaces for the events
- *Person Responsible*
- *Date to Be Completed*

Design a promotion plan for communicating information about the events.
- *Person Responsible*
- *Date to Be Completed*

Schedule and implement pre-registration and registration actions to achieve desired attendance goals
- *Person Responsible*
- *Date to Be Completed*

Sunday School Strategy Plan Sheet:
Fellowship

Objective

To build relationships among all members and prospects through churchwide fellowship events beyond Sunday morning

Goal

Plan and conduct three churchwide fellowship events that brings members, prospects, and their families together on the church campus.

Actions

Develop planning teams for each event using the fellowship leaders from youth and adults classes or departments and a representative leader from preschool and children's department.
- *Person Responsible*
- *Date to Be Completed*

Determine events that would be available and appropriate for your setting.
- *Person Responsible*
- *Date to Be Completed*

Work with each planning team to schedule, budget, and promote each event.
- *Person Responsible*
- *Date to Be Completed*

Determine follow-up plans with prospects and members who are not regular attenders to encourage their participation in ongoing Bible study groups.
- *Person Responsible*
- *Date to Be Completed*

Sunday School Strategy Plan Sheet:
Ministry

Objective

To assist members in identifying and using their abilities in ministry to others

Goal

Begin a "Helping Hand" ministry by May 1, 2000 that uses class/department ministry teams to help people who need assistance with household repairs but are not financially and/or physically able to care for those needs on their own.

Actions

Lead each youth or adult class or department to enlist a ministry leader if they do not have one.
- *Person Responsible*
- *Date to Be Completed*

Secure or develop and administer an abilities inventory in all youth and adult classes or departments.
- *Person Responsible*
- *Date to Be Completed*

Using the inventory results, work with ministry leaders to develop ministry teams in youth and adult classes or departments.
- *Person Responsible*
- *Date to Be Completed*

Develop process for discovering needs and assigning teams to address them.
- *Person Responsible*
- *Date to Be Completed*

Sunday School Strategy Plan Sheet:
Worship

Objective

To lead individuals and families to establish a daily encounter with God through Bible reading and prayer

Goal

Enlist 75 percent of all Sunday School leaders and members to commit to reading the Bible through by December 31, 2000.

Actions

Plan a commitment service or design a commitment card for members to make their commitment to reading the Bible through.

- *Person Responsible*
- *Date to Be Completed*

Provide to all participants age-appropriate resources that may be used as a guide for reading the Bible through.

- *Person Responsible*
- *Date to Be Completed*

Schedule periodic services or identify other ways to highlight the emphasis at various times throughout the year.

- *Person Responsible*
- *Date to Be Completed*

Determine appropriate way to recognize those who read the Bible through by the completion date.

- *Person Responsible*
- *Date to Be Completed*

Budget Planning as Part of Annual Planning

Budget planning is a critical part of the planning process. Budget planning takes on a new perspective when it is related to the annual plan. It becomes more than columns of dollars and cents but represents the financial investments that are necessary to carry out the purposeful actions of a well-prepared annual plan.

Sunday School is not an entity within itself; it is a strategy of the church. The work you do in budget planning is to be done in conjunction with the policies and procedures used in the church. Budget planning is more than just plugging in dollar amounts. The dollars are to represent the plans that have been developed—plans that move your Sunday School to achieve its purpose of helping the church do the work of the Great Commission.

Add to this worksheet and to the budgeting process the needs of special target groups such as Special Education or Young Adult Sunday School ministry.

Budget Planning Worksheet

Literature

Formula for determining cost:

_____ ÷ _____ + _____ = _____
Cost last order / Current enrollment + Anticipated inflation = Cost per person

Enrollment Goal:

_____ x _____ = _____
First Quarter   Cost per person   Total cost per quarter

_____ x _____ = _____
Second Quarter   Cost per person   Total cost per quarter

_____ x _____ = _____
Third Quarter   Cost per person   Total cost per quarter

_____ x _____ = _____
Fourth Quarter   Cost per person   Total cost per quarter

_____
Cost for year

Funds needed for additional teaching aids _____

Total Literature budget requested $ _____

Supplies (*examples: record forms, paper, art materials, refreshments*)
Consider needs for preschool, children, youth, young adults, adult, special education, and other departments.

Total Supplies budget requested $ _____

Furnishings and Equipment (*examples: chalkboards, picture rails, cabinets*)
Consider needs for preschool, children, youth, young adults, adult, special education, and other departments.

Total Equipment budget requested $ _____

Media Resources (*examples: videos, books, maps*)
Consider needs for preschool, children, youth, young adults, adult, special education, and other departments.

Total Media budget requested $ _____

January Bible Study

Resources_____

Refreshments _____

Guest teachers (expenses and gifts) _____

Other JBS expense _____

Total January Bible Study budget requested $ _____

Vacation Bible School

Curriculum _____

Supplies _____

Refreshments _____

Backyard Bible Clubs/Mission Vacation Bible School _____

Other VBS expense _____

Total Vacation Bible School budget requested $ _____

Annual Planning

Lodging, meals _____

Transportation _____

Materials _____

Total Annual Planning budget requested $ _____

Launch Event

Resources _____

Refreshments/Banquet _____

Total Launch Event budget requested $ _____

Leadership Training

Resources_____

Promotion _____

Guest teachers (expense and gifts) _____

Registration/Conference fees _____

Transportation _____

Lodging, meals _____

Total Leadership Training budget requested $ _____

Outreach-Evangelism Planning

Outreach-evangelism events and supplies _____

Promotional materials, postage _____

Outreach meals, fellowship refreshments _____

Total Outreach-Evangelism Planning budget requested $ _____

Other Needs

Worker appreciation banquet _____

Other _____

Total Other Needs budget requested $ _____

GRAND TOTAL BUDGET REQUEST $ _____

Goal-Setting Worksheet Summary

The Strategy Plan Sheets offered suggestions to help you set goals. From that work, develop a goal summary that may be used as quick reference throughout the year. The sheet may be similar to this one. Other goal suggestions are given on this page to stimulate your thinking of other items that may need to be addressed in your planning and goal-setting process. Remember, your goals need to reflect the specific needs and priorities identified to help your church achieve its purpose.

	Completion	Person Responsible
1. Evangelism Goals		
Prospect file created		
Prospect discovery events		
Outreach-evangelism leaders enlisted		
Witness training events planned		
Prospect assignment system developed		
Bible study groups		
•		
Bible study projects		
Vacation Bible School		
Mission VBS		
Backyard Bible Clubs		
2. Discipleship Goals		
New units		
Enrollment		
Attendance		
Bible study projects		
•		
Worker enlistment		
Training events		
•		
•		
3. Ministry Goals		
Class leaders enlisted		
Ministry actions		
•		
•		
4. Fellowship Goals		
Fellowship actions		
•		
•		
Member assimilation actions		
•		
•		
5. Worship Goals		
Prayer ministry		
•		
Personal devotional emphases		
•		

6. Other Goals Specific to Your Sunday School

Sunday School and Organization

The Value of Organization to Church Function

Sunday School strategy is implemented by clustering people into groups, primarily on basis of age. Remember, however, Sunday School is not an organization, but a strategy for doing the work of the Great Commission.

Organizational progression describes how many units (classes or Bible study groups, departments, divisions) and leaders are needed to accommodate member enrollment, particularly as enrollment increases at any point. Organizational progression is the principle a church may use to determine the organization and the progress or movement from one level of organization to the next (see the Steps to Organizational Progression and Growth chart, p. 85).

The individual units are where the personal touch take places in Sunday School. It is where people are mobilized to do the work. The importance of the organizational unit cannot be overemphasized.

An effective Sunday School strategy is one in which a ministry environment exists that encourages unsaved people to come to faith in Christ; encourages believers to be intentional, active soul-winners; facilitates life-changing Bible study; builds fellowship among people; and engages people in pursuing the church's functions—all in an atmosphere of grace, acceptance, love, and support.

The number of participants and prospects for a Sunday School class, department, or other Bible study group; the number of trained and potential leaders identified for service; and available space are important factors that affect organization. Since all of those factors, as well as many others, interact with one another, organizational structures for Sunday School strategy may vary from church to church. Organization is purpose-driven, but not static. It must be flexible.

Organization Supports Evangelism

Organization supports evangelism by assigning every member and prospect to an age-appropriate class. The leaders and members of that class take actions to give an evangelistic witness to the unsaved and make concerted efforts to lead them to know Jesus Christ as Lord and Savior. The class or group provides an atmosphere that encourages unsaved people to faith in Christ and encourages believers to lead others to Christ. Leadership structure for the class or department includes individuals with specific assignments related to evangelism.

Organization Supports Discipleship

Organization supports discipleship (teaching persons that they might grow in maturity in Christ) by providing a context for Bible study that considers the characteristics, needs, and learning styles of the learners assigned to the class. The discipling that takes place through the teaching can be more focused and personal because the teacher, other leaders, and members are able to build quality relationships that nurture one another. The Bible study becomes the focal point for encouraging evangelism, discipleship, ministry, fellowship, and worship. Leadership structure for the class or department includes individuals with specific assignments related to monitoring the discipleship needs of believers and working with the church's Discipleship ministry to provide opportunities focused to address those needs.

Organization Supports Fellowship

Organization supports fellowship by placing people in groups where they can build relationships with others as, together, they build upon their relationship with God. Newcomers are easily assimilated into the larger fellowship of the church as they experience the fellowship of the smaller group.

As important and valuable as fellowship is, the fellowship is not to become the controlling factor in Sunday School classes or departments. Bible study groups (classes or departments) that overemphasize fellowship tend to grow stagnate, or crystallize, because members become content and comfortable with one another. The leadership structure for the class or department includes individuals with specific assignments related to building fellowship.

Organization Supports Ministry

Organization supports ministry by placing leaders, members, and prospects in settings to experience direct care and concern for life's needs. People who are members of a small group like a Sunday School class can communicate more openly and clearly to one another about needs and concerns.

Intercessory prayer is a particularly important aspect of effective ministry that is supported by organization. Organization also provides for leaders, members, and prospects to express their concern for others through identifying and implementing ministry and mission projects that utilize the gifts and abilities of the class. Leadership structure for the class or department includes individuals with specific assignments related to ministry, including responsibilities in missions support and intercessory prayer.

Organization Supports Worship

Organization supports worship by teaching about worship, providing small-group worship experiences that allow for greater participation by members of the class, and encouraging personal worship in home and family settings. The leadership structure for the class or department includes individuals with specific assignments related to worship.

Organizing with Purpose

Organization is a means for getting the work done. Organization enables evangelism, discipleship, fellowship, ministry, and worship to be done well. It is a structure for positioning members in places of service that encourage their growth toward Christian maturity as they do the work of the church, which is ministry in the name of Jesus.

Sunday School seeks to lead people to faith in the Lord Jesus Christ and to build Great Commission Christians through Bible study groups that engage individuals and families in evangelism, discipleship, fellowship, ministry, and worship. The organization that is set in place should be what is needed to fulfill the reason for existence. When the organizational structure ceases to support the strategy, then the structure should be changed. Organization provides the context for attaining the desired results and the most effective behavior out of the people who make up the organization.

In the context of Sunday School strategy, organization helps leaders

- lead members in evangelistic, discipling, fellowship, ministry, and worship actions in the context of open, small-group settings;

- delegate responsibilities to other leaders and potential leaders so that the greatest good can be accomplished;
- meet particular needs of members and prospects with effectiveness;
- effectively manage the time, energy, gifts, and resources available for conducting ministry;
- train and develop new leaders;
- address needs of individuals through Bible study experiences designed to facilitate spiritual transformation; and
- communicate with one another in a spirit of understanding and harmony.

When the proper organization is in place certain desired outcomes can be realized. You/other leaders will be better able to

- discover, understand, and meet age-group and generational needs;
- provide well-trained, God-called leaders to work in all areas where leaders are needed and provide for appropriate leader-learner ratios for each age group;
- provide a variety of opportunities for new persons to participate in the church's ministry;
- discover, understand, and meet specialized learner needs;
- discover, understand, and meet specific goals and objectives related to the evangelism, discipleship, fellowship, ministry, and worship; and
- create and implement an effective growth dynamic by starting new units .

Organizing Bible Study Groups

A Bible study group is a group intentionally formed around the study and living of God's Word. This definition highlights the fundamental distinctive of Bible study groups. Bible study groups are intentionally Bible-centered. The primary question in these groups is, "What is God saying to us through the Bible text?" While there may be other books, tapes, people, and so forth that serve as resources to the study, those resources are not the focus of the event. This is different from a group that gathers for support, fellowship, leadership training, skill development, and so forth. These may study the Bible peripherally or as a part of the agenda, but Bible study is not the primary agenda.

Kinds Of Bible Study Groups

While Bible study groups may be categorized in a variety of ways, nothing shapes the core nature of a Bible study group more than its primary target audience. From the church's perspective, there are two basic target audiences: lost people and saved people. Bible study groups that are designed primarily for reaching lost people are Sunday School groups. Bible study groups that are designed primarily for moving saved people toward spiritual maturity are Discipleship groups.

Sunday School Bible Study Groups

Sunday School is a strategy that accomplishes its purpose through Bible study groups that target lost people. A Sunday School Bible study group is defined by its nature, purpose, and function rather than when or where it meets or the material it uses. Two specific kinds of Bible study groups are suggested for Sunday Schools: ongoing Bible study groups and short-term Bible study groups.

- *Ongoing Bible Study Groups in Sunday School*

Sunday School ongoing Bible study groups have no specified end date and focus on reaching the unsaved, building relationships, and promoting spiritual growth, with the goal of starting new Bible study groups and developing leaders for those groups. Sunday School Bible study groups may be called Sunday School classes or departments. The group should be defined by its purpose, nature, and function rather than by its resources, label, time frame, or location.

Ongoing Bible study groups offer a church a number of advantages.

- An ongoing Bible study group ministry emphasizes the church's long-term obligation and commitment to spiritual transformation and biblical instruction.
- The initial focus of an ongoing Bible study group tends to be more on its purpose, members, and relationships rather than the topic of study or affinity need of the group.
- Ongoing Bible study groups provide a long-term environment for building lasting friendships.
- Long-term curriculum study plans tend to provide greater balance, stronger sequence, and more comprehensive scope.
- These groups typically meet around the time for corporate worship which is convenient for participants and reinforces the essential relationship between worship and discipleship.
- Ongoing Bible study groups typically are easier to maintain for the church leadership. This is true for several reasons.
    * These groups tend to have a fixed location (usually in a public building), time, and facilities.
    * Leader enlistment for these groups is typically annual.
    * A fully age-graded ministry provides a stronger family ministry by offering substantive, age-appropriate Bible study for all family members.
    * Materials are typically dated and ordered rather automatically.
    * Materials are usually less expensive.
    * Curriculum content is usually determined by the publisher rather than the church staff.
    * Most ongoing Bible study ministries offer a fully age-graded program, solving a number of child-care issues.
    * Record keeping is easier in a centralized location.

- *Short-term Bible Study Groups in Sunday School*

Sunday School short-term Bible study groups are started with a specified end date and focus on reaching the unsaved, building relationships, and promoting spiritual growth, with the goal of transitioning participants into an ongoing Bible study group. The group is defined by its purpose, nature, and function rather than by its resources, label, time frame, or location.

Short-term Bible study groups offer several advantages.

- Short-term groups often meet in homes where a more informal and intimate environment can be created.
- These groups often appeal to unreached people who will not attend a group "at the church."
- Study content can be selected to appeal to individuals with specific life needs.
- These groups are not limited by public building space.

- Leader enlistment and member participation may be facilitated by a shorter commitment of time.
- These groups tend to focus more intentionally and naturally on building relationships.

Several target groups may be identified for short-term Bible study groups, including
- reached or unreached adults, youth, or children who may not respond to a Sunday School approach to ongoing Bible study or who may prefer Bible study in a weekday setting;
- unreached persons in apartment complexes, mobile home parks, retirement villages, low-income housing, community centers, businesses, homes, and so forth;
- persons in institutions in the community such as nursing homes and penal facilities;
- Youth and Adult Sunday School members and prospects who desire additional Bible study enrichment.; and/or
- youth involved in equal access Bible clubs in schools.

Relationship Between Ongoing and Short-term Sunday School Bible Study Groups
Ongoing and short-term Bible study groups in Sunday School relate to each other as part of the larger strategy. An ongoing Bible study group has the goal of starting new ongoing Bible study groups and developing leaders for those groups. A short-term Bible study group has the goal of transitioning participants into an ongoing Bible study group. In this context, the two kinds of groups complement each other and build on each other's strengths.

The relationship between ongoing and short-term Bible study groups is similar to a highway system. People select a particular highway and entry point based on their goals and destination. An interstate highway is typically chosen when a traveler wishes to go a long distance with few detours or interruptions. A local highway may be chosen for a closer destination or flexibility. Often, a local highway is used solely as the means to reach the interstate.

As a church establishes its goals and defines its purpose, it may choose to use a combination of both ongoing Bible study groups and short-term Bible study groups. Ongoing Bible study groups are like the interstate highway system; they are best for helping a church achieve its long-range goals. They provide the foundational infrastructure of the church's Sunday School ministry. Short-term Bible study groups are like the local highway system; they provide the church with flexibility and facilitate access to the church's "interstate" of ongoing Bible study.

The diagram on page 76 helps illustrate the complementary relationship of ongoing and short-term Bible study groups. Note some insights that can be made based on this diagram:

- Individuals from the community may enter the ongoing "interstate" system directly or may first enter the short-term "local" system before entering an ongoing group.
- There is no exit ramp from the ongoing "interstate" system. Once they become involved in an ongoing Bible study group, participants also may become involved in a short-term group, but they never leave the ongoing system.

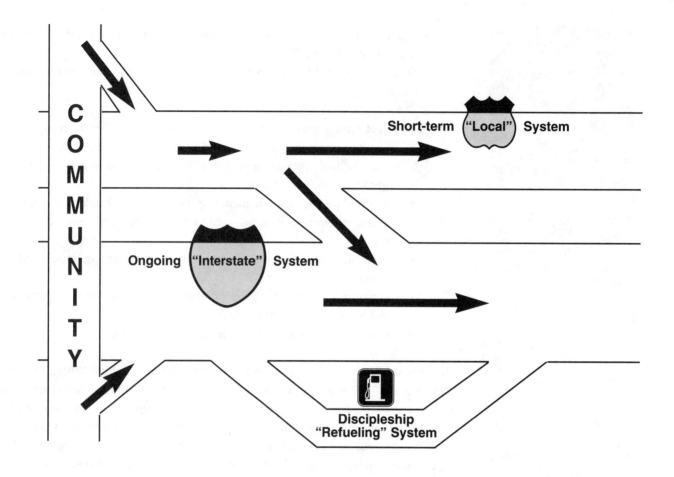

- Discipleship groups support the ongoing "interstate" system by allowing participants to exit the ongoing "flow of traffic" temporarily for the sake of "refueling." They never actually leave the interstate. Note also that discipleship Bible study groups assume the participants already have some relationship to the church and are coming out of the church. They are not designed to be entry points from the community.
- Each "system" coexists with the others as part of the total strategy. The defining and distinguishing element of the various kinds of Bible study groups is not when they meet, where they meet, or the kind of resources they use, but what they do.

Your Time Is Now

If in previous planning you have targeted median adults as a primary target group, how do you position Sunday School as strategy not only to median adults, but also to older children and youth?

Grouping by Age Groups

The guidelines that follow are offered as help for grouping people in ways that facilitates transformational Bible study for each age group. At no time is the organizational structure an end unto itself. It exists to enhance the work of the group. When the structure fails to do that, it has lost its purpose for existing.

Preschool

The preschool organization is for children birth until the first grade. The age and development of the child provide the priority base for grading preschoolers. The suggested maximum enrollment for a preschool department is 12 younger preschoolers (babies—twos), 16 middle preschoolers (threes—pre-kindergarten [pre-K]), and 20 older preschoolers (kindergartners).

Every preschool class or department needs a minimum of 2 leaders. The recommended leader-to-learner ratio for babies is 1:2 and for other younger preschoolers is 1:3. For middle preschoolers the ratio is 1:4, and for kindergartners the ratio is 1:5.

A new department needs to be organized when the existing department approaches the maximum recommended size or when the room has reached its capacity. The basic leadership structure includes a department director/lead teacher and one or more other leaders.

Grouping Preschoolers

Age	Maximum Enrollment	Leader:Learner Ratio
Babies	12	1:2
Ones—Twos	12	1:3
Threes—Pre-K	16	1:4
Kindergarten	20	1:5

Children

The priority basis for organizing children ages 6-11 years is school grades. The recommended maximum enrollment in a children's department is 24, excluding workers. The leader-learner ratio for all children's departments is 1:6. Every children's class or department needs a minimum of 2 leaders. A new department needs to be organized when the existing department approaches the maximum recommended size or when the room has reached its capacity. The basic leadership structure includes a department director and 1 or more other leaders.

Grouping Children

Grade	Maximum Enrollment	Leader:Learner Ratio
Grades 1-2	24	1:6
Grades 3-4	24	1:6
Grades 5-6	24	1:6

Youth

The youth organization in Sunday School, is generally based on school grades 7-12. In addition to school grades, age (12-17 years) and gender also may be used to determine youth groupings. The maximum recommended enrollment for youth is 60 for a youth department and 12 for each youth class.

One adult teacher is needed for every 12 youth enrolled. Every youth class needs a minimum of 2 adult leaders. A new department needs to be organized when the existing department approaches the maximum recommended size or when the room has reached its capacity. The basic leadership structure includes a teacher, an outreach-evangelism leader, and 1 or more other leaders.

Grouping Youth

Grade	Maximum Enrollment	Leader:Learner Ratio
Grades 7-8	12/class; 60/department	1:12
Grades 9-12	12/class; 60/department	1:12

Young Adults

Young adults, ages 18-24 years, make up one of the most diverse and unreached segments of the North American continent. These 6 years are some of the most volatile in a person's life. These are years in which young adults typically leave the home of parents and establish their own households, determine whether to continue to pursue a formal education, decide whether to marry, choose whether and when to begin a family, and make many other major life decisions.

Too often in the past one of those decisions is permanent disengagement from God's people. This group needs special attention and focused efforts to lead them to faith in Christ and build them into Great Commission Christians. Organizational patterns must be flexible, but generally follow those of other adult groups. The basic leadership structure includes a teacher, an outreach-evangelism leader, and one or more other leaders.

Grouping Young Adults

Age	Maximum Enrollment	Leader:Learner Ratio
18-24	25/class; 125/department	1:25 (1:4 all leaders)
Collegians	25/class; 125/department	1:25 (1:4 all leaders)
Young Singles	25/class; 125/department	1:25 (1:4 all leaders)
Young Marrieds	25/class; 125/department	1:25 (1:4 all leaders)

Adults

The basis for grouping adults is more complex because the age range is so broad and adults are so diverse. Such factors as the adult's age, generational segmentation, gender, and marital status may be considered when grouping adults. Common age-group patterns for adults are 25-39 years; 40-59 years; 60-74 years; and 75 and older.

Regardless of the basis for grouping, the suggested enrollment ceiling for adults is 125 for an adult department and 25 for an adult class. However, some churches increase the class enrollment ceiling to 35-40 for coeducational classes made up primarily of married couples. A new department needs to be organized when the existing department approaches the maximum recommended size or when the room has reached its capacity.

The basic leadership structure includes a teacher, an outreach-evangelism leader, and one or more other leaders.

Grouping Adults

Age	Maximum Enrollment	Leader:Learner Ratio
25-39	25/class; 125/department	1:25 (1:4 total leaders)
40-59	25/class; 125/department	1:25 (1:4 total leaders)
60-74	25/class; 125/department	1:25 (1:4 total leaders)
75 and up	25/class; 125/department	1:25 (1:4 total leaders)

People with Special Needs

Within every age group will be some people with special learning needs that require extra attention when designing the Sunday School organization. Some people may be grouped in a special education unit; others may be mainstreamed into existing departments and classes. The key factor is how their needs may best be met.

Consider these examples. People with hearing impairments may require a special grouping, but they also may be grouped with their peers if they are proficient at lip reading or signing. People with visual impairments can be grouped with their peers, but the teacher and others need to be sensitive to their visual limitations. People who speak a language other than that which is dominant in the church may require a group taught in their language. The point is, when a person's needs require special groupings every effort should be made to do so.

See pages 44-46 for additional information on Sunday School ministry for persons with special needs.

Other Specialty Groupings

Other specific teaching units may need to be provided for the homebound; persons who are living away from their church temporarily, such as college students, military personnel, those on job assignments; or gifted persons. Again, the key is providing that which is essential to meeting the needs of unique persons, so that no one is excluded.

Your Time Is Now

How does the "Grouping by Ages" information impact your plans for next year's strategy? for 3 years in advance? for further into the 21st century?

Guidelines for Creating New Units

Steps to Creating New Bible Study Groups

The possibilities for reaching unreached persons are greatly increased by seeking to include them in a new class. A new class can be started anytime.

- Identify a target group (age group, life situation, and so forth) that is not being reached or people who are being overlooked or are not attending even though they could.
- Enlist at least two leaders and two prospective members.
- Identify and allocate space to accommodate the leaders and members in Bible study and fellowship.

Consider some other principles related to the creation of new units. Sharing them may be helpful to others who will be enlisted as leaders or who are affected by efforts to create new classes that seem to be competitive with existing classes.

- A new class will grow faster than an existing class.
- A new class takes more work to get started than is needed to maintain an existing class.
- A new class will grow faster when it receives help from at least one other class and when it is linked organizationally with another class.
- In most instances, as more new classes are started, more new people will be reached and can be the focus of ministry and care.

There is more than one appropriate way to start a new class. However, each class must be based on sound Bible teaching and application and on time-tested principles of growth:

1. Know the possibilities—the people to be reached.
2. Enlist leaders—a minimum of one worker for every six persons enrolled in an adult class; a minimum of two workers for any preschool, children's, or youth class.
3. Enlarge the organization—as existing classes grow, start new classes for Bible study, ministry, and fellowship.
4. Provide space and materials for teaching and learning.
5. Go after the people.

When Should We Start a New Adult or Young Adult Class?

- Classes with too wide an age span (more than 10 years)
- More than 25 enrolled in the class
- Room in which the class meets often is filled
- Single adult prospects but no single adult class
- Young adult prospects but no class
- Adult prospects in a particular age segment but with no class provided
- Unenrolled adult church members
- Classes with more prospects than members
- Classes with more absentees than members present

When Should We Start a New Youth Class/Department?

- All youth in one class or department
- More than 60 youth enrolled in one department
- More than 12 youth enrolled in a class
- A school grade with prospects but little or no attendance
- Class or department with less than 50 percent enrollment in attendance
- A school grade with more prospects than youth enrolled

When Should We Start a New Children's Class/Department?

- Grades 1 through 6 in one class/department
- Grade 1 in class or department with another grade
- Grade 6 in a class or department with another grade
- Class or department with more than 30 enrolled
- Class or department with less than 60 percent of enrollment attending
- A school grade with prospects but none attending

When Should We Start a New Preschool Class/Department?

- Birth through age 5 in one class/department
- Babies in same department with other ages
- Kindergartners in same department with other ages
- Class/department of younger preschoolers with 12 or more enrolled
- Class/department of threes, fours, and pre-K with more than 16 enrolled
- Class/department of kindergartners with more than 20 enrolled
- Class/department where only "baby-sitting" is done
- More prospects than preschoolers enrolled

Determining a Schedule

When should a church's Sunday School ministry meet? The name includes *Sunday* but as we established at the outset, Sunday School is not to be thought of as the sum of the parts of its name. It is not "school" and is not a Sunday only ministry. In fact, the name *Sunday School* may not even work for you and your church. If so, change it. Other options include having "Sunday School" on Saturday night or on a weeknight. There are no rules.

The better question might be, When can we reach more people for Christ? Whenever you can reach people through a systematic Bible study group, that is the best time for you and your church. That becomes the best time for "Sunday School."

Bible Study in the Past

Ongoing weekly Bible study has a long history. It can be traced back to the weekly synagogue worship of the Jews. According to Luke 4:16, Jesus is among those in history who regularly attended a weekly Bible study: "He went to Nazareth, where he had been brought up, and on the Sabbath day he went into the synagogue, as was his custom." Of course, the Scripture Jesus read was the Old Testament only. It was a scroll that was kept in a chest in the front of the synagogue.

With the addition of the New Testament, the Bible has become an indispensable guide for establishing a saving relationship to God and for developing wholesome relationships with others. People need Bible study because they need the Lord. People need Bible study because they need to know how to live in relationship to the Lord and in relationship with one another.

The Sunday schedule of Bible study at 9:45 or 10:00 on Sunday morning followed by the worship service at 11:00 grew out of North America's early agrarian culture. This schedule allowed time for the farm family to complete the early morning chores and get to "Sunday School and church" on time. The question is, Will this schedule continue to be sufficient to provide opportunity for Bible study for everyone?

Bible Study in the Future

In one generation, North America has changed from an agricultural to a high-tech mobile society. One set time a week for Bible study at the church building meets the schedule of fewer and fewer people.

We now live in a 24-hour society. Many churches are adding a second or third Sunday School ministry meeting time on Sunday, Friday night, or Saturday night. Often this second meeting time is targeted to a specific group of people such as college students, single adults, Sunday workers, or the vast number of "seekers."

Small Bible study groups meeting in homes during the week may reach adults, youth, or children who may not respond to a Sunday morning Bible study approach. Unreached target groups in apartment complexes, mobile home parks, retirement villages, low-income housing, community centers, businesses, and institutions such as nursing homes also are potential groups and sites for Bible study beyond Sunday morning and beyond the church building.

Suggestions for Multiple Meeting Times

An inexpensive and available way to reach more people, solve the space crunch, and avoid the struggles associated with a major building project is to make multiple use of the same space. Using space more than once is good stewardship of resources. Moreover, the more time options your church provides for small-group Bible study the more opportunities you have to reach people, because not everyone is available at the same time no matter what time you have it when you have it only one time.

In cases where the church has more worship space available than small group space, the Sunday morning schedule might be:

> Sunday School—8:30—9:30 a.m.
> Worship—9:45—10:45 a.m.
> Sunday School—11:00 a.m.—12 noon.

If the worship space and small group space is essentially equal, the schedule might be like this:

> Sunday School/Worship—9:30—10:30 a.m.
> Sunday School/Worship—11:00a.m.—12 noon.

By using this schedule one-half of the congregation would be encouraged to attend Bible study groups before worship time; the other half would attend Bible study groups following worship. In this arrangement, members do need to commit themselves to a particular meeting time so they can be identified with a class.

Many other issues must be considered before launching into multiple options: schedule, size of leader base, leader enlistment, organization and coordination of the Sunday Schools, prospect assignments, and so forth.

Steps/Timetable for Implementing Multiple Meeting Times

1. Study needs and options—*24 months in advance of anticipated beginning date.*
2. Present the need and rationale to the church—*18-20 months in advance*
3. Orient the church to the concept—*12-14 months in advance.*
4. Prepare a schedule and tentative organization—*8-12 months in advance.*
5. Allocate space; begin enlistment and training of workers—*6-8 months in advance.*
6. Ask members to choose the meeting time in which they prefer to enroll— *4-6 months in advance.*
7. Complete enrollment process and organization—*2-4 months in advance.*
8. Launch and maintain the multiple meeting time schedule.

Advantages of Multiple Meeting Times

- Increase use of education space
- Provide for efficient use of buildings
- Maintain growth with little additional outlay of money
- Offer more service opportunities and utilize more people
- Make funds available for missions and expansion of other ministries
- Give members a choice of times, departments, and leadership
- Extend the outreach potential of Sunday School ministry
- Demonstrate responsible stewardship
- Conserve energy

Additional Guidelines Based on Size of Your Church

Smaller Churches

- Plan for at least one preschool class/department, one children's class/department, one youth class, one young adult class, and at least one additional adult class.
- More than one worker is needed in a preschool or children's class/department, regardless of size. More than one worker is recommended for youth class/department, regardless of size.

Medium-Size Churches

- Decide whether enlisting division directors will contribute to an improved plan.
- Provide organizational patterns that make room for expansion to groups that may not have been addressed specifically in a smaller structure. Examples might include single adults, language groups, college students, homebound persons, and individuals with special needs.
- Remain sensitive to changing enrollment patterns; maintain a flexible organization and be prepared to start new teaching units.

Larger Churches

- Division directors and/or multiple paid church staff members may have overall supervision of the age division.
- Greeters/hosts, classification secretaries, parking-lot hosts, and others are needed to operate a large Sunday School.
- The larger the enrollment, the greater the number of options available. For example, persons who have chosen not to be involved in Sunday School may be reached by alternate Bible studies. Advanced leadership training classes on Sunday morning may be scheduled and may play an important role in the total Sunday School.
- Because of the large organization, special efforts may need to be made to help members in the teaching units relate to and be a part of the larger fellowship.

Your Time Is Now

Size is an important variable, but it is not the only one, especially if Sunday School is strategy. All churches, for example, should consider having greeters in place because of the vital first impression that is made.

Consider whether options "outside the box" of church size might be appropriate. For example, if you serve a smaller church, look now at the suggestions under "Medium-Size Churches." Medium churches, look now at the "Larger Churches" content. Larger churches, you have been blessed with many resources; what new opportunities are you willing to consider?

Is there a "box" in addition to that of size that your team is willing to move beyond?

Steps to Organizational Progression and Growth

Sunday School Organization Progression: the principles a church may use in determining its Sunday School organization and the progress or movement from one level of organization to the next. The function of each unit (class, department, division) is the basis for determining organizational structure. Establishing a Sunday School organization based on function may result in a variety of patterns from age group to age group as well as within the general leadership team. Suggested maximum numbers for each unit (class, department) help in determining the need for additional units.

Step 1

General Leadership
Sunday School Director and Secretary

Adults, Young Adult & Youth: Class
1 class & 1 teacher: 1-25 adult or young adult members
1 class leader for every 6 adult or young adult members

1 class & 1 teacher: 1-12 youth members
1 class leader for every 4 youth members

Children & Preschool: Department
(*some churches may call these "classes"*)
1 department: 1-24 children enrolled
1 leader for every 6 children enrolled

1 department: 1-12 preschoolers enrolled
1 leader for every 3 preschoolers enrolled

A class grows to multiple classes in an age-group department.

Step 2

General Leadership
Sunday School Director, Assistant Sunday School Director, Secretary, or others as needed

All Ages: Department
1 department for 2-6 adult or young adult classes
1-4 leaders for adult or young adult department

1 department for 2-5 youth classes
1-2 leaders for youth department

1 department: 1-24 children enrolled
1 leader for every 6 children enrolled

1 department: 1-16 enrolled in three-year to kindergarten
1 leader for every 4 enrolled in three-year to kindergarten

1 department: 1-12 enrolled in two-year-olds
1 leader for every 3 enrolled in two-year-olds

1 department: 1-9 enrolled in birth to one-year
1 leader for every 3 enrolled in birth to one-year

A department grows to multiple departments in an age-group division.

Step 3

General Leadership
Sunday School Director, Assistant Sunday School Director, Secretary, Outreach-Evangelism Leader, or others as needed in a church's expanded organization

All Ages: Division
2-6 departments for Adult or Young Adult Division
1 worker for Adult or Young Adult Division

2-6 departments for Youth Division
1-2 leaders for Youth Division

2-12 departments for Children's Division
1 leader for Children's Division

2-8 departments for Preschool Division
1 leader for Preschool Division

A division grows to multiple age-group divisions or multiple meeting times.

Sunday School Strategy Growth Worksheet

Age Group	ENROLLMENT				CLASSES				LEADERS			
	1	2	3	4	5	6	7	8	9	10	11	12
	Present Enrollment	Prospects	Total Possible Enrollment (1+2=)	Enrollment Goal	Suggested Maximum Enrollment/Class	No. Classes Currently	Total No. Classes Needed (4/5=)	No. *New* Classes Needed (7-6=)	Suggested Ratio Leaders: Pupils	No. Leaders Currently	Total Leaders Needed (4/9=)	No. *New* Leaders Needed (11-10=)
PRESCHOOL Babies					12				1:2			
Ones–Twos					12				1:3			
Threes–Pre-K					16				1:4			
Kindergarten					20				1:5			
CHILDREN Ages 6-11 years / Grades 1-6					24				1:6			
YOUTH Ages 12-17 years / Grades 7-12					12/ Class 60/ Dept.				1:12			
YOUNG ADULT Ages 18-24 years					25/ Class 125/ Dept.				1:25 (teacher) 1:4 (all leaders)			
ADULT Ages 25 years-up					25/ Class 125/ Dept.				1:25 (teacher) 1:4 (all leaders)			

Section 4

Developing Leaders Who Can Lead

Mentor

Richard Barnes, director, Youth Sunday School Ministry Department, is a leader who is willing to assume the responsibilities of leadership, to entrust leadership to others, and to take the risks involved in venturing into an uncertain future.

Following a stellar performance during the 1988 World Series, Los Angeles Dodgers pitcher Orel Hershiser appeared on "The Tonight Show" hosted by Johnny Carson. As part of the comedian's usual banter, Johnny said to Orel, "I noticed that you were singing in the dugout during the game. Tell me, what were you singing?" To the surprise of the host and the television audience, Orel replied, "I was singing the Doxology, 'Praise God, from Whom All Blessings Flow.'" Amazed, Mr Carson responded, "Are you telling me that in the heat of one of the most important games this baseball season, you were singing hymns. I don't believe it."

Johnny Carson would have believed it had he known Orel as someone other than a great baseball pitcher. Not only is Orel Hershiser one of the most talented baseball pitchers in this generation, he also is a faithful witness of his faith in God.

Not long after signing a professional baseball contract, Orel was assigned to the Dodgers' AA minor league team in San Antonio, Texas. One Sunday Orel and his wife visited the First Baptist Church in that city. As a follow-up, a staff member at the church called upon this new couple who had moved to the city. That staff member was Youth Minister Richard Barnes.

A discipling bond developed between Richard and Orel as a result of that visit. The Hershisers joined First Baptist Church and Orel responded to the spiritual coaching of this leader, much like he responded to the instruction from the pitching coach on the baseball team. Perhaps it was that spiritual coaching that helped Orel to understand where to turn when the pressures of life become ever so intense.

This was just one among many times Richard Barnes has exhibited leadership that God has used in a mighty way. Currently, Richard Barnes is the director of the Youth Sunday School Ministry Department of the Sunday School Group. His responsibilities include designing ministry plans for Youth Sunday School, developing Bible study curriculum resources, and managing field service training assignments.

Richard is admired and respected by youth ministers and young people across the Southern Baptist Convention. Many of the innovative approaches to student ministry during the past 10 years—including *StraighTrak* and *EXTRA!* teaching supplements and other electronic publishing ventures, have been developed under Richard's influence and leadership.

The past few years, something has been amiss among educators and youth pastors who work with young people in the churches. The disruptions in American society are affecting life in all quarters, but perhaps no age group is being as decimated as are youth. They are targeted by every evil tactic of the Deceiver and at times nothing seems to be effective in deterring this onslaught.

The drug culture is pervasive; alcohol abuse is at an all-time high. Families are being torn asunder, so that few youth knew what it is like to grow up in the kind of family

Reflections
Reflections
Reflections

Some leadership experts define leadership as influence. You are a leader to some person or group.

How would you assess your leadership? How would your constituents assess your leadership? What do you need to do to strengthen the leadership you provide?

You may be a key person in discovering, training, and enlisting leaders for your church's Sunday School ministry. For what kind of leaders are you searching? What can you do to avoid getting caught up in the tendency "to fill positions" as opposed "to enlist leaders"?

enjoyed by their parents. Violence has moved its ugly head to the school campuses where youth normally have felt secure.

Even those who produce religious curriculum resources have been baffled. While attending a meeting of the top publishers from across America, Richard listened while one leader commented, "Our approach has been to give them (youth) what they need; wrap it in what they want. In our search to sell materials and to hit the so-called hot spots of discussion, have we missed the target by not providing transformational Bible study resources which made a difference in the lives of our youth?"

The publishers agreed that youth today are taught to be tolerant of everything. We struggle with a leadership crisis, for many youth leaders do not know how to apply God's Word to their own lives, much less how to help teenagers apply biblical truth to theirs. Moreover, everyone struggles with just what application to life means.

These publishing leaders agreed that the teacher is the key; youth will imitate their leaders. Therefore, the question becomes not only "How do youth learn today?," but also "How do teachers teach?" The assignment becomes that of designing resources for teenagers and their gatekeepers.

Furthermore, the group acknowledged that youth are attracted to the Internet, but that the Internet is information chaos. The way things are packaged is important, because many youth will not give truth a hearing unless it's "cool."

Upon his return from this meeting, Richard reported on his impressions. He dared voice this probing question: "Have we turned too much to secular educational models rather than the Bible for developing curriculum plans and Bible study approaches? Shouldn't we focus more on the Gospels and the Book of Acts for designing our Christian education strategies?"

Richard concluded his remarks by saying, "Revival is the key to our publishing woes. Products and plans will not bring revival. Like the Swiss who produce excellent maps for traveling in the mountains, we should produce excellent spiritual maps for youth."

I knew that LifeWay Christian Resources had the right leader in Youth Sunday School work. My two sons are past their teenage years, but I thought, *This is the kind of editor I want preparing spiritual road maps for my church. Hopefully, one day my two grandsons will profit from the wisdom of this dedicated Christian leader.*

Three years ago, plans were being completed for a gathering of Southern Baptists educators in Nashville. We agreed a task force would be needed to process the information and data that would be collected during that meeting. The group would need to be active and able to move forward immediately.

Was there any doubt who needed to convene this group? Richard Barnes was selected because he had consistently provided skilled leadership in all areas of his work and had the confidence of his colleagues.

This task force has formulated the concepts found in this book, *Sunday School for a New Century*. They have challenged our traditions and practices as Sunday School leaders, not to cast aside proven practices but to ensure that they still are the best practices for this generation. The group has been willing to be prescriptive and prophetic when necessary, both of which require courage and demand the best from leadership.

Leadership. The word fills pages of books and it swamps the Internet. It is just like the weather, "Everyone talks about it but no one does anything about it."

Such is not the case with Richard Barnes. He is a leader. He does provide leadership. He encourages other people to give leadership. He is not afraid of leading into risky areas. He wants to be the leader who provides a true spiritual map for youth and the entire family.

The Sunday School Leadership Team

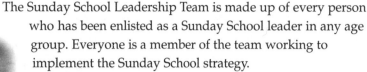

The Sunday School Leadership Team is made up of every person who has been enlisted as a Sunday School leader in any age group. Everyone is a member of the team working to implement the Sunday School strategy.

Each person deserves the benefit of knowing the expectations and responsibilities of the role. Furthermore, a clear statement of basic roles and major responsibilities can be a tremendous encouragement to those who are considering accepting a position of leadership. When leaders understand what they are supposed to do and can see that they are not alone, but are working as a part of a team, they are more likely to respond positively to the call to lead/serve. They also are more likely to be effective and satisfied in the role.

The Sunday School Planning Team

Basic Role

The Sunday School Planning Team is comprised of the leaders with responsibility for the general oversight of a church's Sunday School and/or leaders who provide administrative leadership for a particular age-group division or major affinity group, such as a Special Education Division. As a team, these leaders are responsible for the overall direction, planning, and operation of a church's Sunday School strategy. This team includes the pastor; other church ministers with responsibilities related to Sunday School; Sunday School director; the general outreach-evangelism director (or FAITH director); Sunday School secretary; division directors for each age-group division, and the Discipleship director, missions ministries directors, or others.

Major Responsibilities

- Set goals that lead Sunday School toward fulfilling its objectives.
- Develop action plans for accomplishing the goals.
- Set calendar dates for special events that support the ongoing objectives of Sunday School and contribute significantly to achieving its goals.
- Communicate the overall mission (objective) and message of Sunday School strategy to other leaders and the entire church
- Provide direction for and coordinate the work of age groups, including leader enlistment and leader training, toward the overall objective of Sunday School.
- Evaluate the effectiveness of the Sunday School strategy as implemented.
- Set a positive example for others by living as an authentic witness of Christ and by being thoroughly involved in the life and ministry of the church.

The Pastor/Minister

Basic Role

The pastor is the primary leader for a church's Sunday School strategy. Rarely will a Sunday School stay on its purpose without the visible, vital leadership of its pastor. The pastor and/or other ministers on the church staff are responsible for the overall direction of all of the church's ministries, including Sunday School.

The pastor works with the Sunday School Planning Team to set goals and evaluate the Sunday School's effectiveness in engaging people in evangelism, discipleship, fellowship, ministry, and worship through Bible study groups.

Major Responsibilities
- Provide overall leadership to the Sunday School Planning Team.
- Lead the team in keeping Sunday School focused on its objective.
- Give vital and visible support to Sunday School and its leaders.
- Communicate the overall mission (objective) and message of Sunday School to the entire church.
- Guide team members toward spiritual maturity and assist them in developing skills that enhance their ability to fulfill their responsibilities.
- Set a positive example for others by living as an authentic witness of Christ and by being thoroughly involved in the life and ministry of the church.

The Sunday School Director

Basic Role

The Sunday School director serves as the general administrative leader of a church's Sunday School. This person is responsible for coordinating the work of all Sunday School classes, departments, and other Bible study groups toward the overarching objective of the Sunday School. He leads the Sunday School Planning Team in planning, organizing, enlisting and equipping leaders, and in mobilizing members to achieve goals toward the Sunday School's stated objectives.

As your Sunday School ministry expands in size and scope, additional leaders may be needed or desired to deal with specific responsibilities that are assigned to the Sunday School director. For example, a church may need an assistant Sunday School director or a Bible projects director (such as VBS director or January Bible Study director). These persons may become members of the Sunday School Planning Team and would be responsible to the Sunday School director.

Major Responsibilities
- Meet regularly with the Sunday School Planning Team.
- Communicate goals and actions to leaders and participants and evaluate progress.
- Lead in developing an effective organization that facilitates spiritual transformation.
- Lead in efforts to call participants into service and in enlisting and developing new leaders.
- Lead in evaluating needs related to space, budget, Bible study curriculum, supplies, and other resources; and recommend needed actions.
- Set a positive example for others by living as an authentic witness of Christ and through full involvement in the life and ministry of the church.

The Outreach-Evangelism Director (FAITH Director)

Basic Role

The outreach-evangelism director provides overall direction and leadership toward involving unreached people in Sunday School classes and departments and other Bible study groups. This person gives essential leadership to keeping the focus of Sunday School on evangelism. The Sunday School director assumes this role in churches without an outreach-evangelism director.

In churches using FAITH this position should be filled by the FAITH Director.

Major Responsibilities

- Meet regularly with the Sunday School Planning Team.
- Assist in discovering, enlisting, and training age-group division outreach-evangelism directors and outreach-evangelism leaders for youth and adult departments and classes.
- Promote outreach and evangelism objectives with other leaders and members.
- Guide all actions for outreach and evangelism through Sunday School, and coordinate those efforts with other church outreach and evangelism efforts.
- Lead in keeping the focus of Sunday School on evangelism.
- Ensure that accurate records are kept so that contacts with visitors and prospects can be effectively maintained and Sunday School classes, departments, and Bible study groups can effectively work to meet needs.
- Lead in evaluating the outreach and evangelism efforts of Sunday School.
- Set a positive example for others by living as an authentic witness of Christ and by being thoroughly involved in the life and ministry of the church.

The Sunday School Secretary

Basic Role

The Sunday School secretary assists the Sunday School Planning Team by providing vital support related to record keeping, reports and other communications; securing Bible study curriculum, supplies, and other resources; and coordinating the distribution of resources. The Sunday School director or outreach-evangelism director assumes this role in churches without a Sunday School secretary.

Major Responsibilities

- Meet regularly with the Sunday School Planning Team.
- Process and maintain general records for Sunday School and compile reports, including prospect information.
- Coordinate ordering and distribution of Bible study curriculum materials, supplies, and other resources.
- Set a positive example for others by living as an authentic witness of Christ and by being thoroughly involved in the life and ministry of the church.

The Age-Group Leaders

Basic Role

By far, the majority of leaders in a church's Sunday School relate to specific age groups. These leaders relate to one of the following basic roles:

• *division directors, department directors, and others* who provide administrative leadership for the work of an age group; and

• *teachers, coordinators, apprentices, and class team leaders* who guide participants in Bible study and in doing the functions of evangelism, discipleship, fellowship, ministry, and worship.

Major Responsibilities of Division Directors

Division directors are responsible to the Sunday School director for the total ministry of their age-group division, including planning, organizing, enlisting leaders, and evaluating the work in light of the objectives of Sunday School. Division directors also serve on the Sunday School Planning Team. They must work closely with other members of that team as well as with their age-group division and department leaders.

Their primary responsibilities are to

• meet regularly with the Sunday School Planning Team;

• coordinate the work of the division and determines organizational needs;

• discover, enlist, and train new leaders;

• evaluate, encourage, affirm, and direct age-group leaders in their ministry;

• meet regularly with department leaders for planning and evaluation;

• evaluate needs related to space, budget, Bible study curriculum, supplies, and other resources; and recommend actions related to needs; and

• set a positive example for others by living as an authentic witness of Christ and by being thoroughly involved in the life and ministry of the church.

Major Responsibilities of Division Outreach-Evangelism Directors

Division outreach-evangelism directors work with the division directors for their age groups and the general outreach-evangelism director to lead their divisions in outreach and evangelism. They also work closely with department leaders.

In churches using FAITH Sunday School Evangelism Strategy, these persons should be FAITH Group Leaders or Team Leaders.

Their primary responsibilities are to

• coordinate all evangelism and outreach activities of the division;

• coordinate prospect-discovery efforts for the division;

• assist in training division and department leaders and members in evangelism and outreach;

• evaluate, encourage, affirm, and direct age-group leaders in their evangelism and outreach efforts;

• promote outreach and evangelism objectives with other leaders and members;

• maintain active division and department prospect records;

• greet visitors and guide them to the meeting place for their Bible study group; and

• set a positive example for others by living as an authentic witness of Christ and by being thoroughly involved in the life and ministry of the church.

Major Responsibilities of Division Secretaries

Division secretaries assist the division directors by providing vital support related to record keeping, reports and other communications; securing Bible study curriculum, supplies, and other resources; and coordinating the distribution of resources.

Their primary responsibilities are to

- meet regularly with the division leadership team;
- process and maintain general records for the division and compile reports as requested, including prospect information;
- coordinate ordering and distribution of Bible study curriculum, supplies, and other resources;
- set a positive example for others by living as an authentic witness of Christ and by being thoroughly involved in the life and ministry of the church.

Major Responsibilities of Department Directors

Department directors are responsible to the division director of their age group for the total ministry of their department. Department directors work closely with teachers, encouraging them and assisting them in fulfilling their responsibilities.

Their primary responsibilities are to

- lead in planning and administering the total work of the department;
- meet regularly with teachers for prayer, planning, and making assignments related to evangelism and outreach, fellowship, ministry, and Bible teaching;
- serve as a greeter/host for the department;
- serve as the lead teacher for the department, directing the overall teaching-learning experience, and teaching during parts of the session that involve all participants and teachers together;
- evaluate needs related to space, budget, Bible study curriculum, supplies, and other resources; and recommend actions related to needs;
- maintain attendance records and other participant information that strengthens the groups' pursuit of the overall objectives of Sunday School; and
- set a positive example for others by living as an authentic witness of Christ and by being thoroughly involved in the life and ministry of the church.

Other department leaders, such as a department outreach-evangelism director or department secretary, may be enlisted as needed or desired to assist the department director with administering evangelism and record-keeping tasks.

Major Responsibilities of Department Outreach-Evangelism Directors

Department outreach-evangelism directors work with the department directors for their age groups, the division outreach-evangelism director, and the general outreach-evangelism director to lead their departments in outreach and evangelism. They also work closely with class outreach-evangelism leaders.

In churches using FAITH Sunday School Evangelism Strategy, these persons should be FAITH Group Leaders or Team Leaders.

Their primary responsibilities are to

- coordinate all evangelism and outreach activities of the department;
- coordinate prospect-discovery efforts for the department;
- assist in training department and class leaders and members in evangelism and outreach;

- evaluate, encourage, affirm, and direct age-group leaders in their evangelism and outreach efforts;
- promote outreach and evangelism objectives with other leaders and members;
- maintain active department prospect records;
- greet visitors and guide them to the meeting place for their Bible study group; and
- set a positive example for others by living as an authentic witness of Christ and by being thoroughly involved in the life and ministry of the church.

Major Responsibilities of Department Secretaries

Department secretaries assist the department directors by providing vital support related to record keeping, reports, and other communications; securing Bible study curriculum, supplies, and other resources; and coordinating the distribution of resources.

Their primary responsibilities are to
- meet regularly with the department leadership team;
- process and maintain general records for the department and compile reports as requested, including prospect information;
- coordinate ordering and distribution of Bible study curriculum, supplies, and other resources; and
- set a positive example for others by living as an authentic witness of Christ and by being thoroughly involved in the life and ministry of the church.

Major Responsibilities of Teachers

Teachers are responsible for leading people toward faith in the Lord Jesus Christ and for guiding them to serve Him through evangelism, discipleship, fellowship, ministry, and worship. In pursuing this mission, teachers understand that teaching moves beyond the Bible study session into the daily living of participants. Teachers look for opportunities to mentor participants before and after Bible study sessions. They help ensure that a positive ministry environment is provided during the session that facilitates the work of the Holy Spirit. They invest themselves in building positive relationships with participants, and they involve learners in meaningful Bible study.

Their primary responsibilities are to
- lead a small group in meaningful Bible study;
- build positive relationships with participants and prospects and ensure that they are contacted regularly in order to meet needs;
- maintain attendance records and other participant information that strengthens the group's pursuit of the overall objectives of Sunday School;
- lead participants toward faith in the Lord Jesus Christ and to become Great Commission Christians. In youth and adult groups, organize the class to effectively support those objectives;
- in adult groups—enlist an apprentice from the group for the purpose of teaching a new adult class or working in another age group as a teacher within two years; and
- set a positive example for others by living as an authentic witness of Christ and by being thoroughly involved in the life and ministry of the church.

Major Responsibilities of Class Outreach-Evangelism Leaders

Class outreach-evangelism leaders work with the department outreach-evangelism director to lead the class in outreach and evangelism. In churches using the FAITH Sunday School Evangelism Strategy, these persons work with the department outreach-evangelism leader to administer classes' involvement in FAITH.

Their primary responsibilities are

- coordinate all evangelism and outreach activities of the class;
- coordinate prospect-discovery and prospect enlistment efforts of the class;
- lead class members to create an atmosphere that encourages unsaved people to place their faith in Christ and encourages believers to lead others to Christ;
- maintain class prospect records; and
- set a positive example for others by living as an authentic witness of Christ and by being thoroughly involved in the life and ministry of the church.

Major Responsibilities of Class Coordinators

Class coordinators are adults who may be enlisted for adult or youth Bible study classes to direct the overall work of the class, relieving the teacher of administrative responsibilities. The class coordinator works closely with both the teacher and class team leaders to ensure that all functions are addressed appropriately and that the class is properly organized and mobilized for its mission of leading people to faith in the Lord Jesus Christ and building Great Commission Christians.

Major Responsibilities of Apprentices

Apprentices are enlisted from adult classes by teachers of Bible study classes, departments, and other Bible study groups to assist a teacher in his major responsibilities and/or to prepare to start a new Bible study unit within two years. The apprentice serves as a substitute for the teacher when the teacher must be absent.

Major Responsibilities of Class Secretaries

Class secretaries assist class teachers by providing vital support related to record keeping, reports and other communications; obtaining Bible study curriculum, supplies, and other resources; and coordinating the distribution of resources.

Their primary responsibilities are to

- meet regularly with the class leadership team;
- process and maintain general records for the class and compile reports as requested, including prospect information;
- coordinate ordering and distribution of Bible study curriculum, supplies, and other resources; and
- set a positive example for others by living as an authentic witness of Christ and by being thoroughly involved in the life and ministry of the church.

Major Responsibilities of Class Leaders

Class leaders are enlisted by the teacher of an adult or youth Bible study class to assist with the total work of the group. Class leaders work in one or more of the five function areas in either a leader-based approach or a team-based approach. Generally, the class outreach-evangelism leader heads efforts that address the evangelism function.

- *Evangelism.*—Create an atmosphere that encourages unsaved people to place their faith in Christ and encourages believers to lead others to Christ. In churches using the FAITH Sunday School Evangelism Strategy, members of this team should be on a FAITH Team.
- *Discipleship.*—Create an atmosphere that encourages believers to grow in maturity in Christ; monitor the discipleship needs of believers and work with the church's Discipleship director to provide learning opportunities focused to address those needs.
- *Fellowship.*—Create an atmosphere conducive to members building relationships with one another as together they build upon their relationship with God; lead actions that help new members be assimilated into the fellowship of the class and the team or group to which they are assigned.
- *Ministry.*—Create an atmosphere in which members and prospects can experience direct care and concern for life's needs and avenues through which they may identify and implement ministry and mission projects that utilize the gifts and abilities of class members; lead out in intercessory prayer as a integral ministry and missionary efforts of the class.
- *Worship.*—Create a worshipful atmosphere, encourage participation in the church's corporate worship events, lead small-group worship experiences, and encourage personal worship in home and family settings.

The Participants

Basic Role

The people who attend Sunday School classes, departments, and other Bible study groups are not merely the intended recipients of Sunday School's ministry. They are the grassroots ministers.

Sunday School is concerned with building Great Commission Christians. All of the class leaders, teachers, directors, and pastoral leaders needed for now and in the future may be able to be found on the membership or prospect lists of Sunday School classes. Every participant should receive an opportunity to serve according to the leadership of the Holy Spirit. These opportunities may be provided through their participation in Sunday School.

Major Responsibilities
- Participate in personal and group Bible study regularly, giving attention to the leadership of the Holy Spirit in one's life.
- Be receptive to God's efforts to draw people to faith in Christ through His Word, His Spirit, and His people.
- Actively participate in efforts to lead others toward faith in the Lord Jesus Christ.
- Participate individually and with the class to serve Christ through evangelism, discipleship, fellowship, ministry, and ministry.
- Follow God's leadership in responding to opportunities to grow spiritually and to serve God's people in leadership roles.

Your Time Is Now

How are you developing the leader within you? Within other people?

Prepared by God to S.E.R.V.E.

Leaders know who they are in Christ Jesus. They know how God molded and gifted them for His use. They trust that God can use every experience to prepare them for ministry. They trust that God has prepared them to serve for His glory, not their gain.

God has prepared you for His purposes to bring honor to Him. The Bible says to use the spiritual gifts God gave you to serve others.

According to 1 Peter 4:10, the goal of all God's gifts is service to others. "Each one should use whatever gift he has received to serve others, faithfully administering God's grace in its various forms."

Servant leaders are leaders who serve. The acrostic *S.E.R.V.E.* is an outline for how God has prepared you for His purposes.

S piritual gifts— Those gifts God gives through His Holy Spirit to empower you for service

E xperiences— Those events God allows which mold you into a servant leader

R elational style— Behavioral traits God uses to give you a leadership style

V ocational skills— Those abilities you have gained through training and experience which you can use in service to God

E nthusiasm— That passion God has put in your heart for a certain ministry to others

Your relationship with Christ as well as these five areas—spiritual gifts, experiences, relational style, vocational skills, and enthusiasm—become the raw materials God uses to mold you into a servant leader.

Spiritual Gifts

Leaders know how God has gifted them for service in the body of Christ, the church. Leaders serve out of their spiritual giftedness. They seek to lead from their God-given place in the body of Christ. The church works best when its members know how God has gifted them spiritually and when all members, empowered by their spiritual gifts, are in places of service. Spiritual gifts are the key to understanding how God intends the church to function.

A spiritual gift is a "manifestation of the Spirit" (1 Cor. 12:7). It is not a special ability you develop on your own; that is a skill or talent. You do not seek a spiritual gift. However, you should prayerfully seek to understand how God already has gifted you for His purposes.

God gives you your spiritual gifts for a special purpose in the church when He graces you with salvation through Christ. Understanding spiritual gifts begins with knowing the biblical nature of the church.

Both 1 Corinthians 12:7 and Ephesians 4:12 help us understand why God gives gifts to the church. "Now to each one the manifestation of the Spirit is given for the common good" (1 Cor. 12:7). Ephesians 4: 12 further describes this purpose: "To prepare God's people for works of service, so that the body of Christ may be built up."

Spiritual gifts are for the common good of the church. God gifts members of the church to equip and build up the body of Christ. Spiritual gifts are not for pride but for service. Servant leaders allow God's spiritual gifts to motivate them to serve.

Important to any study of spiritual gifts is God's work in the life of the believer and

Prepared by God to S.E.R.V.E. has been adapted from C. Gene Wilkes, *Jesus On Leadership: Becoming a Servant Leader* (Nashville: LifeWay Press, 1996), 31-84. This resource can lead you to apply the biblical principles of servant leadership to all areas of your ministry. It includes more detailed spiritual gifts and relationship style surveys.

Accountability

the church. You do not decide you want a certain gift and then go get it. God gives the gifts "just as he determines" (1 Cor. 12:11). Spiritual gifts are part of God's design for a person's life and for the life of the church. The Bible says that "God has arranged the parts in the body, every one of them, just as he wanted them to be" (1 Cor. 12:18).

Your goal as a servant leader is to discover how God in His grace has gifted you for service, and to lead others in the same joy of discovery.

Ken Hemphill, president, Southwestern Baptist Theological Seminary, defines a spiritual gift as "an individual manifestation of grace from the Father that enables you to serve Him and thus play a vital role in His plan for the redemption of the world."[4] For this study, we will use this definition: *A spiritual gift is an expression of the Holy Spirit in the life of believers which empowers them to serve the body of Christ, the church.*

Romans 12:6-8; 1 Corinthians 12:8-10,28-30; Ephesians 4:11; and 1 Peter 4:9-11 contain representative lists of gifts and roles God has given to the church. A definition of these gifts follows. Check two or three gifts that seem to fit how God has made you.

- **Leadership**—Leadership aids the body by leading and directing members to accomplish the goals and purposes of the church. Leadership motivates people to work together in unity toward common goals (Rom. 12:8).
- **Administration**—Persons with the gift of administration lead the body by steering others to remain on task. Administration enables the body to organize according to God-given purposes and long-term goals (1 Cor. 12:28).
- **Teaching**—Teaching is instructing members in the truths and doctrines of God's Word for the purposes of building up, unifying, and maturing the body (1 Cor. 12:28; Rom. 12:7; Eph. 4:11).
- **Knowledge**—The gift of knowledge manifests itself in teaching and training in discipleship. It is the God-given ability to learn, know, and explain the precious truths of God's Word. A word of knowledge is a Spirit-revealed truth (1 Cor. 12:28).
- **Wisdom**—Wisdom is the gift that discerns the work of the Holy Spirit in the body and applies His teachings and actions to the needs of the body (1 Cor. 12:28).
- **Prophecy**—The gift of prophecy is proclaiming the Word of God boldly. This builds up the body and leads to conviction of sin. Prophecy manifests itself in preaching and teaching (1 Cor. 12:10; Rom. 12:6).
- **Discernment**—Discernment aids the body by recognizing the true intentions of those within or related to the body. Discernment tests the message and actions of others for the protection and well-being of the body (1 Cor. 12:10).
- **Exhortation**—Possessors of this gift encourage members to be involved in and enthusiastic about the work of the Lord. Members with this gift are good counselors and motivate others to service. Exhortation exhibits itself in preaching, teaching, and ministry (Rom. 12:8).
- **Shepherding**—The gift of shepherding is manifested in persons who look out for the spiritual welfare of others. Although pastors, like shepherds, do care for members of the church, this gift is not limited to a pastor or staff member (Eph. 4:11).
- **Faith**—Faith trusts God to work beyond the human capabilities of the people. Believers with this gift encourage others to trust in God in the face of apparently insurmountable odds (1 Cor. 12:9).

[4] Ken Hemphill, *Serving God: Discovering and Using Your Spiritual Gifts Workbook* (Dallas: The Sampson Company, 1995), 22.

- **Evangelism**—God gifts his church with evangelists to lead others to Christ effectively and enthusiastically. This gift builds up the body by adding new members to its fellowship (Eph. 4:11).
- **Apostleship**—The church sends apostles from the body to plant churches or be missionaries. Apostles motivate the body to look beyond its walls in order to carry out the Great Commission (1 Cor. 12:28; Eph. 4:11).
- **Service/Helps**—Those with the gift of service/helps recognize practical needs in the body and joyfully give assistance to meeting those needs. Christians with this gift do not mind working behind the scenes (1 Cor. 12:28; Rom. 12:7).
- **Mercy**—Cheerful acts of compassion characterize those with the gift of mercy. Persons with this gift aid the body by empathizing with hurting members. They keep the body healthy and unified by keeping others aware of the needs within the church (Rom. 12:8).
- **Giving**—Members with the gift of giving give freely and joyfully to the work and mission of the body. Cheerfulness and liberality are characteristics of individuals with this gift (Rom. 12:8).
- **Hospitality**—Those with this gift have the ability to make visitors, guests, and strangers feel at ease. They often use their home to entertain guests. Persons with this gift integrate new members into the body (1 Pet. 4:9).

List here the gifts you have begun to discover in your life:

1._____
2._____
3._____

God has gifted you with an expression of His Holy Spirit to support His vision and mission of the church. It is a worldwide vision to reach all people with the gospel of Christ. As a servant leader, God desires that you know how He has gifted you. This will lead you to where He would have you serve as part of His vision and mission for the church.

God has gifted you for service in Christ's body, the church (1 Cor. 12:7). His goal is for you to prepare others for service in the church (Eph. 4:12). As a servant leader, you are to use your spiritual gifts for the common good of the body. God gifted you for His glory, not your gain. God gifted you to build up His church, not your ego.

After prayer and worship, I am beginning to sense that God wants me to use my spiritual gifts to serve Christ's body by . . .

I am not sure yet how God wants me to use my gifts to serve others. But I am committed to prayer and worship, seeking wisdom and opportunities to use the gifts I have received from God.

Experiences

Leaders trust that God works in their lives to bring about His plan for their lives. Experiences become God's crucible to mold you into His image. Servant leaders are confident that events which happen to them and around them are part of God's sovereign work in creation.

God can take what already has happened in your life to help accomplish His will. God can mold and make you into a tool of His grace. God can break into your life to make you a new creation for His purposes.

Henry Blackaby calls events like Paul's conversion "spiritual markers." He says a spiritual marker "identifies a time of transition, decision, or direction when I clearly know that God has guided me." [5] Spiritual markers remind you that God is at work in your history. Remembering them helps you see God's work in your life and how He is unfolding His plan for your life.

You have events in your life when God has made His will clear to you. God broke into history, and you know God spoke to you. He may have confirmed a decision you had made. He may have revealed something new about who He is.

Take a moment to describe in the space below some of your most important encounters with God. Write as if you are telling a friend about these life-changing moments. Start with your salvation experience. Don't worry if you do not have a dramatic desert story. God works in everyday events to shape you into His likeness. Spiritual markers can be any life experience, from a burning bush to a child's gentle touch.

Let me tell you about my most important encounters with God . . .

Relational Style

Every person has a natural style of how he or she relates to others. Every style has its strengths and weaknesses. God can use any relational style that is submitted to His will to serve His purposes.

How you relate to others is basic to how you serve as a leader. To know your relational style is to know how God has molded you to serve people through your relationships with them. Servant leaders know how they naturally relate to others and how others relate to them.

Since leadership involves influencing others for the common good, knowing how God has molded your temperament is key to knowing your leadership style. Knowing the style of others' also allows you to meet their relational needs. Moreover, understanding the relational needs of other people helps you communicate with and

[5] Henry Blackaby and Claude V. King, *Experiencing God: Knowing and Doing the Will of God* (Nashville: Convention Press, 1990), 104.

lead them more effectively.

God will help you understand your role as a servant leader as you assess the strengths and weaknesses of your relational style. A four-category model has been proven over time and has strong scientific support. The primary source for understanding this model is Ken Voges, an author of *Understanding How Others Misunderstand You*. Voges uses the letters *DISC* to represent the four primary relational styles. [6]

• **D** stands for the "dominance" style—Works toward achieving goals and results; functions best in active, challenging environments.

• **I** stands for the "influencing" style—Works toward relating to people through verbal persuasion; functions best in friendly, favorable environments.

• **S** is the "steadiness" style—Works toward supporting and cooperating with others; functions best in supportive, harmonious environments.

• **C** represents the "conscientious" style—Works toward doing things right and focuses on details; functions best in structured, orderly environments.

Using the descriptions above that best describe you, personalize your DISC style by completing the following statements:

Because of my special, God-given style of relating to others, I tend to work toward . . .

and I function best in . . .

But I also see these additional qualities of my God-given personality:

The most important part of the above activity is to reflect on these questions: *How does my relational style relate to servant leadership? How can my own God-given temperament be used by God to make a difference in my church and community?*

As you think about these questions, note the following chart that summarizes possible strengths and weaknesses of each leadership style.

Dominant		Influencing	
Strengths	*Weaknesses*	*Strengths*	*Weaknesses*
Direct	Too controlling	Gregarious	Forgets the goal
Active	Hates routine	Enthusiastic	Poor follow-through
Decisive	Hates details	Extremely flexible	Overlooks details
Steadiness		**Conscientious**	
Strengths	*Weaknesses*	*Strengths*	*Weaknesses*
Cooperative	Fails to confront	Detailed	Inflexible
Deliberate	Dislikes change	Conscientious	Rigid
Supportive	Too compromising	Cautious	Indecisive

[6] Ken Voges and Ron Braud, *Understanding How Others Misunderstand You* (Chicago: Moody, 1990)

Note that each style has strengths *and* weaknesses. No single style can meet every need. God intentionally created a variety of styles, none being more important or more needed than another. All gifts and strengths are important to the overall servant ministry of your church. At the same time, each strength, when out of control, can become a weakness. And weaknesses should not become excuses for failure. A person and a church constantly must strive to accomplish without excuse the ministries received from God.

This diversity of styles within the church may at times produce conflict, but it provides the important balance needed to accomplish what God gives the church to do. It reminds us of the important lesson that God needs each one of us, and that we need each other.

Churches function best when members accept the relational styles of others and seek to meet the needs of those persons, never compromising the message of Christ. Relationships remain strong when members follow God's pattern for living together as His body with all its diversity (1 Cor. 12:14-26).

God's Word offers clear teaching on how we are to serve one another in love. Colossians 3:12-14 says, "Therefore, as God's chosen people, holy and dearly loved, clothe yourselves with compassion, kindness, humility, gentleness and patience. Bear with each other and forgive whatever grievances you may have against one another. Forgive as the Lord forgave you. And over all these virtues put on love, which binds them all together in perfect unity."

Remember that your natural relational style is not an excuse to sin. God's indwelling Spirit balances your natural tendencies with God's temperament. Regardless of your style, the fruit of the Spirit (Gal. 5:22-23) is always a vital part of a servant leader's relationships. God's Spirit molds your temperament for His glory.

Vocational Skills

Our English word *vocation* comes from the Latin word *vocare*, which means "to call." A vocation, then, is what one feels called to do with his or her life. In previous generations, a sense of divine calling was part of a person's place in the world. A vocation was part of God's plan for a person's life. God called, and you responded by gaining the skills necessary to live out that calling.

Vocation has come to mean any profession or occupation. A vocational skill is any ability you have learned that enhances your calling in life.

In today's secular world, people often prefer to use the word *career*. A career is your choice. Instead of looking for God's plan, the world teaches you to choose what you want to do and, then, to plot a course of training to accomplish your career choice. A career, then, is what you choose for yourself.

In the New Testament, Paul encouraged the Christians in Ephesus to "live a life worthy of the calling you have received" (Eph. 4:1). He was not talking about their jobs. He encouraged them to adopt a lifestyle consistent with who they were in Christ. Calling in the Bible is one's position in Christ, not one's position in the world.

Whatever your vocation, your calling is to live worthy of the salvation God gives you in Christ Jesus. In Colossians, Paul wrote, "Whatever you do, work at it with all your heart, as working for the Lord, not for men. . . . It is the Lord Christ you are serving" (Col. 3:23-24). Whatever you do, God calls you to live like a child of God and to bring honor to God through your actions. It matters less what you do in life than it does what you do with your life.

For the sake of our study, let's define *vocation* as what you do to provide for your needs in society, recognizing God's work in your life to lead you to that choice. *Calling* is God's call to salvation in Christ Jesus and to a special mission in your life for His purposes.

Vocational skills are those skills you have acquired to do your career and/or hobbies. Let's make an inventory of your skills. Use the following table to create your skill inventory:

Name of Skill   *How I Use This Skill in My Vocation*

1._____

2._____

3._____

God used Paul's vocational skills for his life's calling. God can do the same for you. Take time to imagine how God can use the skills you listed above for His work of spreading the gospel. For example, if one of your skills is carpentry, you can use that skill to build shelves in your church's preschool rooms or for a local mission or ministry. Be creative as you consider how you can use your skills for the glory of God.

Name of Skill   *How God Can Use This Skill in His Mission*

1._____

2._____

3._____

Enthusiasm

The word *enthusiasm* comes from a Greek word that literally means, "in god." The Greeks believed that a god could enter a person and inspire or enthuse him. Our word enthusiasm takes on the meaning, "God in you." While the Greek word for *enthuse* is not found in the New Testament, the emphasis on God's presence which energizes the believer is a recurring theme (John 14:20; 20:21-22; Matt. 28:18-20; Acts 1:8).

The Bible is clear that God's Holy Spirit is the source of passion for God's mission within the believer. Paul declared it is "Christ in you" which is "the hope of glory" (Col. 1:27). We do not generate hope on our own. God energizes us with His living Holy Spirit. Jesus promised that the Holy Spirit will be our Counselor and "guide you into all truth" (John 16:7,13). He is our counselor and guide as we follow the Lord. Passion and enthusiasm for ministry come from God.

Scripture tells about people who were enthusiastic about what they did. This is not a self-generated thrill. Enthusiasm is a God-given desire to serve Him by meeting the needs of others. Servant leaders have a God-given passion to serve.

A servant leader's joy comes when he sees God at work and he is a part of it. Servant leadership is a God-given passion for the success of God's plan. Servant leaders find joy when God's will is done.

Your God-given enthusiasm is sometimes your only source of joy in ministry. As you lead, you will face obstacles and disappointments. People will criticize you. Sometimes they will question your motives. But the sincere desire to know God's will and the passion God puts in your heart for His work absorb these negative reactions and allow you to move forward with your ministry. Your enthusiasm is the beginning of a fruitful life in Christ.

What has God burned in your heart to do for His mission on earth? Take a moment to consider what that may be. Prayerfully write your responses to the following statements. Complete them with honest, heartfelt statements.

The one thing I do for God that makes my heart beat fast is . . .

If I could do one thing for God, it would be to . . .

My S.E.R.V.E. Profile

Believing God has prepared me for servant leadership. I am discovering that He has molded me in the following areas. (Pull together what you have written on the previous pages to complete the following statements.)

- *God has gifted me with the spiritual gifts of:*

- *God has allowed these experiences to guide me for His purposes:*

- *God has created me to relate most often to others naturally in this way:*

- *God has given me the opportunities to develop these vocational skills that can be used in His service:*

- *God has burned in my heart the enthusiasm to serve in this area of ministry:*

How does your experience with the S.E.R.V.E. inventory/profile translate to worker enlistment—to what we say and how we say it when we enlist workers? How should this information be discussed during an enlistment visit? What other information or resources are needed for people to make the best decision? Why is a personal visit more important than ever?

Making a Leader Enlistment Visit

Properly enlisting a person is the first step toward good leadership.

- Pray for God to lead you to the one person whom He wants you to enlist for a position. You already have identified potential leaders who have specific gifts; pray over this list and ask God to select a person for the position. As you pray, ask God to start moving in the person's heart.

- Make an appointment for a visit with the prospective leader. Schedule the appointment for a time and place most convenient for the person to be enlisted. Often this will be in the person's home. Be sure to be on time for the visit.

- Explain up front why you want to visit. Let the person know you feel God is leading you in a particular direction, and that you want to discuss it with him.

- Provide the prospective leader with a written list of duties for the position you are asking her to consider. Make sure the list includes all expectations, such as participation in visitation, leadership team meetings, witness training, and so forth.

- Inform the prospective leader of the term of service intended. In most cases, except when someone is enlisted to fill a vacancy during the year, the term of service would be one year. Indicate also that service for this year is no guarantee of being in that position next year. Explain that your goal is to give every person an opportunity to serve God in a position that makes best use of his/her talents and spiritual gifts.

- Provide the prospective leader copies of essential materials that will help in doing the work. Teachers and members Bible study materials, resource kits, maps, and information about other available resources should be provided. If the prospective leader declines to serve in this position, you can ask him to return the materials.

- Give the person adequate time to discuss with you what is expected of leaders serving in this position. Explain what support systems are available and who will be working in similar capacities. Encourage the prospective leader to ask questions now, but also provide your telephone number for contact later when other questions arise. Be honest. The prospective leader has the right to know as much as possible about the responsibilities.

- Ask the prospective leader to pray about the position, and promise to do the same. Live up to that promise. Your objective is for the person and you to discern God's direction for the situation.

- Set a time (usually a week later) when you can contact the person for a decision. Setting a time to call back takes pressure off the person from feeling a decision must be given immediately.

- Accept the person's answer. Do not try to force the person to accept responsibilities he or she really does not want to accept. If the person accepts the position, provide additional details about planning, worker enlistment, and training. If this new leader is responsible for enlisting others, train him to use the same techniques in enlisting others that you modeled in his enlistment.

Developing the Leadership Team

Potential Leader Training

Potential Sunday School leader training includes a basic orientation to the ministry of Sunday School, transformational Bible teaching, and age-group work including observation of age-group sessions. Potential leader training also includes a Bible survey, helps for developing a personal devotional life, a foundation in servant leadership, an introduction to outreach and evangelism techniques, an overview of effective planning skills, and an understanding of purposeful leadership team meetings. Potential leaders can even do practice teaching.

The training is to equip potential Sunday School leaders to serve effectively in an area best suited to them. Participants are exposed to ministry techniques appropriate to each age group through a mentoring/modeling process. The participants receive technical as well as practical training, including practice on the job. The goal is to develop a readiness and sensitivity to a particular age group area in hope that the participant will discover a place of service.

The *Christian Growth Study Plan Catalog* lists leadership skills and personal growth diploma study plans that can be used in designing a potential Sunday School leader training course for your church. Other undated resources can be incorporated into a plan to address specific needs you identify.

Ongoing Training for Sunday School Leaders

Sunday School leaders need opportunities to improve their work through training, which will sharpen their skills, improve their understanding of methods, and expose them to new insights. That is the purpose for ongoing Sunday School leadership training. A church needs to create a climate that encourages training or leaders will not be likely to see its importance. Training becomes part of the church's expectation for its leaders and a way leaders are held accountable.

Training is to address felt needs among the leaders. Moreover, a continuous focus on mission, vision, and action statements can help perpetuate the desire for additional training. Some ways of discovering training needs are through observing leaders at, conversing with leaders, discussing training needs during Sunday School Planning Team meetings, using evaluation instruments, and reviewing Sunday School leaders' progress toward their own individual training goals. Because all the training needs cannot be met in one year, strive to provide training that meets priorities and that contributes to greatest improvement in performance.

Just as with potential leader training, budget is a factor in developing an ongoing training plan. Funds will need to be allocated for resources and leaders for training events conducted at the church. Training fees and travel expenses may be included in the budget for leaders attending state events or national conference centers.

Leader training is not always dependent on assembling a training group. Individualized study using books, study modules, audio, video, or other electronic means is a valid and convenient means for leaders to develop skills needed for their job assignment. In fact, more persons may be willing to do individualized training than may commit themselves to a series of group training sessions.

The *Christian Growth Study Plan Catalog* suggests leadership skills and personal growth diploma study options.

Perhaps one of the most overlooked opportunities for ongoing training is to make full use of dated curriculum resources for Bible study leaders, especially the age-group leader guides. Each leader guide includes a section for leader and ministry development, providing help throughout the year to develop leaders into more effective practitioners of Sunday School strategy. Other resources such as *The Sunday School Leader* monthly magazine supplement ongoing training for all Sunday School leaders.

Ongoing training needs to address the relationship of church functions to Sunday School strategy, curriculum understanding, age-group characteristics, learning styles, tools and techniques for transformational teaching, spiritual growth and development, a foundation in servant leadership, evangelism and outreach techniques and tools, fellowship, relationship-building skills, ministry ideas, and helps for class members.

Assessment of Training Needs

Any number of approaches can be used to identify training needs. Here are a few to consider in addition to those currently used by your planning team.

Make training a regular topic of discussion in Sunday School Planning Team meetings.

This type of discussion may occur naturally as the planning team considers its work in evangelism, discipleship, fellowship, ministry, and worship; its progress toward goals, and so forth. In case it does not surface periodically, keep training needs as an agenda item.

Listen to workers.

Times of informal conversation can reveal valuable information. You also can learn a lot by "listening" to situations as well as to words. Does worker turnover in a certain area tell you something? Are workers frustrated? Are once-happy members becoming chronic absentees? Look at records for what they indicate about training needs.

Periodically survey all workers.

In addition to times of informal listening, provide formal times in which you ask workers to identify their training needs.

Listen to members.

Talk with age-group division/department directors about needs they observe.

These leaders are the closest to their area of work. Rely on their impressions, and follow up on their input.

Evaluate training events and use the information comments or insights to shape future training.

Responses will help bring to completion a training event. Such evaluation also can indicate other areas in which training is needed.

Observe how workers are doing in Christian Growth Study Plan activities.

Encourage those who are involved to continue and provide the assistance they need. Help other workers see how this approach can help them achieve training goals. Provide the resources all workers need to participate fully.

Look at job descriptions.

Change in job responsibilities indicate potential training needs. Training will be a priority to make Sunday School for a new century become reality.

Use items such as Sunday School Strategy Checkups, items in the Planning and Training Pack, and other evaluation tools to assess areas of training need.

Observe in classes and departments.

An Annual Training Calendar

Consider developing an annual training calendar. A training calendar might include the dates of the following events:

- Sunday School Launch event;
- January Bible Study;
- Spring training event (between New Year's Day and Easter, for a midyear focus on a specific function or area of Sunday School);
- Associational Training Schools;
- Sunday School Leadership Events at Glorieta® and Ridgecrest® Conference Centers and at Green Lake, Wisconsin;
- Potential Sunday School leader training; and
- Associational and state convention sponsored conferences.

Consider several different training approaches in planning your annual leader training calendar.

- *One-day training extravaganzas*

Many churches are finding that adults will give a Friday evening or a Saturday morning, even a Saturday afternoon, to training. One approach, called "Midnight Madness," begins with a banquet, followed by a training event, and ends with prayer at midnight.

- *Quarterly training*

Choose a yearly theme and then develop a detailed, age-graded training plan for each quarter. Each event could include dinner followed by a short training event. Potential leaders are included in this event to introduce them to the nature and scope of Sunday School ministry.

- *Semiannual preparation*

The events are tightly focused on such needs areas as caring skills, evaluating and using records properly, team building, or creative teaching methods.

- *Ongoing weekly leadership team meetings*

Often overlooked as training opportunities, the weekly leadership team meeting provides a natural time to train leaders in specific areas of effective Sunday School ministry. Training in how to use the lecture method properly, how to be a good listener, how to witness using the Roman Road, how to plan an effective fellowship, and so forth can be covered in 15 to 20 minutes with all leaders together. Age-group leaders meet in age-group meetings to debrief and dialogue how the material applies to their work.

- *"Home-Grown" training packets*

Many church members have video cameras and audiocassette tape recorders. Leaders can create their own training resources by staging a training session or recording parts of a planned training event. Additional copies of these audio and video clips could be made and written activities or assignments included with the clips. These could be packaged and checked out through the church office.

- *On-the- job training*

Few training experiences are as effective as on-the-job training. Don't confuse this with "trial by fire" training. The latter is sending an unsuspecting novice into a class and telling the novice to learn the hard way. On-the-job training is giving potential leaders opportunities to serve as apprentices under effective leaders in each age group.

The FAITH evangelism training process relies heavily on this approach by linking two first-time Learners with a Team Leader already trained in FAITH. As a Team, three people train and make home visits together and experience the dynamics of sharing the gospel firsthand.

Being an effective leader requires dedication, consistency, training, and a lot of hard work. Never underestimate the value of training. It can save you and the leaders in your Sunday School from struggles later. And it will move toward greater effectiveness in helping the church do the work of the Great Commission.

Your Time Is Now

How knowledgeable are you of the training needs of your leaders? How is the choice of events and calendar influenced by training needs? How will your strategy address training needs next year?

Key Leader Training Opportunities

Sunday School Launch Weekend, 1999

Leadership and motivational events for workers in your own church can launch a new year based on the theme Sunday School for a New Century.

National Sunday School Leadership Training Events

What better way to discover the full implications of Sunday School as strategy than by attending as a group one of the National Sunday School Leadership Training Events in Summer 2000? In settings that facilitate team-building, fellowship, and responsiveness to God's guidance, Sunday School practitioners will provide training that is focused on the opportunities and challenges of a new century. Activities for all ages make conference center events appropriate for the entire family. Each site offers unique beauty and recreational opportunities.

Information about National Sunday School Leadership Training Events will be posted on LifeWay Online at www.lifeway.com. Under "Conferences" you will find information about events at both Glorieta® (New Mexico) Conference Center and Ridgecrest® (North Carolina) Conference Center. One Sunday School Leadership Training Event is held at Green Lake, Wisconsin, Conference Center during the Summer 2000. Information about Sunday School leader training at all three locations will be available at www.lifeway. com/sundayschool/faith.

Christian Growth Study Plan

The Christian Growth Study Plan assists churches in providing a systematic approach to leadership and skills development and Christian growth. Two categories of diploma plans are available: (1) Leadership and Skill Development; (2) Christian Growth.

Leadership and Skill Development Diplomas are available to help train leaders in various ministries. The same course titles are given for leaders of a specific audience.

For example, the course "Administration of Preschool Ministries" is one course for all preschool leaders; Preschool Sunday School leaders can choose either to read *Preschool Sunday School for a New Century* or attend a preschool leadership conference at Glorieta, Ridgecrest, or Green Lake. Courses in addition to "Administration" include "Understanding Preschoolers and Their Families," "Teaching Preschoolers," and "The Preschool Leaders' Role in Ministry, Witnessing, and Reaching People." Similar choices exist within each course and among other diplomas.

Diploma plans are available for the other age groups, special education, and general officers. A Reaching People Through Bible Study Projects and Groups Diploma Plan allows trainees to focus on off-site Bible studies, Vacation Bible School training, and other special projects.

Information about the Christian Growth Study Plan can be obtained from state Sunday School offices. Ask for the current *Christian Growth Study Plan Catalog*. You may also secure information about Christian Growth Study Plan, including your church's member list/summary, by accessing the Web site at: http//www.lifeway.com./cgsp.

Associational and State-Sponsored Training Events

The local Baptist association and state convention offer worker training events that many churches may not be able to provide for themselves. Contact the associational director of missions or the state Sunday School department office for a schedule of events. Insert the dates for these events in your planning calendar.

Online Resources and Information

EXTRA!—weekly updates of lesson-related current events, illustrations, teaching approaches, and other timely tips for users of Youth, Adult, Children's, and Preschool Six (Kindergarten) Sunday School materials—illustrates the difference technology can make for both the teacher and the participant. This and other information may be secured by accessing the age-group Web site.

Web surfers around the world can access information about LifeWay Christian Resources products, services, and personnel through LifeWay Online. The site is located at: http//www.lifeway.com. LifeWay Online serves as the gateway to all LifeWay-related sites on the Internet. Here are locations of other Web sites that relate specifically to Sunday School. Other sites are currently under development.

- *For Preschool Sunday School Leaders: PRESource*

At PRESource, leaders can be introduced to Bible study resources, learn about new products and services, and read articles. One section contains ideas for teaching preschool sixes. The site is located at: http//www.lifeway.com/presource.

- *For Children's Sunday School Leaders: KidTrek*

KidTrek provides information about children's resources and services. This animated site has something for Sunday School leaders, parents, and children. The site is located at: http//www.lifeway.com/kidtrek.

- *For Youth and Youth Sunday School Leaders: YouthScape*

YouthScape features information for youth leaders, parents of youth, and youth. Topics include: Bible study, evangelism and missions, leadership development, and more. The site is located at: http//www.youthscape.com.

- *For Adults and Adult Sunday School Leaders: Bible Insites*

Bible Insites, the adult biblical studies Web site, provides resources and support for resources that focus on Adult Sunday School. The site for adults is located at : http//www.lifeway.com/bibleinsites.

- *For General Sunday School Leaders and FAITH Information*

The site offering information of interest for FAITH church leaders, general Sunday School leadership, pastors, ministers of education, and others is located at: http://www.lifeway. com/sundayschool/faith.

Security Issues in Leader Enlistment

The current social climate has created special concerns that need to be raised when enlisting persons to work with preschoolers, children, and youth. To protect young children and youth and the church, the church needs to develop screening procedures that provide background information on anyone who would work with any of these age groups.

Consider these tips from *Reducing the Risk of Child Sexual Abuse in Your Church*. These tips apply to enlisting or hiring any persons who may encounter young children or youth, such as Sunday School leaders, staff members, childcare workers, custodians, and so forth.

- Confirm identity. If an applicant is unknown to the church leadership, look for ways to confirm the person's identity.
- Screen all workers. The screening procedure should apply to new members as well as current staff members.
- Lower the risk. Think of the screening procedure in terms of risk reduction. Consider other actions that need to be taken to reduce risks.
- Use professional help. The services of a local attorney should be solicited in drafting an appropriate screening form to ensure compliance with state law.
- Use well-prepared forms to secure appropriate and acceptable information.
- Fulfill legal requirements. Be aware of any additional legal requirements that apply in your state.
- Maintain confidentiality. Churches are required to treat applications, records of contact with churches, or references as strictly confidential information. [7]

[7] Richard R. Hammar, Steven W. Klipowicz, and James F. Cobble, *Reducing the Risk of Sexual Abuse in Your Church* (Matthews, NC: Christian Ministry Resources, 1993), 34.

Volunteer Leader Screening Form

This application is to be completed by all applicants for any position involving the supervision or custody of minors. It will help our church family provide a safe and secure environment for all preschoolers, children, and youth who participate in our ministries and use our facilities.

Personal

Name _____ Date _____

Present Address _____ Social Security #_____

City _____ State_____ Zip_____

Day Phone (____)_____ Evening Phone (____)_____

Occupation _____ Marital Status _____

On what date would you be available to begin?_____

What is your minimum length of commitment?_____

Do you have a current driver's license? ___Yes ___No   Please list your license number:_____

Have you ever been charged with, indicted for, or pled guilty to an offense involving a minor? _____ Yes _____ No

If yes, please describe all convictions for the past five years: _____

Were you a victim of abuse or molestation while a minor? _____ Yes _____ No

(If you prefer, you may refuse to answer this question. Or you may discuss your answer in confidence with one of the ministers rather than answering it on this from. Answering yes or leaving the question unanswered will not automatically disqualify you.)

Church Activity

When did you make your profession of faith in Christ? _____

When were you baptized?_____ Are you a member of our church? _____ Yes ___ No

If no, where are you a member?_____

List (name and address) other churches you have attended regularly during the past five years:

_____
_____

List all previous church work involving preschoolers, children, or youth:

Church Name	Address	Type of Work Performed	Dates

List all previous nonchurch work involving preschoolers, children, or youth:

Organization	Address	Telephone No(s).

List any gifts, calling, training, education, or other factors that have prepared you for teaching preschoolers, children, or youth:

_____
_____

Personal References (not former employers or relatives)

Organization	Address	Telephone No(s).

Applicant's Statement

The information contained in this application is correct to the best of my knowledge. I authorize references or churches listed in this application to provide information (including opinions) they may have regarding my character and fitness for working with preschoolers, children, or youth. I release all such references from any liability for furnishing such evaluations, provided they do so in good faith and without malice. I waive any right I may have to inspect references provided on my behalf. Should my application be accepted, I agree to be bound by the bylaws and policies of this church and to refrain from unscriptural conduct in the performance of my services on behalf of the church. I further state that **I have carefully read the foregoing release and know the content thereof and I sign this release as my own free act**. This is a legally binding agreement which I have read and understand.

Signature _____

(**Disclaimer**: This form is solely for illustrative purposes. State and local laws may vary. It is recommended that each church solicit the advice of an independent and qualified attorney. LifeWay Christian Resources and the Southern Baptist Convention assumes no liability for reliance on this form.)

Your 1999-2000 Sunday School Planning Team

SUNDAY SCHOOL PLANNING TEAM			
Position	**Name**	**Address**	**Phone**
Pastor/Church Staff			
Sunday School Director			
Outreach-Evangelism Director			
Sunday School Secretary			
Adult			
Young Adult			
Youth			
Children			
Preschool			
Others as Needed			

DIVISION/DEPARTMENT/CLASS LEADERSHIP TEAM			
Position	**Name**	**Address**	**Phone**

Section 5
Implementing the Strategy

Jay Johnston, director, Sunday School/FAITH Ministry Department, is a leader who calls others to be and do their best to meet the challenges and needs of the 21st century.

As we said at the end of Section 1, *Sunday School for a New Century* has been written from the perspective of Sunday School "best practices." *Best practices* is a strong phrase. It asserts that while there may be several ways of doing something, one way is proven to be better and more effective.

The challenges of a new century will require the best. No longer can we be satisfied to linger in the crowded corridors of complacency. Instead, we must step forward with solutions for the future. Such times demand decisive leadership and intentional action.

The principle of excellence is important to all phases of Sunday School ministry: from organization to personnel, from record-keeping to ministry visitation, from evangelism to Bible teaching. The people reached or to be reached through Sunday School deserve the best practices possible.

Jay Johnston, director, Sunday School/FAITH Ministry Department at LifeWay Christian Resources, exemplifies best practices as well as anyone. Jay has been at LifeWay for more than 10 years. Prior to joining the Sunday School Group, he managed a component in the Discipleship and Family Group with major responsibilities related to men's and women's ministries, senior adult work, and so forth. His work has brought him into contact with such popular writers and lecturers as Henry Blackaby, Beth Moore, and Anne Graham Lotz.

In his current assignment, Jay has responsibility for the design and development of Sunday School principles and practices that potentially can influence work in more than 40,000 Southern Baptist churches and among thousands of pastors, ministers of education, age-group ministers, and Sunday School leaders.

Jay has attributes that make him a valuable asset to our ministry. He is disciplined—seen in his frequent practice of rising at 3:30 a.m. to spend time with the Lord. He is sensitive—seen in his deep concern for people. With quiet dignity this young man, who was reared in New Orleans at the feet of a godly mother and father, has himself become a dedicated practitioner of the faith.

Not long after I became director of the Sunday School Group, I became convinced of the need to reexamine the basic design and traditional approaches of Sunday School ministry. Over a period of time, Sunday School had evolved into an organization that reflected an educational approach to ministry. While the learning that takes place in Sunday School is invaluable, it is not to be a substitute for the evangelistic vitality that long has been part of Sunday School's heritage.

My concern was heightened by knowing that some church leaders were looking for other paradigms. The conviction was growing among some that Sunday School ministry could no longer be the primary strategy for reaching people in the local church.

Armed with those concerns, I included in the 1996 strategic plans of LifeWay Christian Resources an intentional thrust to help Sunday School ministry strengthen the spirit of evangelism. Frankly, even as I submitted the idea, I did not know how or in what direction we should turn to ensure that the desired result would be accomplished in the churches. However, I would soon learn that God knew and already was at work in this endeavor.

Identify some leaders in your Sunday School who model best practices. Why did you think of them?

Through a series of events and relationships, we entered into dialogue with Bobby Welch, pastor, and Doug Williams, associate pastor with responsibilities for evangelism/education, both serving First Baptist Church, Daytona Beach, Florida. For several years this congregation had been working in a blended process that brought together the best of Sunday School with the best of evangelism training and practice. They called this process *E/S*, or *Evangelism/Sunday School.* Out of these conversations and meetings with leaders at LifeWay, we joined together to develop a new Sunday School evangelism strategy that has become known as FAITH.

In January 1998, pastors and other leaders from 28 churches located strategically across the nation were trained in the FAITH Sunday School Evangelism Strategy. These churches have taken the proven "best practice" modeled at First Baptist, Daytona Beach and made it work in all types of locations. The results have been phenomenal. These 28 "originator" churches have trained more than 1,500 other churches. Hundreds of people have come to know Christ. The goal is for more than 9,000 churches to be trained in the FAITH process over the next 4 years.

What can you do as a Sunday School leader to become a model of best practices?

Jay Johnston and the department he directs have the responsibility for introducing FAITH to churches, training participants, and supporting its implementation across the nation. This is a major assignment that requires the keenest attention to detail and a close walk with the Lord. He and his department personnel must deal with a myriad of situations reflecting great intensity, yet maintain a spirit of helpfulness and courtesy. One reason they do this work well is because it is modeled well in Jay's work and leadership style.

In a recent year, as many as 10,000 of our 40,000 churches reported no baptisms. Further examination revealed that this report was no exception but part of a trend in Southern Baptist life over the past two decades. As many as 70 percent of our churches are either plateaued or declining in membership. These statistics tell a tragic story but, even at that, they do not tell the entire story.

If these trends continue consider potential answers to these questions:

How many people will remain lost without Christ?

How many potential leaders will vanish from service in our churches?

How many families will be torn asunder because they do not know Christ?

How many classes will go without teachers?

As you overview the best practices described in this section, which ones are at work in your Sunday School ministry? Which best practices do you and your Sunday School Leadership Team need to address during this year?

Recently Jay talked with Anne Graham Lotz about FAITH and told her about the results that were beginning to be realized. In response, Anne mused, "I wonder what state the world would be in today if there had been a ministry such as FAITH to capture and assimilate into the life of the Body, the people who made decisions for Christ in my father's many evangelistic crusades?"

The posture of espousing "best practices" is a bold move, but a necessary one. Some may misunderstand our intent, but the work of the kingdom is too great to stand idly by. If you think you have the best, it must be shared, it must be put into practice.

"Best practices" in Sunday School for a new century—Our *best* is needed because nothing less is worthy of our service to our Lord while *practices* reminds us that we must move beyond talk to effective actions.

"Best practices" in both ministry and minister—Jay Johnston, our leader in FAITH, is one who mirrors both. May the Lord increase his tribe among us.

Launching the Plan

In Section 3 you were given help for developing annual details for implementing Sunday School as strategy. If you followed those suggestions, you have set goals and determined actions that will move you to accomplish the goals and meet the needs that precipitated the goals.

But consider, what if action ceased? What a waste of time and effort that would have been. So it is time to launch the plan. Here are some suggestions to help you plan a Launch Weekend.

A Launch Weekend includes several events designed to prepare individual Sunday School leaders and mobilize all members for the challenges and opportunities of the new year. The weekend becomes a time to celebrate accomplishments, communicate plans, train leaders, commission leaders for service, challenge the church about the potential of Sunday School strategy, and create a sense of excitement and purpose for what lies ahead.

Some elements of a Launch Weekend are described below. Use your own creativity in planning and promoting the event.

A Sunday School Rally

The rally is for all Sunday School leaders and may be a Friday evening kickoff event for the weekend. The rally may be held in conjunction with a banquet hosted by the church. Once again, be creative in presenting the information. Make the event one every Sunday School leader will be talking about in anticipation of next year.

Leader Training Event

Continue the weekend by conducting a leadership training event. This training my be done on Saturday. Promote it as a training spectacular that will equip all Sunday School leaders to function more effectively.

The training may include a general session with all leaders together. During this time the pastor, Sunday School director and/or minister of education may do an over view of the annual plan, review the structure, discuss other training events, preview the annual calendar, and so forth. However, this general session need not be long, probably less than one hour.

The majority of the time needs to be spent in age-group leader training. The training needs to address a specific need that will improve the effectiveness of your Sunday School in helping the church do the work of the Great Commission. The age-group books in the *Sunday School for a New Century* series would be an appropriate resource for use in this training. Some churches may need to provide training that strengthens teaching improvement, that builds Sunday School classes as caring communities on mission with Christ, or that improves outreach and evangelism.

See the leadership training curriculum resources listed on pages 178-179 for suggestions.

Sunday Morning Worship and a Sunday School Leader Commissioning Service

The excitement and purpose of the weekend continues with Sunday morning worship. If you are the Sunday School director or minister of education, talk with the pastor about the worship service. The service is not to be a promotional event but a focus on the work of the church and the calling of God's people to share the good news. Sunday School is highlighted as the strategy for leading people to faith in the Lord Jesus Christ and for building Great Commission Christians through Bible study groups.

The service may include a member giving a brief testimony about the importance of Sunday School, music and Scripture reading that support the emphasis of the day and/or the annual theme. The pastor's message could place the emphasis in a biblical context.

Conducting a commissioning service for Sunday School leaders will accomplish several things. First, it will indicate to the leaders the significance of the commitment they are making. Second, such a service emphasizes to the congregation the importance the church places on the ministries conducted through Sunday School and the people who conduct them. Third, a commissioning service can be a meaningful time of dedication.

You may elect to devote a full worship service or part of one to the commissioning. Here are some ideas.

Scripture
Some possible selections:
> Deuteronomy 6:4-7
> Deuteronomy 31:12-13
> Matthew 28:16-20
> 2 Timothy 2:15
> > • Ask individuals of varying ages to read the Scripture verses.
> > • Ask the pastor to use the verses to form the basis for a sermon.
> > • Combine verses and read responsively.

Music
"Take My Life, Lead Me, Lord" (*The Baptist Hymnal, 1991*, No. 287) or"Share His Love" (*The Baptist Hymnal, 1991*, No. 567) sung
> • By the congregation
> • By a choir or a soloist
> • As a poem.

Testimonies
Ask an experienced leader to give a testimony on what serving through Sunday School has meant to her.

Ask a new leader to talk about his expectations.

Bulletin Insert
Ask various Sunday School members to write testimonies on the subject "What My Sunday School Teacher Has Meant to Me," "My Favorite Sunday School Teacher," or a similar topic.

Other Suggestions

•Invite all leaders to wear a ribbon indicating that they are leaders in Sunday School. Representatives of each age group would wear a different color.

•Recognize all leaders during the service by asking them to stand during a special prayer. They could stand as a group or by the age group in which they will work.

•Ask all leaders to come to the front of the worship center for commissioning. Use the responsive reading on page 120.

•Follow the service with a luncheon for leadership.

•Distribute "My Commitment" sheets (see p.121) during the luncheon. Encourage each worker to fill one out and place it in his or her Bible.

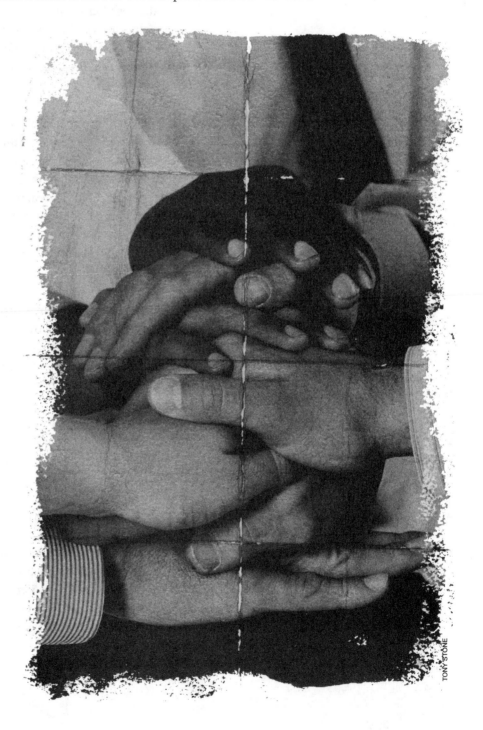

Sunday School Leader Commissioning Service Responsive Reading

Pastor: Following our Lord in service is a a high calling. As His church we affirm that calling and renew our commitment to His service.

Congregation: We, the members of _____ acknowledge that as God's children by faith in Jesus Christ, we are to be witnesses for Him. We do not give away that responsibility to our ministers or Sunday School leaders. We gladly accept the privilege and responsibility to stand for Christ in His power and by His grace.

Pastor: Yet God does specifically call out some to particular roles of service and leadership. Sunday School leaders, you stand before us today because you have responded to His call and this congregation's confirmation to serve as a leader through Sunday School. The call is to be a servant leader—called, surrendered, committed, and able. I challenge you to serve faithfully and by example to show us how to love God, love others, and reach out with the good news to people who are lost and seeking.

Sunday School Leaders   We affirm that we have answered the call of the Lord. We commit our lives to love and serve Him with our heart, soul, mind, and strength. We accept the challenge of service and in Christ's power will do our best to share the good news that has the power to change lives.

Pastor: Do you, members of _____ commit to pray for, encourage, and support these leaders during this year before us?

Congregation: We do commit to pray for, encourage, and support these who serve among us and with us.

Pastor: As pastor of this church and colaborer with all of you in the high calling of Jesus Christ, I urge you to keep the commission of Christ foremost in your minds and the love of Christ foremost in your hearts as you serve Him by reaching out to others with the good news.

All: Amen.

My Commitment

This commitment is made between you and God and no one else. After prayerful consideration, sign your name. Keep the commitment form in your Bible as a reminder throughout the year.

I, _____, because I feel called by God, commit to the following as a Sunday School leader for the _____ year.

As a Sunday School leader, I am committed to

Our God
- I have a personal relationship with Jesus Christ that I desire to model for others.
- I enjoy study of the Bible, pray regularly, and desire to grow in my faith and my commitment to Him.

Our Church
- I worship regularly with our church family.
- I support God's work in the total church ministry by giving of my time, talents, and money.

My Students
- I enjoy (preschoolers) (children) (youth) (young adults) (adults) (persons with special needs) and desire for them to know of God's love and purpose for their lives.
- I will take the necessary time to prepare, incorporating my own God-given gifts into each session.
- I will care for my members individually, through prayer, telephone calls, cards, and in other ways.
- I will follow up with mailings, cards, or visits to absentees and prospects.
- I will be faithful in attendance, arriving at least 15 minutes before the session begins. If I must be absent, I will secure a replacement and notify my department or division director as soon as possible.
- I will participate in at least one training event during the year to improve my teaching skills.

My Teaching Team
- I will participate in scheduled leadership team meetings.
- I will communicate regularly with the other leaders on my team.

Signed _____ Date _____

The Value of Annual Promotion Day

Annual Promotion Day recognizes the natural laws of growth and development that occur within people and an organization. Therefore, Promotion Day should be regarded as a necessary factor in the normal growth of Sunday School ministry.

Consider significant benefits of observing Annual Promotion Day in every age group—including adults. Annual Promotion Day

- Keeps the Sunday School structure dynamic.
- Provides for normal advancement through the natural stages of life.
- Equalizes the enrollment of classes and departments.
- Keeps classes from becoming too self-centered and closed to others who need to be reached.
- Provides an opportunity for members to change class membership without embarrassment as they move to new teachers and other new class members.
- Allows members to experience the wider range of teaching and influence of a larger number of consecrated Sunday School leaders.
- When coupled with beginning new classes and departments, opens the way for new paths of service for more people.
- Brings fresh interest in prospects by reassigning them to new leaders.
- Creates greater possibilities for members to develop new relationships.
- Gives everyone a fresh start.

When a person moves into a new class, renewed interest is generated for that person's well-being. When members refuse to promote, the profile of the existing class becomes static, and the bulk of the enrollment tends to move toward the upper end of the age range of the class. That refusal, in turn, discourages the people in the class below this age group to want to promote into it.

Observing an annual Promotion Day can be difficult in those churches where it has not been an ongoing practice. Several objections arise or challenges may come. However, we should not be deterred from doing the best thing because it is difficult or challenged.

Communicate clearly the benefits of observing Annual Promotion Day. Most people, when they understand the reasons for an action, will be cooperative and supportive. Focus attention on the value of Promotion Day for reaching people. Place it in the context of the Great Commission mandate, not rules and regulations from a book or an institution.

Even so, some people still will be uncooperative. Some people—and some classes—will want to be an exception. Let them be exceptions by their choice. You cannot coerce people into action. In time, as they see the benefits of advancing, they may make the choice themselves.

In the case of a class that does not want to observe Promotion Day, assign it a place in the organizational structure. Continue to begin new classes around it that will intensify your efforts to reach people. This is not to say, ignore the older class; people still need to be promoted into it. New members in the class can help others acquire different attitudes toward promotion as a practice.

Annual Promotion Day makes good sense when seen from the perspective of the purpose of Sunday School and the significance of organization for reaching people.

Monthly Sunday School Planning Team Meetings

All the planning required for effective, ongoing Sunday School ministry and its implementation as foundational strategy cannot take place at an annual planning event. Plans change. New situations arise that need to be addressed.

To stay apprised of new situations and to manage implementation of the plan, a monthly Sunday School Planning Team meeting needs to be set in place. This team usually will be made up of the same people as the annual planning team.

By meeting regularly, the Sunday School Planning Team positions itself to be proactive—addressing matters related to implementing the annual plan and purposefully looking ahead for other actions that can move the plan toward fulfillment—rather than reactive—addressing issues in the midst of crisis. Even so, the best annual plan needs to be flexible enough to accommodate unanticipated needs, issues, and problems.

Select an Appropriate Meeting Time

A regular Sunday School Planning Team meeting following the last Sunday of the month is ideal because statistical data for the month usually is available. The members of the team need to select a time most convenient for them. Usually about one hour is enough time to do the work.

Use an Agenda

A valuable tool for an effective monthly planning meeting is a meeting agenda. Some benefits of preparing and distributing an agenda in advance of the meeting are to
- remind participants of the time and place of the meeting;
- identify the focus of the meeting;
- provide a summary of the work to be completed; and
- clarify who is responsible for various elements of the meeting.

Plan the Elements of the Agenda

A model plan sheet to help you develop an agenda is on page. 124. A version of the plan sheet with monthly update information is provided in each issue of *The Sunday School Leader*. The plan sheet is built around these elements of the meeting:
- *Inspiration.*—Set the meeting within a spiritual context and relate the work to the commission of Christ and the mission of the church.
- *Information.*—Provide pertinent information that can help leaders improve the effectiveness of the Sunday School.
- *Evaluation.*—Discuss the effectiveness of events that have been completed and consider ways they could have been improved.
- *Communication.*—Report on current activities or on upcoming events.
- *Preparation.*—Initiate efforts related to future or new projects.

Follow Up the Meeting

Send members a summary of the meeting. Absentees will know what occurred during the meeting and those who attended will be reminded of assignments.

Suggested Monthly
Planning Team Meeting Agenda

Date of Meeting_____

Focus of Meeting_____

Preparing for the Meeting	Person Responsible
• Plan, prepare, and mail a copy of the agenda to all members one week before the meeting.	Sunday School director or minister of education
• Contact every member.	General secretary

Suggested Agenda

A Time for Inspiration
  Devotional
  Pray for:

_____

A Time for Information
  Review pertinent articles in *The Sunday School Leader* or other pertinent resource.

_____

A Time for Evaluation
  Discuss events and activities concluded.
  Consider how they could be improved or whether they should be repeated.

_____

A Time for Communication
  Receive progress reports on
  • Evangelistic results
  • Church calendar
  • Age-group concerns
  • Leadership training
  • New units

_____

A Time for Preparation
  Schedule, plan, and assign responsibilities for future projects and/or emphasis.

_____

After the Meeting

• Prepare a summary of the meeting; mail to absentees.	General secretary
• Follow up all assignments.	Sunday School director/ minister of education

Weekly Sunday School Leadership Team Meetings

Sunday School is a weekly ministry. Therefore, to increase the effectiveness of the work, a church needs to have weekly Sunday School leadership team meetings to enhance communication, planning, and implementation.

The leadership team meeting is to help all Sunday School leaders to be more effective in all aspects of Sunday School ministry. The meeting provides a regular time for Sunday School leaders to focus on the mission of the church; on relationships with people, both members and prospects who are related to the Sunday School; and on life-changing Bible study that is critical to effective Sunday School ministry. Here are other reasons a weekly Sunday School leadership team meeting can be beneficial.

- *Encourages and strengthens leaders.*—Sunday School leaders have high accountability to God and to their church. The content of leadership team meetings needs to be designed to encourage leaders to live out their calling from God, strengthen their own character as they model what it means to be a people of faith, and improve their competency as leaders in ministry.
- *Strengthens outreach and evangelism.*—Weekly leadership team meetings provide a wonderful opportunity for leaders to discuss outreach and evangelism efforts. Reviewing the names and needs of prospects, discussing ways to involve members in outreach, determining how to enroll and win to Christ lost prospects, and praying for prospects lead to greater effectiveness.
- *Focuses on evangelism, outreach, ministry, and efforts to build fellowship.*—Many churches depend only on the promotion of a visitation night for the involvement of their people in witnessing, reaching, and ministry. Built into leadership team meetings is time to discuss witnessing to the lost, reaching prospects, ministry to Sunday School members, and making plans for assimilation actions that involve members and prospects in loving and caring relationships.
- *Improves administration in the department and class.*—Sunday morning is not the time to deal with administrative concerns that may arise such as receiving and completing records, addressing space problems, adjusting Sunday schedules, determining starting and stopping times, previewing resources, and ordering materials. These concerns can be better dealt as a team during a weekly leadership team meeting.
- *Promotes stronger team spirit.*—Establishing common goals, developing plans, hearing and understanding the same information, dreaming together, sharing burdens and concerns, understanding what other people in the department or the other age group departments are trying to accomplish, and praying together contribute to a team spirit.
- *Includes evaluation, leading to better work.*—Leadership team meetings allow leaders to evaluate their work and the work being done in their classes and/or in their departments. Ongoing evaluation allows for continual improvement.
- *Improves coordination and communication.*—Weekly leadership team meetings provide a time to coordinate aspects of the work and to communicate information pertinent to other leaders.

- *Improves teaching as leaders prepare for Bible study.*—Preparing for Bible study on Sunday includes more than each teacher studying the lesson and making individual plans. The Sunday morning session is to be the culmination of the joint effort of all the leaders in a class or department to prepare to accomplish the goal that has been determined for the session. An effective weekly leadership team meeting brings together all the elements of a Sunday morning session and moves them toward a common purpose.
- *Increases involvement of members and prospects in Sunday Bible study sessions.*—Leadership team meetings not only focus on the content of the Bible study, but also provide leaders a time to determine how the Bible will be taught. Methods can be discussed and a plan built for maximizing the involvement of members and prospects in Bible study that changes lives.
- *Makes better use of space and equipment.*—The weekly leadership team meeting will help leaders determine the best way to use the space and equipment to create the best environment on Sunday.
- *Calls attention to enrollment and attendance goals and reports.*—A leadership team meeting is a time to make leaders more conscious of the progress being made in the department or class in attaining enrollment and attendance goals. Records can be studied and appropriate actions determined.
- *Leads to greater involvement of departments and classes in the work of the church.*—Leadership team meetings provide opportunities for departments and classes to determine ways they will support events, emphases, projects, and other concerns of the church, such as mission offerings or revivals.
- *Provides for ongoing training.*—The ongoing evaluation, planning, and preparation included in weekly Sunday School leadership team meetings also provides an opportunity for ongoing training. As leaders evaluate teaching sessions, they can discuss how the session could have been improved. Planning for future sessions involves discussions of the best procedure for teaching the session.

Choosing a Time

The best meeting time is that which fits the needs of the church and the people who are to participate. The meeting time chosen need to be coordinated with other church leaders. Generally, a minimum of one hour needs to be available for the meeting.

- Discuss thoroughly with the Sunday School Planning Team the advantages of a weekly Sunday School leadership team meeting. The Sunday School director may choose to review the benefits of the meetings and the positive effect they can have on the work of the church.
- Interview churches that have an effective weekly leadership team meeting.
- Secure the commitment of the pastor and staff. The pastor can help to promote the advantages of a leadership team meeting.
- Work through regular church processes to bring a proposal to the church.
- Provide training for those who will lead the meetings. Allocate space and other resources. Curriculum materials for each age group and Sunday School administrative materials contain suggestions for conducting the leadership team meetings.
- Promote the meetings and encourage attendance. During leader enlistment, stress the value of the meetings and the expectations for participation.

Some churches may find it impossible to schedule weekly leadership team meetings.

Even so, every church needs to allocate some time. Monthly leadership team meetings may be a viable alternative. All the items that are included in the weekly leadership team meeting schedule need to be covered during a monthly meeting. Note: This monthly leadership team meeting for all Sunday School leaders is different from and in addition to the monthly meeting of the Sunday School Planning Team.

Content of a Weekly Sunday School Leadership Team Meeting

Regardless of the schedule, the leadership team meeting has some common content. A brief general promotion period with all leaders together may be desired. Following that segment, age-group department leadership team meetings are conducted by the respective department directors to focus on the church's mission, relationships with members and prospects, and life-changing Bible study. In churches without departments the focus areas become the object of class planning. Class leaders gather with the class teacher to discuss focus areas.

General Period (15 min.).—This period is a brief gathering of all Sunday School leaders led by the Sunday School director, pastor, or minister of education. The purpose of the general period is to motivate and inform leaders in areas of concern to all age groups. Help for leading this period is found in *The Sunday School Leader.*

Department/Class Leadership Meeting.—This period is the primary focus of the weekly leadership team meeting. Generally, it is led by the department directors or class teacher. Each segment is to contribute to the achievement of the objectives of Sunday School. Instead of a segmented prayer period in which prayer tends to become generic, prayer is to permeate the discussion in each area of work. This will allow for more specific and focused praying about issues and people.

• *Focus on the Mission* (10 min.).—This portion of the meeting is an opportunity to relate the work of the Sunday School departments and/or classes to the mission and the ministry of the church. Information is shared concerning the church's ministry. Leaders are made aware of churchwide emphases, needs, and concerns.

• *Focus on Relationships* (25 min.).— During this time relationships with members and prospects are discussed, individual needs assessed, and, as appropriate, plans are made to involve members in responding to them. Approaches are determined for being involved with members and prospects beyond the Sunday morning session, especially ways to involve members in evangelism. Specific plans are made for following up on ministry needs of members and prospects. Plans are made for fellowship activities and various assimilation actions to involve members and prospects in caring relationships. Visitation assignments and reports can be shared.

Churches using the FAITH Sunday School Evangelism Strategy will use this time to review assignments, give reports, and make follow-up assignments. Occasionally during this time, a study and review of witnessing approaches may be conducted.

• *Focus on Bible Study* (25 min.).—Teaching for spiritual transformation is facilitated when leaders work together to plan the best way to bring members into a life-changing encounter with the Bible message. Bible study is not seen as an independent task but is the focal point around which people are reached for Christ and becomes the foundation for leading people to evangelism, discipleship, fellowship, ministry, and worship. During this time, previous Bible study sessions may be evaluated and assignments made for subsequent studies, in particular plans deciding how the Bible content for subsequent Sundays will be taught.

Sample Meeting Schedules

Following are three model schedules for weekly leadership team meetings. Model 1 is for smaller churches or churches that choose to have all leaders meet together for most of the meeting. Models 2 and 3 are for churches who choose to have age-groups departments meet separately after a brief general session. Model 3 adds a department directors' meeting to the schedule preceding both the general session and the department meetings.

Model 1: For Smaller Churches or Churches with All Leaders Meeting Together
Minimum 60 minutes
- Sunday School General Period (5 minutes)
- Focus on the Mission (5 minutes)
- Focus on Relationships (25 minutes)
- Focus on Bible Study (25 minutes)

Model 2
Minimum: 75 minutes
- Sunday School General Period (all workers together, 15 minutes)
- Department Planning Period (by departments)
    Focus on the Mission (10 minutes)
    Focus on Relationships (25 minutes)
    Focus on Bible Study (25 minutes)

Model 3
Minimum 75 minutes
- Department Directors' Meeting (in separate room)
- Sunday School General Period (all workers together, 15 minutes)
- Department Planning Period (by departments)
  Focus on the Mission (10 minutes)
  Focus on Relationships (25 minutes)
  Focus on Bible Study (25 minutes)

Beginning a Successful Weekly Sunday School Leadership Team Meeting

Taking several actions in advance can ensure a successful weekly leadership team meeting.

Prepare the people.—When beginning a leadership team meeting, or seeking renewed commitment to the meeting, allow sufficient time to prepare people for the change. Don't announce one Sunday that meetings will begin the following Wednesday. Lay a foundation by helping leaders understand the value of the meeting and training those persons who will conduct them.

Become familiar with resources.—Resources can help leaders better understand their roles and the kind of activities that need to be taking place in the age-group meetings.

Build support for the meeting.—The pastor, other staff, Sunday School director, and the Sunday School Planning Team need to demonstrate strong initial support for weekly leadership team meetings. Their support will be useful in leading the church to establish this meeting as a priority and in strengthening the position that attendance is required as part of the leader's responsibility.

Establish an appropriate schedule.—A successful weekly leadership team meeting is dependent on an acceptable meeting time.

Secure church approval.—While church approval may not be required, taking this action demonstrates the value and support the church places on the meeting.

Make provisions for children.—Child care needs to be age-graded, ongoing, and self-sustaining, which means materials and leaders do not have to be secured week-after-week. Ongoing organizations such as children's music and missions are ideal ways of providing for children during weekly leadership team meetings.

Publicize the value of the meeting.—The value of the leadership team meeting needs to be clearly communicated before securing commitments from leaders to attend them. Describe the meeting's purpose, agenda, and benefits.

Enlist workers with a commitment to attend.—When enlisting department directors, clearly outline the director's role in leading a leadership team meeting and the priority of the meeting to the work. Information about leadership team meetings needs to be available to those who will be enlisting other leaders as well.

Train department directors to conduct planning meetings.—The department director is a key person to the meeting's success. Don't assume he knows how to lead the meeting.

Establish a reporting (record) system.—A simple reporting system that records those present and absent is sufficient. Such a reporting system will establish accountability for attendance and enable general officers to be aware of struggling departments.

Recognize those who effectively conduct leadership meetings.—Share success stories from departments that have effective leadership team meetings. Tell about ways the meetings are strengthening the work of the departments. Describe what the directors are doing to keep the leadership team meetings alive and productive.

Give help to struggling departments.—Giving attention to a department with a struggling leadership team meeting is easier than reviving a failed meeting later.

How to Keep a Weekly Sunday School Leadership Team Meeting Strong

Some churches are careful in their effort to start a weekly leadership team meeting; however, once the meeting has begun, the church and its leaders turn their energies to new projects. This often results in struggling, ineffective meetings that eventually fail. Even churches with ongoing leadership team meetings do not derive full benefits if they do not continue those actions that were used in beginning the meeting. The following actions will help the meetings stay strong.

Provide the necessary resources.—Leaders need curriculum materials and access to member and prospect records. Remember, these meetings are about improving the work as it relates to the Great Commission with its focus on people.

Check with department directors about weekly leadership team meeting needs and/or problems.—Ask department directors how they feel about their leadership team meetings. Listen for the good things happening in the meetings and share them with others. Be sensitive to weaknesses or needs and assist the director in overcoming them.

Clearly communicate church and Sunday School plans.—Clear communication enables departments to plan support actions for emphases that involve the entire church.

Continue to train leaders.—Never assume training is complete. Veteran leaders need to be updated on changes; new leaders need the support of continual training.

The Pastor's Role in Weekly Sunday School Leadership Team Meetings

The pastor is the leader of Sunday School. Here are some ways he can be involved.

The pastor's presence.—By his presence at leadership team meetings the pastor shows his leadership and commitment to them. By his participation the pastor can encourage the highest quality Bible study.

The pastor needs to be heard as well as seen at the meeting. He does not have to be on the agenda every week, but from time-to-time time he needs to speak to all Sunday School leaders. During this time the pastor can

- support the concept of Sunday School being the foundational strategy leading people to faith in the Lord Jesus Christ and building Great Commission Christians;
- encourage the workers;
- highlight the progress being made through Sunday School;
- update workers on progress being made on annual goals: new members, total attendance, contacts, and so forth; and
- emphasize special events, such as revivals, or churchwide emphases.

The pastor's encouragement.—By encouraging the leaders the pastor declares his commitment to Sunday School and expresses his gratitude for all the team members do week-to week. He needs to be sincerely positive, happy, and excited.

The pastor's heart.—The leadership team meeting is a good place for a pastor to share his heart for evangelism, discipleship, fellowship, ministry, and worship.

The Sunday School Director's Role in Weekly Sunday School Leadership Team Meetings

The weekly leadership team meeting must be a high priority for the Sunday School director. Here are some specific areas in which that high priority can be expressed.

High priority in understanding what should take place.—The Sunday School director is the leader of the weekly leadership team meetings.

High priority in providing resources.—The director needs to see that the department directors have the resources they need to plan and conduct an effective meeting.

High priority in communicating with the church's total ministry leadership team.—The director needs to discuss with the pastor and other staff members (minister of music, minister of education, and so forth) the value of weekly leadership team meetings for the effectiveness of Sunday School. Discuss ways Sunday School can be more supportive of the other ministries of the church.

Identifying Prospects for Your Church

Ministry Prospects

For our purposes, *ministry prospects* are people already members of classes and departments and who have a specific need to which the class or department may respond. They may be nonattenders or absentees toward whom efforts are being made to restore them to active participation. Some may be active members of the class who would benefit from an encouraging visit by another member of his or her class. Others may be members or nonmembers who are experiencing a critical life experience for which specific care and nurture would be appropriate.

Ministry assignments are not to be taken lightly. Specific assignments for ministry are communicated on a visitation assignment form. Results from ministry visits are compiled and reported during during the weekly leadership team meeting.

Evangelistic Prospects

An evangelistic prospect is any unsaved or unchurched person who is in such proximity as to be reached by a church. For most churches, this definition means their neighborhoods, communities, towns, and cities are filled with prospects.

More specifically, however, an evangelistic prospect is any unsaved or unchurched person who is in such proximity to be reached and cared for by a church and for whom the church has a name, address, and other pertinent information that will enable that person to be assigned to an appropriate class for a visit. By receiving assignments to visit specific unsaved or unchurched people, each class has opportunity to encounter them personally so they can hear and respond to the gospel.

Many churches are not calling the people they are seeking to reach, *prospects*. Many churches are beginning to refer to prospects as *V.I.P.'s*, guests, or some other term that communicates that prospects are extremely important to us and to the Lord.

This importance is communicated in other simple yet subtle ways: by staffing a welcome center with friendly, knowledgeable members who escort guests to the rooms where the Bible study group meets; by greeting guests in the parking lot; by wording prospect information cards in user-friendly ways (for example, asking guests to indicate the most convenient time to call); and by how guests are welcomed in Sunday School classes and worship services. Consider how your church views prospects now, and make any adjustments needed.

Sources for Evangelistic Prospects

Evangelistic and unchurched prospects are everywhere. It is a matter of identifying who they are and how to follow up with them. In many cases, people already have had some contact or relationship with your church. As a result, they already may have indicated an interest in the church, religion, or spiritual matters. Do not overlook them.

- *Church members not enrolled in Bible study*
- *Visitors in worship services*
- *People who attend special-emphasis events, revivals, or seasonal presentations at or sponsored by the church*
- *Parents and siblings of preschoolers, children, and youth enrolled in other Sunday School classes or departments*

- *Parents and siblings of preschoolers, children, and youth enrolled in Vacation Bible School, Backyard Bible Clubs, or mission Vacation Bible School*
- *Extended family members, friends, neighbors, or associates of people who are members of your church or are enrolled in other Sunday School classes or departments*
- *Unsaved members of Sunday School classes or departments*

Prospect-Discovery Actions

Conduct prospect-discovery events through the church. While prospect discovery is an ongoing action, periodic emphasis needs to be given to this important work. At least once each quarter, work with Sunday School leaders and members to conduct a prospect-discovery event that will provide information about people who have not been reached through the ministries targeted by your (or any other) church.

Some of the events described may be community-wide. Others may focus on a geographical area of the community or a particular target group, such as single adults, senior adults, homebound adults, parents of preschoolers, and so forth.

- *Gather names of people who attend special events and ministries through the church.*—These include but are not limited to worship services, Vacation Bible School, special concerts, bus ministry, recreation, or socials.
- *Conduct a direct-mail opinion survey with a return card providing the name and address of the responder.*
- *Conduct a neighborhood door-to-door religious survey.*
- *Conduct a telephone survey.*
- *Obtain information from a newcomer welcoming organization or other agencies on individuals or families who have recently moved into the community.*
- *Designate a Sunday in which all members are asked to complete a card providing information on people they know.* —Ask members to list the name, address, and phone number of a family member, neighbor, work associate, and others who are evangelistic, enrollment, or ministry action prospects. Give the day a theme or special name (for example, Friends Day).
- *Organize a "Prospect Watch" in member neighborhoods, encouraging members to look for persons/families moving into the area.*
- *Conduct community or neighborhood Scripture distribution visitation during which members are on the lookout for prospects.*
- *Invite the community to seminars and workshops addressing community issues, family concerns, or personal needs.*—Follow up on registrants or participants who are prospects.
- *Locate demographic data available through online people search engines.*
- *Develop a corps of members to survey the newspaper for potential prospects.*—This process may include reviewing birth records, hospital lists, death notices, new-home purchases, announcements about new professional and businesspersons who have moved into the community, marriage announcements, and other such public information. Determine appropriate ways to respond to or follow up to learn more about people and their life needs.
- *Conduct community surveys to make contact with and get information from people who have had no contact with the church.*—A community survey can be a nonthreatening way to discover new names and to assess community interest in ministries sponsored by the church.

Process for Making Visitation Assignments

Develop and maintain a prospect file and membership file as part of the system for recording, distributing, and receiving information about people. The prospect file will help you determine the growth potential of your church. The number of prospects on file needs to be equal to the total enrollment.

Your church may choose one of several options: card files and preprinted assignment forms, a pocket-and-card system, or electronic files and electronically generated assignment forms. Whichever you choose, here are some elements that need to be part of your file system.

The Master File

The master file is a permanent file in which all information about each prospect or member is logged and tracked. The file should include such information as name, address, phone number, class/department to which assigned, spiritual condition, and other information you determine to be helpful. This file may be arranged alphabetically by family units or by individual names.

Other options for arranging the file include geographical areas, age groups, among others. You may choose to use more than one approach for master files. For example, you may have a family file and an age-group master file. Remember, these are master files, not working files for making assignments.

Keep a separate file for prospects and for members. Make sure the member file can be accessed by Sunday School division, department, and class.

Working Files

These are the files from which assignments are made and on which members make notes about visits attempted or made. New or corrected information about the prospect needs to be recorded so both the working file and the master file can be updated. No information needs to "sit in a file" but ought to be used regularly and updated for visitation and follow-up. Each Sunday School class and department must have access to information regarding people who would relate to that class.

Maintenance of master and working files needs to be assigned through the church office to someone who can receive and update information each week, distribute up-to-date outreach information in time for weekly leadership team meetings, prepare visitation assignment cards based on updated information, and assign prospects to the appropriate class or department. See the visual on page 134 for a possible "flow" of information.

A Basic Assignment Process

Every prospect discovered should be assigned to a Sunday School class or department for follow-up. In the case of family prospects, assignments can be made to adult classes and classes of preschoolers, children, or youth. Leaders in all age groups related to the family can coordinate visits and contacts and may make some visits together. Here are some other suggestions related to assignments.

- Enter information about the prospect into the master prospect file.
- Based on the age of the prospect and the Sunday School structure, complete an age-group prospect assignment record and forward it to the outreach-evangelism leader for the class/department working file.

- Give the assignment to a member of the class or department to make the contact. Give the member a date by which the visit should be made, with instructions to return the assignment material to the person making the assignment.
- Following the contact, receive the member's report on the outcome. Forward information on the outcome of the visit to the Sunday School outreach-evangelism director for updating the master prospect file.
- Make other contacts based on the initial results and the needs of the person.

EVANGELISM VISITS

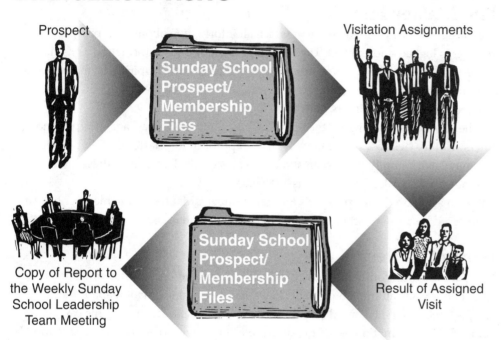

This visual shows a possible flow of information between a prospect visit and the different church or Sunday School groups who need or can share updated information. Similar information is provided for Sunday School ministry visits.

MINISTRY VISITS

Using Records to Learn About People

Records are more than numbers. Records are written or electronic reports on the involvement and growth of people. When used properly, records reflect the life and health of classes and departments by revealing information about members and prospects. Individual records should be compiled by each Sunday School class, department, or other Bible study group. The total record of smaller units, such as classes, within an age group make up the records for larger units, such as departments or divisions, within the age group. The total record of those larger units should be summarized on a churchwide basis by the Sunday School secretary or other designated leader. Every individual associated with a Sunday School class, department, or other Bible study group should be represented by a record in the general, churchwide record system.

A good record system begins in an up-to-date member roll and an up-to-date prospect file. Every name in the member file and prospect file represents a person who needs a regular systematic encounter with God and the ministry of a concerned, compassionate teacher and group of Sunday School class members. The member and prospect data tell who people are, where they live, what their spiritual condition is, and to which group they have been assigned. Weekly individual member and class records tell who is and who is not present.

A record-keeping system is a tool that helps identify people and their needs, track their participation, and give some indication of spiritual growth. A record system takes the efforts of Sunday School out of the realm of generalization and personalizes it. Record keeping becomes a way in which leaders have accountability for members and members become accountable for the commitments they have made to their class, church, and God.

If we only have records that constitute a head count, we will know how many came on a given Sunday, but we won't know who came, or perhaps more importantly, who did not come. Over an extended period we may know how many came on an average Sunday, but we won't know how often any one person came during that time.

In a class, for example, 10 people may have been present each Sunday for Bible study, but were they the same 10 or a different 10? Were visitors included? Of those visitors, were any prospects who needed follow-up? With only an attendance count, we cannot answer these questions. Therefore, complete records should be kept on every member and prospect every week. Records should be taken and compiled whenever and wherever Sunday School classes, departments, or other Bible study groups meet.

Set Up a Record System

Select a system (manual or computerized) that fits your church's needs and that provides for recording pertinent personal, family, spiritual development, and church participation information for every individual. Train all leaders with responsibility for record keeping in effective use of the system. Provide appropriate forms to participants, and provide all necessary forms for those with record-keeping responsibilities in classes, departments, and other Bible study groups. Some record-keeping systems are available through LifeWay Christian Resources. See page 177 for ordering information.

Use Records Effectively

Leaders with responsibilities related to record keeping in a class, department, or other Bible study group should use records to build up people and strengthen the work of the church through Sunday School.

Use Records to Strengthen Ministry

Keeping accurate records is more than busy work; that is, unless the records are never put to any practical use. Use records with people in mind. Here are some ways.

To Evaluate

By analyzing class, department, and school records over a period of time, leaders can note areas of advancement or decline. Records can indicate spiritual decline or indifference on the part of members. Thorough records can help leaders answer questions about the effectiveness of the Sunday School as a strategy for helping a church do the work of the Great Commission. Here are some examples:

- What has happened to the total Sunday School class and department enrollment this year? Are unsaved persons being added to classes? These questions speak to the evangelism, discipleship, fellowship, ministry, and worship functions of the church.
- What has happened to total attendance this year? This question speaks to the evangelism, discipleship, fellowship, ministry, and worship functions of the church.
- How many members also participate in Sunday worship? Are members reading their Bibles and praying daily? These questions speak to the worship function of the church.

Notice that the use of records helped to answer questions about people. When leaders use records in this way, they can see where people's needs exist, plan actions that address those needs, and work to bring about improvement where it is needed most. The Sunday School Planning Team depends heavily on records to plan for the future. The outreach-evangelism director can rely on the record-keeping system to assess how effectively class leaders are involving members in penetrating the community with the gospel. Churches and leaders who are genuinely interested in reaching people will learn to keep and make wise use of records.

To Motivate

Records can be motivational tools for members. As they record their own achievements in whatever areas information is requested, they may be inwardly convinced of the need to improve a certain spiritual discipline.

As leaders review records, they may identify areas where improvement is needed. These may be areas in which the leaders themselves need to make improvements, or disciplines in which the leaders need to challenge members to make improvements.

To Enable

Accurate records provide leaders with direction in planning. Having the facts at hand adds credibility to the concerns and efforts of leaders as they lead Sunday School to accomplish its objectives. Records give leaders the information needed to set priorities and goals with authority and confidence.

The Importance of an Enrollment Policy

A discussion about record keeping would be incomplete without addressing some questions about enrollment. A study of growing churches continues to show some correlation between enrollment, growth, and evangelistic potential. Sunday School growth expert E.S. (Andy) Anderson offers these insights from his experience:

- When open enrollment (enrolling a person anytime, anywhere) is practiced, one-half of the total number enrolled will be unsaved.
- Of that number of unsaved persons, one-half will be saved and baptized into the church within 12 months.

Inviting people to become members of classes or departments is a way of saying we want them to be part of us. It becomes an expression of interest and concern. Because our mandate is to reach all people, there is a need for openness in the enrollment process. Rather than making it difficult to become a member of a Sunday School class, we need to make it easy. The basic requirement for a person to enroll is a desire to do so. No attendance requirements are necessary.

It is easy to join; on the other hand, it ought to be difficult to be dropped as a class member. Sometimes leaders have the tendency to drop persons in an effort to "clean out" the roll. Dropping names is a sure way to lose contact with nonattending members and evangelistic prospects. Purging the roll seems to indicate more concern for records than people.

Remember, records are about people. Sunday School is about people. Church is about people. We do not want to do anything that results in lost contact with people.

Enrollment is not to be perceived as a list of people who have proved their worth. A class roll is a ministry list, not a list of dedicated Christians. The class roll ought to include persons who need to study the Bible and receive ministry and grow in the Lord. Actually, healthy adult and youth Sunday School classes should include people who have not professed Christ and who may not be regular attenders.

Some churches still are influenced by the desire to have 100 percent attendance to enrollment. That is a worthy goal, but we have learned the easiest way to achieve it is to delete the names of those who do not come. Those people usually are the lost, the uncommitted, the spiritually immature—the people we are trying to reach.

So what do we do with the records of those people? Here are some things *not* to do: *Don't* move their enrollment cards to the back of the record book or their names to the bottom of the list, as if to hide them. *Don't* write *inactive* across the card as if providing a warning sign to any who would be looking at the records. *Don't* move their cards to the prospect file, for usually the newest prospects get all the attention.

Instead, keep the records intact, in a place where they can be seen. Look for ways to encourage these people to more faithful participation. Assign FAITH teams or other class representatives to visit these individuals. Here are some other positive actions that can be taken:

- Pray for members regularly.
- Organize class members to communicate with one another.
- As a leader, communicate regularly with members.
- Involve people in caring for one another.
- Provide relationship-building fellowship opportunities.
- Make it easy for absentees to come back without calling unreasonable attention before others to their presence or to their extended absences.
- Conduct projects designed to involve absentees.

Four valid reasons exist for dropping people from class membership (1) the person died; (2) the person joined another church; (3) the person moved out of the ministry reach of the church; and (4) the person asked to be removed. Aside from these reasons, a person continues to be the responsibility of the class to which he/she is assigned.

Records and Reporting

Occasionally some Sunday School leaders ask if and when Bible study events beyond Sunday morning can be counted in Sunday School ministry enrollment and attendance records. Actually the decision is a local church decision, but the chart below offers some suggestions that may help you decide.

You may want to differentiate between how many persons you have participating each week in ongoing Sunday School classes and departments and how many persons you have participating each week in your total Sunday School ministry at any level. Remember, ongoing small-group Bible study may not meet just on Sunday morning. You may have "Sunday School" that meets on a day other than Sunday. A Sunday School class is defined by its reason for existing, not its meeting time or designation as a small group, class, department, cell group, or any other name. The question is, Is this group focused on leading people to faith in Christ and building Great Commission Christians? That is what Sunday School is all about.

Enrollment/Attendance Status Chart

Project	Included in SS Enrollment	Registration Recorded	Recorded in SS Attendance
VBS	Not in SS until transfer	Yes; Pre-register	No
Mission VBS	Not in SS until transfer	Yes	No
Backyard Bible Clubs	Not in SS until transfer	Yes	No
New Sunday Schools	Yes, when non-duplicating	No	Yes
Bible Conferences	No	Yes	No
January Bible Study	No	Yes	No
Short-term Bible Study Groups	No	Yes	No
Homebound	Yes	Yes	Yes
Adults Away	Yes	Yes	Yes (when home)
Campus Clubs	No	No	No

Assimilating People into a Class

Assimilating new members begins with a plan to welcome, include, and actively involve people in Bible study and in the entire life of the class. Until people feel they have been accepted, not enough has been done to assimilate them. Folks who come to Bible study groups may be turned away by the feeling that no one is interested in them. The interest of another person, particularly someone who has influence with other people, can make a tremendous difference to a new member.

Assimilation is a process for enabling members to express their interest in a new member and for the new member to experience that interest from others. The goal is to lead the person to that point where he or she begins to assimilate new members into the life of the Sunday School class and church.

Here are some ways that Sunday School classes in particular can create opportunities for expressing interest and concern for others and can build personal relationships with new members.

- *Sunday morning Bible study*

Sunday mornings provide an opportunity for members and guests to enjoy regular Christian fellowship. They may visit informally before and after the session. During the session participation in Bible study becomes a common bond that can draw people together.

- *Get-acquainted activities*

Occasional get-acquainted activities can stimulate relationships. In the case of adults and youth, groups of three or four members (or couples) can be formed for informal get-togethers during a given quarter. These get-togethers can be anytime other than Sunday mornings. Participants can use open-ended comments like, "I came to Sunday School the first time because . . ." and complete the statement with personal information. Participants can share favorite experiences, hymns, holiday stories, childhood memories, and so forth.

- *Name tags*

No one wants to be addressed by, "Hey, You!" But failing to call people by name is not much better. Knowing people's names indicates you have enough interest to remember who they are. Being addressed personally says that someone considers the person significant; it is a way of saying, "You are special, so I have made an effort to remember your name." Name tags can help everyone get to know one another, and help leaders in calling everyone by name in every class session.

- *Words of encouragement and affirmation*

Giving a positive, affirming word is a simple and but impressive way to let people know they are appreciated. Affirm good answers to difficult questions. Let newcomers know their contributions are appreciated. Affirmations can be given outside class as well. Make a phone call during the week to express appreciation to a newcomer for attending a class.

- *Celebration of special occasions*

Birthdays are something all people have, whether they want them or not. When everyone's birthday is celebrated in simple ways, everyone is affirmed. Monthly birthday activities can build fellowship.

- *Social events*

Do not overlook the obvious. Every newcomer and guest should be invited to every social event. Social events allow relationships to grow and barriers to disappear. When newcomers are included in fellowship events, everyone's "comfort zone" grows. Make sure that prospects are not ignored during the events. Enlist someone to "adopt" newcomers during social events. Encourage this person to introduce the newcomers to others and involve them in different aspects of the event.

- *Newsletters and printed information*

Regardless of whether newcomers enroll immediately, including them on class mailing lists will let them know someone considers them part of the group already. Add newcomers and prospects to the list for at least six months. After this "trial period," ask prospects whether they want to continue receiving the newsletter.

- *One-on-one mentoring*

In adult and youth classes, a spiritually mature member of the class may be assigned as a mentor to a new member to encourage spiritual growth and development. The mentor and new member may meet together regularly for prayer and additional study periods.

FAITH: Best Practice for Sunday School Evangelism

FAITH is an evangelism process and training system linked directly to Sunday School. By incorporating FAITH into Sunday School, a church will have multiple opportunities and incentives to strengthen its ongoing Bible teaching and reaching ministries. By implementing FAITH, a church can mobilize its army of Sunday School leaders and members to share the gospel, give unsaved persons an opportunity to accept Christ, and enable believers to grow through its ministries.

The Philosophy of FAITH

Second Timothy 2:1-2 is the key to understanding the strategy and success of FAITH. Others are to be taught so they can teach still more people to share the gospel. FAITH is an intentional multiplying approach of evangelism training through Sunday School. It also supports Sunday School ministry, by providing opportunities to keep in touch with members and meet their special needs; worship and discipleship functions, by providing opportunities to grow in Christlikeness; and fellowship, by uniting the church in a common goal and in celebration of results.

FAITH is not a program, but a process and a means for growing Great Commission Christians. The FAITH evangelism strategy is built around important ingredients designed to help someone investigate, understand, apply, and pass on the gospel message. Great Commission Christians are not made overnight; the process takes time. A person easily can learn the gospel presentation that is part of FAITH, but more is involved.

In one sense, FAITH calls for a high level of commitment from leaders and members. At the same time, it takes people where they are—willing to obey—and helps build their commitment as Great Commission Christians. FAITH does not require persons to start off knowing everything—only that God will cause them to grow in grace as they practice those things which Scripture teaches.

The Primary Components of FAITH

An awareness of the key components of FAITH provides some important background and context.

• *The Sunday School class.* FAITH focuses on the work assigned to the class of each age division. As a result, three-person FAITH Teams are enlisted from a Sunday School class or department. The Teams are assigned visits to prospects and members of their class or department. FAITH Team members should serve as outreach-evangelism or other ministry leaders in their classes.

Giving Sunday School ministry high visibility, some FAITH visits are to members who need caring or maintenance; others are to members who have short- or long-term crises or concerns; and some are to members who may have dropped out of ongoing participation or involvement in Sunday School.

Other visits are to people targeted for the class, people who do not know the Lord or may not be participating in any ongoing Bible study. Who better to try to reach them than persons of similar age, needs, and life situations?

• *Sunday School leadership team meetings.* Sunday School leadership meets regularly to deal with people issues as they are impacted by God's Word and the ministry of caring believers. As prospects are discovered and people are visited, follow-up actions are planned and implemented. These actions affect both members and prospects. This ongoing meeting focuses on a Sunday School class accomplishing all of its functions.

• *Coordination meetings.* Those persons who relate to multiple FAITH Teams/Team Leaders are called FAITH Group Leaders. They should serve as department or division outreach-evangelism directors. They meet regularly to coordinate assignments and follow-up. The leaders build accountability and motivation into the FAITH ministry. They also are among FAITH's strongest and best promoters.

• *Evangelism training.* Integral to FAITH is an intentional process and plan to train persons to share their faith using a simple visitation sequence and easy-to-remember gospel presentation. *FAITH* as an acronym is used in making the presentation. Training includes classwork, home study, and on-the-job training by individuals who already have been trained and are mentoring others in the process.

Sixteen sessions of training, visitation, and home study provide enough information, practice, and modeling for learners to put into practice a recommended sequence for visits and to learn the specific FAITH gospel presentation. During this time of equipping, trainees experience firsthand opportunities to learn the gospel and share it personally as they visit Sunday School members and prospects.

• *Public profession of faith and assimilation into the church.* There is a big difference between leading a person to make a personal commitment to Christ and that person making a public profession of faith. FAITH intentionally links persons through the nurturing ministry and ongoing fellowship of Sunday School classes and helps them come to the point of making a public declaration of faith.

One reason many converts do not follow up on their profession of faith is because church leaders have not helped them relate to the church and other Christians. When we connect new converts to Sunday School classes, we increase the possibility of their being baptized and discipled. The second semester, FAITH Advanced, gives strong emphasis to assimilation, follow-up, and baptism as a next step of obedience.

• *Discipleship of those being trained.* One of the intentional distinctives of the training materials and process is to help participants in their personal journey of Christian faith. Learners and Team Leaders model the process that helps them see personally how God is at work in their lives and in the lives of those who are being visited.

Strategic Assumptions About FAITH Training

1. The FAITH Sunday School Evangelism Strategy is, first and foremost, a Sunday School strategy. FAITH is done in and through Sunday School.

2. FAITH equip participants to become soul-winners.

3. FAITH training centers around 16 consecutive sessions of training in evangelism, one session each week, and conducted during a fall or a spring semester. Most churches do two training semesters a year.

4. All participants in all age groups are required to complete the first 16-week basic course of study (FAITH Basic) before advancing to additional semester courses of study (FAITH Advanced and FAITH Discipleship).

5. A semester of training requires a commitment by FAITH Learners to participate in classroom study, on-the-job training, and home study. It also encourages faithfulness in Sunday School.

6. Participants include Team Leaders, who have been trained and are equipped to lead a Team in FAITH home visits; and Team Learners, who have committed to receive training. The only persons who can teach FAITH in the local church are individuals who have participated in a FAITH Training Clinic at a host church certified to teach FAITH and persons trained in the local church under the leadership of the pastor who was certified in a clinic. Even these trainers are encouraged to attend a clinic to gain a wider scope and understanding of the FAITH ministry.

7. Each FAITH Team is comprised of a Team Leader and two Learners. Ideally, the Team Leader and Learners are members of the same Sunday School class or department visiting prospects assigned to the class or department in order to integrate evangelism through Sunday School. Some visits will be class ministry contacts or visits to take a neighborhood opinion poll.

8. Each Team should have both male and female representation. A man and a woman not married to one another should not visit together without a third person. The three-member makeup of each Team each week is essential to protecting the integrity of the ministry as well as the safety of the person(s) visiting and being visited.

9. Team Leaders are responsible for leading their Team Learners to put into practice the parts of the FAITH Visit Outline for which they have received training.

Team Leaders are responsible for leading Team Time, when Learners are reciting memorization from home study and previous sessions. Team Leaders and Learners have separate Teaching Time sessions in different rooms. Team Leaders gather with their Teams immediately after Teaching Time for home visits during Visitation Time, a sequence that maximizes learning. Teams return to the church for reports during Celebration Time.

Team Leaders are expected to participate as appropriate in two essential weekly meetings: FAITH Group Leader meetings (if a Group Leader) and weekly Sunday School leadership team meetings (if a member of the class or Sunday School leadership team).

10. Team Learners are responsible for memorizing the entire FAITH Visit Outline, including a gospel presentation built around the word *FAITH*. The entire presentation requires approximately 30 minutes to present. Learners participate in home visits, expanding their role each week to practice presentation elements studied in the classroom and at home. The Team Leader assesses his/her Learners' readiness and encourages them to take part in the visit, while being ready to help as needed.

11. By the conclusion of the second 16 weeks of FAITH training (FAITH Advanced), Team Learners should be equipped to be soul-winners—acceptable and confident in conducting a FAITH visit, in presenting the gospel of Jesus Christ, and in sharing their faith in any life-witness opportunity.

High Attendance Days and Enrollment/Attendance Emphases

High attendance days can provide exciting times in the life of a church. More people may be in Sunday morning Bible study and worship than any other time. That is a worthy goal only if the motive for doing so is right. Some reasons for having a high attendance day or enrollment/attendance emphasis are to

- bring honor to Christ by focusing on a specific day of Bible study and evangelistic harvest in the church;
- demonstrate the potential of the church when members engage in a concerted actions designed to reach others; and
- challenge members to make intentional efforts to lead the spiritually lost to faith in Christ and to serve Him through ongoing Bible study, fellowship, ministry, and worship.

When planning a high attendance day or an enrollment/attendance emphasis, the planning team needs to determine a clear objective and communicate it to the leadership team and members. Make the day or emphasis worthy of the effort. In other words, the sustained value of a high attendance day or emphasis that is focused only on the numerical goal is questionable. Determine what the leadership team and members can learn from the event that will assist or encourage them in their ongoing work.

For example, an attendance goal is set for high attendance day. Use the goal to generate interest and excitement. But focus much attention on the kind of actions that will lead to the attainment of the goal. The emphasis may need to be on contacts, the intentional efforts to make contact with every member and prospect. These contacts, however, are not just to focus on the high attendance day. The specific day may be an impetus for making the contacts, but the encounter with absentees, irregular attenders, and prospects should communicate genuine concern for the person. Don't leave the impression that a person is just a way of attaining a goal.

By the same token, unapologetically emphasize attendance. Make concentrated efforts that say, "We want you to be part of our group who will meet for Bible study next Sunday." Be prepared to say why the Bible study is important and what the group can offer to the individual. Help the person see some reasons for their participation beyond helping the church reach a goal on one Sunday.

High attendance days and enrollment/attendance emphases usually are more effective when all classes and departments have had part in determining the goals for the event. For example, each class may be asked to set a goal for the event. The cumulative total may become the overall goal for the day. Some churches have good results by developing friendly competition between classes or department. In these cases, churches in adjoining communities have challenged each other on high attendance day. But whatever you do, remember the focus is on the people and on helping members learn good practice, such as developing the habit of regular contact of members and prospects.

To help in the promotion of high attendance days, you may want to consider some campaigns that are available. For example, the North American Mission Board produces an annual emphasis to be used in October in relationship to On Mission: To

Tell the Gospel Sunday (formerly Soul-Winning Commitment Day.) The emphasis for the month concludes with a high attendance day for worship and Sunday morning Bible study. An emphasis packet for this event is mailed from the North American Mission Board to all Southern Baptist churches in late summer.

Steps to Preparing for a High Attendance Day

1. *Bathe the effort in prayer.* —This is a spiritual emphasis, as are all efforts to reach others for Christ. The plans and efforts will be incomplete without the powerful presence of the Holy Spirit.

2. *Place the emphasis date on the church calendar.*

3. *At least 6 to 8 weeks in advance of the event, provide details to all Sunday School leaders about the high attendance day.*—Lead workers to commit their support. Contact workers not present and enlist their commitment as well.

4. *Approximately 4 to 6 weeks before the event, ask Sunday School leaders to guide their classes and/or departments to set contact and enrollment goals for the emphasis.* —Encourage them to establish a goal that is at least one more than the high attendance in a previous year. Leaders in younger children's and preschool departments may work with adult class leaders to encourage parents and their children to be present for the high attendance day. Poster board with a emphasis graphic and theme could be preprinted and distributed for making posters to display class/department goals.

5. *Develop a plan in which classes/departments contact every Sunday School member and prospect at least three times before the event culmination day.* —Contact members and prospects by a personal visit, a phone call, and a card or letter. During these contacts, present an evangelistic witness as appropriate, enroll prospects, and obtain commitments to attend Sunday morning Bible study and worship on the emphasis day.

6. *Promote enthusiastically!* —Use announcements, newsletters, church bulletins, banners, posters, and word-of-mouth.

7. *Prepare to receive guests who will attend.* —Ask every class/department to have someone in place (outreach-evangelism leaders, class leaders, so forth) to welcome guests. If the church does not have a welcome center at the primary church entrance, consider creating one. Train persons to receive guests, complete guest forms, and accompany visitors to the appropriate classroom area. Remind Bible study leaders to prepare to teach evangelistically. Do not presume that guests know about the Bible so be cautious in asking them questions or calling on them to read aloud.

8. *Plan to celebrate the victories of the day.* —Recognize class/departments that reach contact, enrollment, and/or attendance goals. Expect a harvest to occur. Just as you began the emphasis in prayer, conclude it with a prayer of thanksgiving to God.

Bible Study Projects

Bible study projects include all-age January Bible Study; all-age Vacation Bible School; mission Vacation Bible School for preschoolers, children, and youth; and Backyard Bible Clubs for preschoolers and children. These projects are targeted to both the unreached and reached and occur during a set time span, such as a five-day Vacation Bible School.

A church may choose to conduct a Bible study project to

- provide an annual Bible study event for members and prospects that focuses on a Bible book, or portion(s) of a Bible book, or major Bible truth;
- contribute to a church's work in accomplishing one or more of its functions through Sunday School ministry.

Preparation Actions

1. *Identify intended participants in the Bible study project.*

Consider all outreach and evangelism opportunities, including all Sunday School prospects, age-group target groups (single adults, senior adults, and so forth), and community target groups (apartment dwellers, mobile home park residents, ethnic groups, business community, and so forth).

2. *Consider how participants will be grouped (by separate age groups, geography, language, special needs/interests).*

3. *Determine the approach and schedule to fit the church's needs and personality.*

Studies for age groups may be conducted using same/different approaches at the same/different times.

- The *Teaching Approach* may be on consecutive days in one week or one day per week in consecutive weeks.
- The *Preaching/Worship Approach* may be on consecutive days in one week or one day per week in consecutive weeks.
- The *Retreat Approach* may be one or two days, either at church or in a retreat setting

4. *Look at the church calendar and select dates and times that best meet the needs of intended participants and provide for the best use of church resources, including leadership.*

5. *Include as part of the Sunday School ministry budget support for the project.*

Budget for the following items: (1) planning and promoting the event; (2) leader and study material; (3) compensation for guest leaders, if needed; (4) refreshments, if desired; (5) additional expenses incurred with optional approaches, such as facilities away from the church.

6. *Determine who will lead the study.*

Possibilities are (1) the pastor; (2) faculty from within the church for any/all age groups; (3) guest leaders for any or all age groups.

7. *Set the organization.*

Separate classes are recommended for each age division so biblical content and teaching approaches will be consistent with the needs and interests of learners or develop other forms of organization, such as geographical or special needs/interests, necessary to implement the chosen approach effectively or to reach the specified target group.

8. *Obtain materials.*

9. *Enlist leaders and train leaders.*

Enlistment Ideas:
- Involve leaders from Sunday School and/or other ministries of the church.
- Partner with other churches to share leadership. For example, schedule January Bible Study at different times and use a combined faculty in both churches.
- Enlist a guest preacher, Christian educator, or other outstanding Bible study leader to guide the study.

Training Ideas:
- Participate in a preparatory training event provided by the association, state convention, or LifeWay Christian Resources. For example, attend a VBS clinic conducted by your local association.
- Provide a training event in your church for your own faculty.

10. *Promote the emphasis.*

11. *Assign space appropriate to each group.*
For off-campus approaches, secure and assign space.

12. *Complete final details.*
These include conducting faculty meeting(s), setting up rooms, arranging for breaks and/or fellowship meals, securing attendance records for study recognition credit, or arranging lodging and transportation for guest faculty.

13. *Conduct the study.*

14. *Conduct follow-up actions.*
- Within one week, send letters to participants not enrolled in ongoing Bible study inviting them to enroll in Sunday School class or department.
- Transfer the names of nonmembers to prospect files. Assign prospects to classes or department for contact.
- Consider the need for follow-up Bible studies to prospects. Are weektime Bible study groups needed? Refer ideas to the Sunday School Planning Team.
- Mail applications for study recognition credit.

Your Time Is Now

Of the best practices summarized here and developed throughout this book, which one most needs attention? To which best practice will you direct your planning team to give focused attention 1999-2000?

1. Identify the Strategy
2. Organize with Purpose
3. Build the Leadership
4. Train Effective Leaders
5. Provide Space and Equipment
6. Value Record Keeping
7. Develop Soul-winners
8. Teach to Transform
9. Conduct Special Events
10. Choose Sound Curriculum

Section 6

Teaching That Transforms

pioneer

Nearly 100 years ago, P. E. Burroughs, a pioneer Sunday School leader among Southern Baptists, wrote a classic Sunday School book, *Building a Successful Sunday School*. In discussing the value of Sunday School in encouraging members to do personal Bible study, he wrote:

> "The Sunday school is the chief agency of the church for the promotion of Bible study. Apart from the Sunday school, how much Bible reading and study would there be among our people? If the Sunday school should go out of existence, how much Bible study would we have? Many would read their Bibles; how many would study them? The Sunday school offers the only practicable effective means of promoting popular Bible study . . . ." [8]

That was then. How about now?

I am eager to declare that, as we prepare to enter a new century and a new millennium, Sunday School still holds center-stage in the churches. The new definition of Sunday School set forth in this book may not be new after all; it echoes the principles put forth by Dr. Burroughs and many others who have gone before us:

> Sunday School is the foundational strategy in a local church for leading people to faith in the Lord Jesus Christ and for building Great Commission Christians through Bible study groups that engage people in evangelism, discipleship, fellowship, ministry, and worship.

One key phrase in this definition is that Sunday School is "a foundational strategy" implemented "through Bible study groups that engage people." The effectiveness of Sunday School for a new century is dependent on a people who are involved in studying the Word of God. His Word challenges each believer to share the good news of Jesus Christ. Through a study of the Bible that engages, convicts, and instructs, believers grow in maturity in Christ.

Hight C Moore, the first editorial secretary of the Southern Baptist Sunday School Board (now LifeWay Christian Resources), influenced much of what Southern Baptists studied in Sunday School because the material passed across his desk for review and analysis. Today another generation of biblical scholars and editors give their lives to producing quality Bible studies.

David Morrow, director of the Children's Sunday School Ministry Department, is one of those leaders. The target audience for David's work is children, first through sixth grades. Because so many life-changing experiences happen during this span of a child's life, it is so important that children learn early how to study God's Word and to build into the disciplines of their lives a hunger for studying the Scriptures.

David Morrow served on the task force that strategized the kind of resources needed for Sunday School in the new century. His contributions have been significant. Because of his background in discipleship, his voice has been lifted in support of Bible

David Morrow, director, Children's Sunday School Ministry Department, is a leader who is committed to paying the price to provide Bible study that transforms lives.

[8] P. E. Burroughs, *Building a Successful Sunday School* (Fleming and Revell Co., 1921).

Think about the teaching that takes place in your Sunday School classes and departments.

Is it teaching that focuses on facts, or is it teaching that focuses on changing lives? What kind of steps need to be taken during this year to improve the quality and focus of teaching through Sunday School?

Think about the people in your life or in your church who are effective Bible teachers.

What contributes to their effectiveness? How has that person helped you to be changed in the power of the Holy Spirit, or how does that teacher influence her class members to be transformed by Christ?

study that transforms lives rather than just communicates facts.

David has helped to influence a new instructional design and approach to Bible study in the 21st century. Three words will provide the framework for guiding Bible study through Sunday School: *prepare, encounter,* and *continue.* Their use, which will be described more fully in the pages that follow, will yield a purposeful seven-day-a-week Sunday School ministry.

Over the years one of the struggles faced by many teachers has been how to effectively apply the Bible teachings for a particular lesson. Sometimes the application appeared only to be an addendum to the session, a summary that took place within the closing 10 minutes or so.

Personally, I have not always felt comfortable with this approach. For example, in a lesson on being honest a person can choose to "tell the truth" because he has studied a passage related to honesty. That is *application.* But I believe that biblical truths should be *integrated* into the lives of a believer so that the person tells the truth because he has been transformed by the power of Christ. A person is honest because of who he is in Christ rather than because he has applied a certain lesson to his everyday dealings.

David also has helped to influence concepts that lead to spiritual transformation through an encounter with God's Word in a Bible study group. Seven Bible teaching elements—common concepts for all Sunday School age groups—guide the Bible study process. A key word summarizes each concept. All seven concepts will be described more fully in subsequent pages of this book.

- *Acknowledge Authority* (control).—What authority, power, or rule guides the life of each learner?
- *Search the Scriptures* (content)—What did God say in the Scripture to the first readers or hearers?
- *Understand the Truth* (concept)—What abiding biblical truth(s) is the Holy Spirit teaching to you in your life situation from the Scripture?
- *Personalize the Truth* (context)—Based on the abiding biblical truth(s), what is God teaching you about thinking, feeling, and living today?
- *Struggle with the Truth* (conflict)—What conflict or crisis of belief is God bringing about in your heart and life to challenge what you think and value and how you live? What life questions, problems, issues, or struggles compel you to seek answers and promises in the Bible?
- *Believe the Truth* (conviction)—What new truth is God leading you to receive and integrate into your life? How is the Holy Spirit leading you to repent or to change your mind, your values, or the way you live?
- *Obey the Truth* (conduct)—To what extent will you love, trust, and obey the Lord in what you think and value and the way you live?

David Morrow understands those concepts and is committed to providing them for every family in the world. This commitment comes with a price, but it is one worth paying.

The new century is going to be filled with thrilling moments for Sunday School teachers who grasp the opportunities before them. Hopefully, you can see the possibilities of what will happen in the lives of those who will be part of your Sunday School in a new century.

Bible Teaching That Leads to Spiritual Transformation

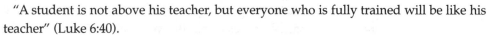

"A student is not above his teacher, but everyone who is fully trained will be like his teacher" (Luke 6:40).

"Whatever you have learned or received or heard from me, or seen in me—put it into practice. And the God of peace will be with you" (Phil. 4:9).

Why Teach People the Bible?

The central command in Jesus' Great Commission is to "make disciples" (Matt. 28:19). Jesus gave a three-part plan for fulfilling the commission: "Go," "baptizing," and "teaching." All three parts are essential to Sunday School ministry: go to the people and share the gospel, assimilate them into the fellowship, and teach them to obey Jesus' commands. This section focuses on teaching for 21st-century Sunday School.

If one word were to capture the goal for teaching people the Bible, that word might be *Christlikeness*. The goal of Bible study and biblical instruction is transformed lives that exhibit love for God and others (Matt. 22:37-40; 1 Tim. 1:5). Such lives glorify God because they are Christlike in nature (Ps. 119:1-16,105-112; 2 Cor. 3:18; Col. 3:16-17).

To accomplish this vision, we, as leaders, must model the truth that God transforms lives day-by-day. Then as we teach people God's Word, we move beyond transferring biblical information and calling for discussions about application to walking with our learners in obedient, Christ-centered living.

Spiritual transformation is defined as God's work of changing a believer into the likeness of Jesus by creating a new identity in Christ and by empowering a lifelong relationship of love, trust, and obedience to glorify God. Spiritual transformation begins when a lost person repents and places personal faith in Christ and continues as that believer "works out" his or her salvation through obedience to God in His power (Phil. 2:12-13).

As Jesus indicated in His prayer (John 17:17), it is God's Word that sanctifies—sets believers apart from the world for service to the world. Exposing God's Word to the hearts and minds of people, both lost and saved, so that they may be transformed in Christ is what Sunday School is about! We must do more than deal with "felt needs" where people make mental assent to biblical relevance for a "hot topic" or pressing issue. As must the people we teach, so too must we integrate intimately into our minds and hearts biblical truth that sets the course for living.

How, Then, Should We Teach People God's Word?

Simply stated, here are three best practices for Sunday School teachers to use in the 21st century:

- Before the teaching session, *prepare* the ministry environment for spiritual transformation.
- During the session, guide the learners toward spiritual transformation through an *encounter* with God's Word in a Bible study group.
- After the session, *continue* to guide learners toward spiritual transformation in daily living and family relationships.

Prepare

How do you prepare a ministry environment? A ministry environment includes the teaching-learning setting, but it is much more. Think of the environment in terms of relationships. Yes, you will want to give attention to the physical setting—walls, chairs, visuals, for example. But you will want to create an environment in which everyone feels welcome and wanted—including the Holy Spirit.

More on the ministry environment later, but begin by accepting the fact that the first essential for all effective Sunday School leaders is to be prepared. The apostle Paul called for preparation in 2 Timothy 2:15, "Do your best to present yourself to God as one approved, a workman who does not need to be ashamed and who correctly handles the word of truth." Great Commission Sunday School leaders recognize that, in a real way, the leader is the lesson. Learners will long remember the character of the leader more than the content the leader presents. (Note how the apostle Paul addressed this principle in Phil. 4:8-9.)

Teachers and other leaders are accountable to be authentic examples of Christianity in personal living and in what they teach (Jas. 3:1). What's the best way to get ready for such a ministry? There are two tried and proven strategies—Sunday School leadership team meetings and personal Bible study.

Through the Sunday School Leadership Team Meetings

Sunday School leadership team meetings help teachers and other leaders plan through praying together and reporting on three essential areas of Sunday School ministry. Each area contributes to the ongoing ministry of Sunday School. Prayer should permeate each focus area.

• *Focus on the Mission (10 min.)*

During this portion of the leadership team meeting, the department director guides teachers and other leaders to relate the work of their department and classes to the overall vision and mission of the church. Everyone finds out about churchwide and age-group events and emphases. Also, organizational issues, records, and other administrative concerns are addressed.

• *Focus on Relationships (25 min.)*

During this time the needs of members and prospects are assessed and, as appropriate, plans are made for responding. Approaches are determined for being involved with members and prospects beyond the Sunday session, especially ways to involve members in evangelism and ministry. Fellowship activities and assimilation actions could be planned.

Witnessing and ministry approaches also should be reviewed. Churches using the FAITH Sunday School Evangelism Strategy will use this time to review assignments, give reports, and make follow-up assignments.

• *Focus on Bible Study (25 min.)*

Teaching for spiritual transformation is facilitated when leaders work together to plan the best ways to bring participants into an encounter with God's Word in the Sunday

morning Bible study group. As teachers and leaders plan together, what is planned in department time interfaces with what will be done in class time. Such intentional planning maximizes the impact of God's Word on the hearts of individuals and the group as a whole.

In addition, teaching methods can be previewed and adapted. New approaches can be created. Previous Bible study sessions can be evaluated and assignments made for the upcoming study.

Not to be overlooked is the value of this Bible study and prayer time for the adult leaders. Sometimes adults say they do not want to work with preschoolers, children, or youth in Sunday School because their Adult Sunday School class is so meaningful to them. Yet, what a rich Bible study and prayer time the weekly leadership team meeting can be just for the adult leaders, regardless of the age group they teach!

Finally, the weekly leadership team meeting is a good time to claim Jesus' promise that as we bear fruit, we can ask what we need (John 15:16; Matt. 18:19-20). Praying for each other as leaders and teachers in a weekly leadership team meeting will do wonders to improve the Sunday morning Bible study experience!

Through Personal Bible Study

Beyond the Sunday School leadership team meeting, you must *first prepare personally for God to use you to teach His Word*. Just as did the first-century leaders in Acts 6:4, 21st-century leaders have a "ministry of the word." Use God's Word as the textbook for Sunday School and for personal spiritual development. As you prepare for the Bible teaching session, ask God to speak to you personally about your own walk with Him. When God creates personal conflict and conviction in your preparation to teach or lead, surrender to the Lord's leadership in your life. Practice personal repentance and obedience as you prepare to teach His Word.

Plan to depend on the Holy Spirit. The depth of the ministry environment is directly related to your own depth of spiritual transformation. Just as the "ministry of the word" worked together with prayer (Acts 6:4), you should begin with prayer, making yourself available to God to depend upon Him. Then, intercede on behalf of others and about needs within your department, class, and their families. Also include prayer for your fellow leaders.

The Holy Spirit is already at work in the lives of your participants, convicting them of sin and drawing them to God (John 16:8-11). The Holy Spirit is present in believers, revealing spiritual truth and enabling them to understand this truth, discern its application to their lives, and become transformed into Christ's image (2 Cor. 3:18). While selected facets of secular educational theories are useful in Christian education, following these alone will not achieve the Spirit's work of transforming human hearts, minds, and lives.

Second, prepare for learners to encounter God's Word. By yourself you cannot create a ministry environment. The good news is God can create it through you. Using information and ideas from your Sunday School leadership team meeting, do as much as you can to magnify caring relationships among participants. When teachers lead people to experience New Testament fellowship—sharing the common life found in Christ—during the Bible study session and throughout the week, then, like Jesus, they will find opportunities to communicate biblical truth in a variety of settings, dilemmas, and crises. The depth of relationship with the learner can affect how well that learner will be motivated to participate in the Bible study session.

Here are some factors to consider to help you prepare to lead your learners into an encounter with God's Word.

1. *Learn to enjoy the people you teach.*

If people hear you affirm and accept them, they will be more likely to be responsive to your guidance from the authority of God's Word.

New Testament teachers related to their learners, both personally and creatively in language, culture, and life needs. Jesus was open and approachable, allowing questions and challenges to His teaching. Jesus taught individuals, small groups, or large groups in any setting at any time. He used everyday objects and stories to grab the attention of His hearers. He loved people, even His adversaries.

Peter, at Pentecost, began with what the people were experiencing. In Athens Paul started with what his hearers knew from secular philosophy. In short, Peter and Paul illustrate what many Bible teachers have to do today—start where people are, unfocused, and focus their attention on spiritual truths.

2. *Make sure that ministry to the individual's needs takes place.*

One practical reason to keep classes small in order to personally attend to individual needs. After all, Jesus chose only 12 disciples. Within the class or department, you can organize individuals in such a way that participants can care for one another and can receive care.

As the teacher-leader, you are responsible to move beyond teaching Bible content to building up lives that God wants to spiritually transform. People will care more for what you teach when they know how much you care for them.

3. *Be prepared to teach people God's Word in and through their family.*

The home is the first place where God desires that Bible teaching for spiritual transformation to occur (Deut. 6:6-8; Prov. 1:8-9; 3:5-6). Because the Bible emphasizes the primary responsibility of parents and families in spiritual instruction, Bible teaching sessions and the resources used before, during, and after the sessions should support and encourage spiritual growth and understanding within the context of the home. For example, intentionally challenge participants to share what they learn with their family members.

4. *Prepare to teach people in a variety of ways.*

It is incumbent, then, to teach to change lives. The role of the teacher is to guide learning in ways that facilitate the work of the Holy Spirit to transform learners' lives. This includes recognizing the ways in which learners learn best (1 Cor. 3:1-2; Heb. 5:11-14). Teaching people God's Word more likely will bear fruit when teachers relate to them with teaching-learning approaches they prefer. Teachers must seek to connect not only with the learner's intellect but also with the learner's heart.

Begin by preparing the physical setting. What the room looks and sounds and sometimes smells like is the first thing people will notice when they come to Bible study. Arrange the room from session to session so that it teaches visually and creatively.

With regard to choosing teaching-learning methods, examine the following list of ways people prefer to learn. Can you think of a time when Jesus employed each of these teaching-learning approaches? Read carefully Luke 22:1-38 and Luke 9:57-59. You will find each of these teaching-learning approaches at least once in these passages:

- *Relational.*—People who prefer to learn through relationships are highly social, make friends easily, and may be "good talkers."

- *Musical.*—Some people enjoy listening to music and often find it easy to express themselves through music—composing, playing, and performing.
- *Logical.*—Others prefer to learn by seeing patterns and reasoning through difficult situations.
- *Natural.*—These folks enjoy being outdoors and can readily appreciate elements of the natural world.
- *Physical.*—These learners are usually very active and prefer to get involved through such methods as drama, field trips, and sports.
- *Reflective.*—Others prefer to learn by seeking to understand who they are and how they feel. Such people may prefer to work alone.
- *Visual.*—Those who prefer to learn visually can "see" in their minds as well as in the concrete world. They also enjoy creating their own pictures and visual representations.
- *Verbal.*—These learners like to use words—either reading, writing, speaking, or listening. They often enjoy poems, stories, debates, monologues, and essays.

Think about the people you are assigned to teach. Try to write a name by each approach; it's OK to use a person's name more than once.

The truth is that your Bible study group may have every one of these learning approaches represented during any given Bible study session. Also, no one individual learns only through one of these approaches. As the leader, don't limit how the Holy Spirit can break through in a person's life by choosing only one or two approaches to teaching and learning. Seek the Lord's guidance and trust His Holy Spirit to teach through you.

You can learn to relate creatively to any generation's language, culture, and life issues. Ask the group to help you. The key here is variety. The death knell for any Bible study group is the label "boring." Avoid doing anything—even the "most fun things"—the same way every Bible study session. In case you haven't heard, a rut is a grave with both ends kicked out. And no one wants to be in a dead Sunday School class or department! So vary your teaching-learning approaches.

Encounter

During the session, guide people toward spiritual transformation through an encounter with God's Word in a Bible study group. Never forget that the Bible is the truth that transforms. Centuries before sending His Son, God promised to transform human hearts:

> "This is the covenant I will make with the house of Israel after that time . . .
> I will put my law in their minds and write it on their hearts. I will be their
> God, and they will be my people. No longer will a man teach his neighbor,
> or a man his brother, saying, 'Know the Lord,' because they will all know me,
> from the least of them to the greatest . . . for I will forgive their wickedness
> and will remember their sins no more" (Jer. 31:33-34).

In the New Testament, Paul described God's work of spiritual transformation as "the renewing of the mind" (Rom. 12:2). Peter asserted, "For you have been born again, not of perishable seed, but of imperishable, through the living and enduring word of God" (1 Pet. 1:23).

Can we discern from Scripture how God uses His Word to transform lives? Yes, we can in several places.

For instance, let's do a Bible study from John 4:1-42. Verses 1-6 set the historical background for Jesus' journey through Samaria. The disciples and the Samaritans allowed prejudices to control their hearts and attitudes. Verse 4 implies that Jesus' journey through rather than around Samaria was a conscious decision Jesus felt compelled to make. Jesus' heart was controlled by the Father's will for His life. He was under the authority of His Heavenly Father.

In verse 7, Jesus' call for a drink of water accomplished more than expressing a weary desire to quench a physical thirst. Jesus was calling for the woman to engage in conversation with Him, something He may not have been able to do when the disciples were with Him (v. 8).

Acknowledge Authority

Verses 1-6 and 7-8 reveal the first element of teaching God's Word in such a way that God can transform lives. This principle is *Acknowledge Authority,* and the key word is *control.* Teachers must discern as far as humanly possible what authority, power, assumptions, presuppositions, worldview, or rule guides or controls the life of each participant. Ultimately, teachers want to address the fundamental life questions common to all people: *Where did I/we come from? How do I/we fit in? Where am I/we going?*

Knowing where people are "coming from" will help you choose teaching approaches that will motivate them and engage them more readily in the Bible study session. Key questions for discerning the authority in participants' lives are questions such as these: *Where is your heart—what is the most important authority in your life—as you approach Bible study (Matt. 6:21)? What grips your life—including developmental issues associated with "growing up" or generational issues associated with living in this era? What assumptions—maybe prejudices—do you have about the Bible, this subject, or the people in the Bible study group?*

This element identifies an assumption that you must make for every session, specifically that every participant comes to a Bible teaching session with an authority—recognized or unrecognized—that controls his or her life. As the leader, you are engaged in a spiritual warfare for people's hearts and lives. Your ultimate goal is to lead participants to accept the authority of God and His Word as the sovereign rule over all of life.

Ideally, you and your learners should perform a spiritual "heart check" before and during each session. Many discipline or attention problems are the result of not discerning where your heart is as the leader and where the individual's heart is as the learner. Knowing each participant and what controls his or her heart will give you insight in how to guide the person to participate in the Bible study.

Emotions also are vitally important to how much teaching and learning takes place, especially at this point of acknowledging authority. Do all you can to communicate unconditional love to every person. Using Jesus as your model, seek to make the Bible study an experience with lighter moments as well as the "heavy" times. For example, try bringing in a log or a two-by-four piece of lumber and holding it up to someone's eye to make the point of Matthew 7:3!

Search the Scriptures

John 4:9 indicates that immediately the woman felt internal conflict. She could not get past the fact that Jesus, a Jewish man, was speaking publicly to her, an outcast Samaritan. Then in verse 10, Jesus presented the content of His message: God has a gift, He is there to offer it, and she could have "living water." These two verses reveal the second element: *Search the Scriptures.*

The key word related to *Search the Scriptures* is *content.* Searching the Scriptures is what most people associate with Bible teaching—reading, examining, and communicating the content of the Bible. And this element of Bible teaching is probably what most Christians have done best. As we search God's Word, ask, *What did God say in the Scriptures to the first readers or hearers?*

To answer this question most effectively, Bible teachers should examine:

- *The linguistic factor*—the intended meaning of words and phrases, the relationship of words, and the kind of literature in a particular part of the Scriptures.
- *The historical factor*—the setting, including the customs of the time, the land, and the people of the Bible, the language of the Bible, and the archaeology of the Bible.
- *The holistic factor*—Scripture compared to Scripture in light of how the entire Bible treats the truth or concept.

Careful study of what the Bible said to its original readers begs us to ask another question: *What abiding truth(s) for all generations is the Holy Spirit teaching from the Scripture?* Answering a question such as this leads to the third element.

Discover the Truth

Continuing to look at John 4:9-10, we see the third element of Bible teaching: *Discover the Truth.* The key word for this element is *concept.* The Bible is much more than a book of history. It has eternal truths and principles that we can relate to today's life issues and life questions. In other words, *How do we understand these truths and communicate them?* There are two different ways, both of which can be found in the New Testament.

First, the teacher can begin with a single "Biblical Truth" or "Central Bible Truth," study the Scriptures, and then call for the learners to apply the truth to their lives. The concept of Bible story-telling—presenting the message of the Bible in historical narrative sequence—uses this approach. Stephen reflected this strategy when he defended himself before the Sanhedrin in Acts 7, and Paul utilized this approach when he taught in the synagogue in Acts 13:13-42.

The teacher's role is to communicate effectively the biblical truth and to create a climate for learners to engage the biblical truth. Some people call this approach direct instruction or expository teaching. For the most part, the teacher controls the pace, sequence, and content of instruction to cover.

Second, the teacher can begin by selecting a passage and calling upon learners to read it and name the truths they understand are in the passage. Jesus' use of parables reflects this way of calling for listeners to identify the truth He was teaching. Philip's session with the Ethiopian eunuch was begun with the Scriptures and the eunuch's questions (Acts 8:25-40).

The teacher's role in this approach is to guide learners effectively so they can discover personal biblical truths and help them apply biblical truth and principles to their daily lives. Some people call this approach "guided discovery." The teacher does not simply tell the learner the biblical content or truth but seeks to guide the learner to express what he or she thinks it says and means. Through individual study and through group discussion, each person is given an opportunity to respond and to take steps toward changing or transforming the way he or she thinks and acts.

Such guided discovery questions usually follow this pattern:
- An approach question to introduce the lesson (ice breaker).
- An observation question to discover the facts of the passage.
- An interpretation question to discover the writer's basic meaning of the text.
- An application question to discover the personal, life-transforming message.

Which approach is best for helping people "discover the truth"? The Holy Spirit can use either or both approaches effectively. Both should be viewed as two different paths to the same objective. You could select elements from both teaching-learning approaches to create a blended plan that is right for the group. Or you may choose one approach based on your personal giftedness, the context in which the Bible teaching session is conducted, the preferred learning approaches of the participants, and/or the content of the study. As stated earlier, the key is variety. You will show people how much you love them by teaching them in ways they learn best.

Finally, teach as a coworker with the Holy Spirit. The Holy Spirit is the ultimate Teacher (John 14:26). Paul set a good example for all Sunday School leaders. He spoke "in words taught by the Spirit" (1 Cor. 2:13) and saw himself and his colleagues as "God's fellow workers" (1 Cor. 3:9). Great Commission Sunday School teachers and leaders depend on Jesus' promise, "I am with you always" (Matt. 28:20).

Personalize the Truth

The key word for this fourth element of Bible teaching could be *context*. Important questions to answer are these: *Based on the abiding biblical truth(s), what is God teaching me personally about thinking, feeling, and living today? What could God be teaching people in their personal lives?*

John 4:11-12 indicates that the woman continued to experience conflict in her mind, perhaps because she was taking Jesus literally. In verses 13-14, Jesus returned to the content of the subject of "living water" and added to it the eternal concept that anyone can ask for living water. But in verses 15-18, Jesus personalized His teaching about "living water" by directing the woman to call her husband. The woman continued to experience personal conflict as Jesus' teaching became increasingly real to her.

In this part of the Bible study process, your understanding of the life context of the learners plays a critical role. Is the person lost or saved? If the learner is not a Christian, how can the truth be understood from his or her point of view? How does the person's cultural, generational perspective, age, or life stage influence how he or she will personalize this truth? If the teaching method is not connecting, perhaps due to a disability, what is another approach that you could use to help the participant to personalize the truth?

Again, here is where you as teacher are totally dependent upon the Holy Spirit's presence with you, in you, and through you in the teaching process. The learner also has to determine how open he or she will be to the Spirit's ministry. And this brings us to the next element.

Struggle with the Truth

The key word is *conflict*. Any time sinful humans encounter the truth of God's Word there will be a struggle. Some questions to ask are these: *What conflict or crisis of belief is the Holy Spirit bringing about in my heart and life to challenge what I think and value and how I live? What life questions, problems, issues, or struggles compel me to seek answers and promises in the Bible? What aspect of my thinking and belief system needs to be changed?*

As noted, throughout the Samaritan woman's encounter with Jesus, she had been experiencing internal conflicts and struggles. In John 4:9-24, the woman tried to change the subject to places of worship, but Jesus tactfully took the conflicts within the woman and turned them into the concepts He wanted her to learn. Jesus came back to personalize His message to her by identifying Himself as the Christ (vv. 25-26). When the disciples returned in verse 27, they struggled with what Jesus was doing—speaking with a Samaritan woman! Jesus' teaching and actions led to conflicts for the woman and for the disciples.

Conflict is the work of the Holy Spirit. He may use what you teach, how you involve the learners, or your testimony; but you cannot create this internal spiritual conflict on your own. Real "application to life" intensifies when we allow ourselves—and lead our learners—to be honest with how God's Word creates conflict in our hearts, minds, and lives.

Believe the Truth

Its key word is *conviction*. These questions arise: *How is the Holy Spirit leading me to live and repent—to change my mind, my values, or the way I live—or to resolve the struggle or conflict in my life? What new truth is God leading me to receive and integrate into my life?*

Upon the return of the disciples (v. 27), the woman went quickly to share her growing conviction about Jesus being the Messiah (vv. 28-30). The Samaritan woman had a growing conviction, one that she believed and acted upon. While the Samaritan woman was deepening her conviction, the disciples (vv. 31-38) continued to struggle with Jesus when He did not eat. In response, Jesus tried to teach them to understand and personalize the truth about doing His Father's will by joining with Him in the spiritual harvest.

Conviction is the point at which spiritual transformation becomes most intense, for conviction addresses the human will. At this stage—if the learner has been open to the leadership of the Holy Spirit—the learner is confronted or convicted with a change that needs to be made in his or her life in order to become a Christian or to become more Christlike. When a person accepts God's Word as truth and repents, such repentance is without regret (2 Cor. 7:9-10). People who place their trust in God will not be disappointed (Ps. 22:5; Rom. 10:11).

In John 5:39 Jesus commended those who opposed Him for searching the Scriptures, but He also said in verse 40 that they were unwilling to come to Him to receive the life they sought in the Scriptures. In John 5, the Jews recognized the elements of control, content, concept, context, and conflict; but they were not willing to surrender to the conviction that Jesus is God's Son.

Obey the Truth

Its key word is *conduct*. The "bottom line" question is this: *To what extent will I obey the Holy Spirit's leadership in what I think and value and the way I live?*

Our study of Jesus and the Samaritan woman concludes with John 4:39-42. The woman believed in Jesus and demonstrated her faith by bringing townspeople to Him. Many others believed when they heard Jesus personally. He stayed two more days with them; He could not leave them.

In the Bible, the word *believe* carries with it more than intellectual assent. In the Bible believers showed their faith by acting on their faith. In recent years, almost everyone has insisted that Bible study resources "apply the Bible to life." Yet, experienced Bible teachers realize that application means more than merely making a mental connection of biblical truth to a life issue.

Faithfulness to obey God's Word is the ultimate application. "You are slaves to the one whom you obey," wrote the apostle Paul in Romans 6:13. People who are being spiritually transformed depend upon the Holy Spirit to provide the power for living in obedience to God. Because their old human nature has been crucified with Christ, believers set their minds on Christ who strengthens them (Gal. 2:20; Col. 3:1-17; Phil. 4:13).

When does a believer really understand the meaning of God's Word? Jesus said, "Everyone who hears these words of mine and puts them into practice is like a wise man who built his house on the rock" (Matt. 7:24). "If you love me," Jesus said, "you will obey what I command" (John 14:15). Both leaders and learners recognize that people do not complete their Bible study until they obey the Bible in life.

During a 1998 chapel address at LifeWay Christian Resources, Jimmy Draper commented on Luke 6:46, where Jesus asked, "Why do you call me, 'Lord, Lord,' and do not do what I say?" Jimmy said simply, "You can say 'No' and you can say 'Lord,' but you cannot say 'No, Lord.' "

What if everyone—leaders and learners together—said "Yes, Lord!" from one Bible teaching session to the next—seven days a week!

Review of the Seven Bible Teaching Elements

The seven Bible teaching elements of control, content, concept, context, conflict, conviction, and conduct will rarely be completed before the end of a 60-minute Bible study session. For the Holy Spirit to transform lives, however, all elements should be experienced by leaders and participants before, during, and after the session. In addition, the amount of time devoted to the seven Bible teaching elements will vary based on the different life situations. While some people may need these elements in specific, sequenced steps, other learners may prefer that the elements occur in a different sequence or repeatedly throughout the session. The elements can be repeated throughout a session or over a period of several lessons in a unit, much like a spiral advances upward through a series of repeated movements.

Twenty-first-century Sunday School teachers and other leaders recognize that there is more teaching to do when the closing prayer ends the Bible study session.

Continue

Because God uses His Word to transform lives after the session concludes, teachers continue their teaching ministry 24 hours a day, 7 days a week. Continue to guide participants toward spiritual transformation in daily living and family relationships. Actually, spiritual transformation into the image of Christ is a lifelong process. Plan to lead learning that continues to facilitate the Holy Spirit's ministry for as long as the Lord allows a ministry to the person or his or her family.

Continue means helping the learners connect the everyday experiences with the larger picture of what God has planned for their lives. *Continue* also means getting the Word of God off the page and bringing it to life in the minds and hearts of the participants.

Learning occurs all the time. Some of the best learning experiences are spontaneous. Try to continue teaching by helping people connect new truths with what they already

know. When people see that God's "abundant life" for them is spiritual transformation into Christlikeness, they will have a framework that the Holy Spirit can use to help them make sense of their day-to-day problems, questions, victories, and joys.

People desperately want to make sense of what is happening with God, their friends, their family, their church, their careers, and their world. Lead Sunday School teachers to continue their teaching ministry in many different settings—in the workplace, at school activities, in conversation with parents and other family members, on church trips, in one-on-one times. Encourage youth and adult teachers to enlist participants as class team leaders to help "continue" to teach.

Based on the Bible study and in obedience to the Holy Spirit, teachers could use in conversations, cards, letters, or emails to members such questions as these to further explore after the session:

- What command did God present?
- What promise did God make?
- What truth did God teach?
- What attitudes, behaviors, or values will you make a part of your life?
- What relationships are you developing in your life that are a part of your journey of becoming a Christlike believer?

As teachers continue to teach, they will have opportunity to work with the families of participants. Much of what influences the people in Sunday School classes, especially the amount of support participants receive from their families and the kind of acceptance and affirmation they get from others, is beyond our control. Nevertheless, we must do all we can to connect with home, friends, and school or work. Teachers do have control over the environment at church or in their Bible study group. We must create positive ministry environments there and maintain seven-day-a-week instruction based on the truth that learning can occur anytime and anywhere. Love for teaching people God's Word has no limits (1 Cor. 13).

Your Time Is Now

In light of what you have read, how can you as a general leader
- be more aware of the kinds of preparation being done by classes/departments?
- enable your team to lead participants to consistently encounter God through life-changing Bible study?
- communicate that learning can and does continue?

Choosing Curriculum for Sunday School

First of all, exactly what is curriculum? Essentially, curriculum refers to the course, track, or path on which a person runs. Curriculum is similar to running a race toward a finish line, much as the author of Hebrews encouraged his readers to "run with perseverance the race marked out for us" (Heb. 12:1). Note that Hebrews 12:1 calls for the race to be run "with perseverance" and that the race is on a track that is "marked out for us."

Choosing *Bible study* curriculum means pursuing the course that *the Bible* sets for life—Christlikeness, transformation into the image of Christ (2 Cor. 3:18; Rom. 8:28-29). Sunday School curriculum is the continuous course, process, or system for Bible study groups to use in order to guide unbelievers toward faith in Christ and believers toward Christlikeness through the transformational power of the Holy Spirit. Sometimes curriculum can be a sprint, like a 100-meter dash—a short course. Ultimately, however, curriculum should be viewed as a marathon, for in the final analysis the track of study the leader and learners choose shapes people's worldview.

There are two aspects of curriculum: the curriculum plan and the curriculum resources. The curriculum plan sets the course for *wha*t is studied. The curriculum resources contain the curriculum plan and set forth *how* to study it.

Getting on the Right Curriculum Track

A curriculum plan, or "curriculum map" as some call it, is an orderly arrangement of Bible study content organized so that Sunday School leaders can engage the learner in the study of God's Word to meet spiritual needs through planned teaching-learning experiences.

An ongoing Sunday School ministry built from the **1•5•4** Kingdom Principle begs for an ongoing Bible study curriculum plan. What guidelines should you use to select or develop an ongoing curriculum plan for your church, and why will such a plan keep you on an exciting and fruitful track?

1. When choosing a curriculum plan, choose one that covers all of the Bible's content, not just selected or "favorite" parts. "

All Scripture," Paul wrote, "is . . . useful for teaching, rebuking, correcting and training in righteousness" (2 Tim. 3:16). That is, make sure the curriculum plan is comprehensive of all of the Bible and of all life concerns that people face over a speci-fied length of time.

2. Choose a plan that has a balance of biblical content, Bible study approaches, and life issues.

For example, the plan should contain a balance of Old Testament studies, the life of Christ, and New Testament epistles. The plan could contain a balance of approaches to studying the Bible, such as studying through a book of the Bible, a character in the Bible, or a topic or life issue in the Bible.

Why not just choose whatever people want to study, or whatever the "hot topic" or "felt need" is? By following a systematic, comprehensive plan, ongoing Bible study points repeatedly to the fact that the Bible, not developmental life needs and human issues, must guide and shape believers' lives. If a Sunday School leader selects studies that only address age-group needs and issues, then the leader risks supplanting the Bible's goal for believers with contemporary perceptions of age-group needs and issues. Occasional topical, issue-oriented studies are necessary and included in ongoing curriculum plans, but the ultimate goal of the Bible and Sunday School curriculum is to lead people toward faith in Christ and transformation toward Christlikeness.

While He was responsive to immediate physical, emotional, and spiritual needs, Jesus did not always teach on subjects the people wanted—their "felt needs." Jesus was aware there were deeper issues of the human heart that went beyond the current issues of the day—ceremonial washing of hands, Sabbath laws, and getting caught in adultery. Jesus' curriculum plan focused on redemption, the cross, and transformation of human lives beginning with the human heart.

Make sure that the plan has a balanced diet of biblical truth and life issues. Yes, the curriculum plan needs to address head-on where people are. However, a balanced curriculum plan will not only address the "hot topics" and "felt needs" but also studies that will place people on the race toward mature biblical faith, such as being in Christ, being empowered by the Holy Spirit, being a faithful witness, caring for a lost world, and developing a biblical worldview.

3. Confirm that the curriculum plan is properly sequenced so that learners can build on what they already know.

A systematic approach to Bible study facilitates the integration of biblical truth into the learner's life as a lifelong ongoing process. Jesus built on what His hearers already knew and took them to a new level when He said, "You have heard that it was said . . . But I tell you . . . ." (Matt. 5:43-44).

Remember that spiritual transformation into Christlikeness is a lifelong process. Because curriculum is best viewed from the perspective of a marathon, appropriate repetition of biblical content and life concerns in different ways and at different times strengthens learners, much as a fresh cup of water reinvigorates a marathon runner. The Hebrews 12:1 principle of perseverance for believers applies here.

At the same time, open Bible study groups will always have new people joining the curriculum race—new learners who need the basics the veteran learners could help teach. Do a quick survey of Jesus' teaching in the Gospels, and you will discover how frequently He repeated themes—and how slowly His disciples caught on.

Interestingly, brain researchers speak of the way the human brain organizes knowledge into "natural categories" of patterns. [9] "Experts" in any field are those who (1) are able to "fit into place" new information; (2) have the ability to see the "larger" picture; (3) grasp the context of new information; and (4) possess a different way to remember information, not just random facts, but an orderly arrangements of those facts. Properly sequenced studies help the brain relate new truths to previously learned truths.

A properly sequenced Bible study plan is one expression of the principle of renewing the mind found in Romans 12:2. The ministry of the Holy Spirit is one of helping believers recall what Jesus taught, of helping believers become "experts" in living and bearing witness for Christ. Curriculum can support your goals for transformational Bible study.

4. A planned, ongoing Bible study strategy is most conducive to creating a ministry environment that fosters strong relationships and regularly invites the lost to believe in Christ.

Ongoing groups have a more fixed organizational structure that provide more stable leadership over a longer period of time. A ministry environment of grace and acceptance takes time for God to create.

[9] Renate Nummella Caine and Geoffery Caine, *Making Connections: Teaching and the Human Brain* (Alexandria, VA: Association for Supervision and Curriculum Development, 1991), 100-101.

In addition, one important aspect of creating a ministry environment is helping prepare the participants to hear God's message for a particular time. A planned, ongoing Bible study strategy is a wise discipline for the person who wants to hear God speak and is seeking to obey God's direction. By submitting to a disciplined, lifelong approach to listening to God through His written Word, we do not presume to know exactly what God would speak to us. Instead we demonstrate a commitment to love God and His Word—all of it; to trust God and His Word—all of it; and to obey God and His Word—all of it. Teaching and studying an ongoing, well-designed curriculum plan demonstrates a heart that is ready to be transformed.

With regard to curriculum planning or "curriculum mapping," God knows the timeliness of any study for any individual's life, as well as for a people's time and circumstances. Through the leadership of the Holy Spirit, He will guide those He has placed in strategic places of leadership in discerning the lessons and messages He has for those who will receive them. Curriculum planners carry a tremendous accountability to actively seek God's direction; and then to receive, and faithfully obey, His direction.

The Holy Spirit can work in the hearts of curriculum planners months and years in advance to design studies that are truly God's message for a particular time. Those who design comprehensive, balanced, and properly sequenced Bible study plans will always seek to hear God's voice to choose Bible studies that help believers come face-to-face with God's message in order for them to take it to their communities, culture, and world.

Choose the Best Curriculum Resources

With regard to the curriculum resources, make sure the resources you choose express the curriculum plan that meets these four principles and accomplishes the ministry goals you and your church believe God wants you to fulfill. Materials produced by LifeWay Christian Resources contain Bible study curriculum plans that are comprehensive, balanced, properly sequenced, and conducive to ongoing ministry and address the 1•5•4 Principle of Kingdom Growth. In addition, LifeWay curriculum resources, whether print, video, audio, electronic, or multimedia

- guide churches to fulfill the Great Commission through the five essential functions for church growth—evangelism, discipleship, fellowship, ministry, and worship;
- provide sound, reliable interpretation of the Bible from a conservative point of view;
- offer clear support for evangelism, including the FAITH Sunday School Evangelism Strategy;
- provide a variety of age-appropriate, timely, and relevant teaching-learning approaches, all of which lead learners toward faith in Christ and spiritual transformation into Christlikeness;
- supplement teaching-learning plans with resource kits and leader packs containing creative posters and teaching aids and free online *EXTRA!* teaching supplements containing the latest news, research, and other ideas on this Web site, www.lifeway.com;
- provide choices of Bible study options that feature comprehensive, balanced, sequenced, and ministry-conducive curriculum;
- offer a variety of reasonably priced, easy-to-use, and attractive learner and leader resources in print, audio, electronic, and/or multimedia formats;

- feature biblical insights and teaching approaches written by Southern Baptists experienced in Sunday School ministry in churches;
- provide financial assistance for various Southern Baptist ministries;
- offer an optional devotional and reading guide to deepen participants' daily commitment to love, trust, and obey God based on the Bible study participants study on Sunday; and
- contain leader, teacher, and learner development features to engage and equip persons in the full ministry of evangelism, discipleship, fellowship, ministry, and worship through Sunday School.

Think carefully about which track you want to run on . . . and then "run with perseverance the race marked out for us" (Heb. 12:1).

Why Use a Learner's Guide?

The teaching-learning process is a two-sided coin. On the one hand, people have certain expectations of Sunday School teachers and leaders. On the other hand, Sunday School leaders also have certain expectations of the participants. Most often people arrive for Bible study with little or no personal preparation for the Bible study experience or for ministry opportunities. This lack of preparation and anticipation is rooted in a wide range of issues, from low motivation for spiritual growth to time limitations. Could the most significant factor be traced to the leader's low expectations and lack of planning for participants' involvement before, during, and after the session?

To help people get the most out of Bible teaching-learning before, during, and after the session, Sunday School leaders should take advantage of the most strategic tool other than the Bible itself—the learner's Bible study guide, called everything from a "quarterly" to a student book.

Bible study learner guides are designed to
- provide readers with features on how to become a Christian and live for Christ. What other resource, week in and week out, better communicates the primary purpose of an "open" Bible study group than a well-designed learner's guide that prominently features the plan of salvation?
- help people develop Bible knowledge and Christian convictions based on sound biblical exposition. Where else can people learn more consistently what the Bible teaches on the Christian faith? Bill Taylor in his book, *21 Truths, Traditions, and Trends*, addresses the importance of a learner guide as a "constant monitor of doctrine." [10] He stresses that today's learners are being bombarded with many varieties of false teachings and adds that many churches have almost abandoned leadership training for teachers, leaving teachers to teach tenets that could be detrimental to sound biblical doctrine. LifeWay learner guides provide the true compass north on biblical doctrine.
- encourage learners to develop lifelong Bible study skills and Christian disciplines by providing Bible study helps. What better way is there to help people learn to study the Bible, pray, and feed themselves spiritually than through a well-planned learner guide?
- provide attractive visuals that engage people in reflective questions and biblical

[10] Bill L. Taylor, *21 Truths, Traditions, and Trends: Propelling the Sunday School into the 21st Century* (Nashville: Convention Press, 1996), 158.

insights. How often do people find photography and illustrations that beg them to examine and integrate God's Word?

- challenge readers to make a personal commitment to obey what God is teaching them. What tool will you provide after the session for God to use to reinforce the truths you teach on Sunday morning to help them to love, trust, and obey God in their daily lives?
- support a diversity of learning preferences. How will people "learn it all" during a single Sunday session? When will those who prefer to learn alone have their best opportunity to learn and obey the Scriptures?
- provide leaders with an economical tool for involving people during the session for Bible research and response. How much does it cost in time and church resources to prepare or duplicate handouts in comparison to multi-page full-color resources that are economically priced?
- assist people in preparing for Bible study sessions. Where is the easiest place for participants to discover what the Scripture passage is for the next session?

To strengthen your Bible study experience, provide a Bible study guide for each Bible study participant and prospect. Use the learner guide in the Bible study session as a tool for exploring the Bible passage. Show participants how to use the learner guide as a spiritual growth resource after the session. Finally, hold learners accountable for obeying what God teaches from Sunday to Sunday.

Every Bible study participant expects the teacher and other leaders to come prepared to teach God's Word. What if every Bible study participant came prepared to report on what God taught them or how God used them in ministry during the preceding week? That would be a transformed church and people!

Determining Space and Equipment Needs

A church needs to provide the best possible space for small-group Bible study. Exquisite space with the latest equipment and furnishings may not be available, but the space can be clean, appealing, and functional. Here are some suggestions related to determining space needs.

- Analyze all available space using the guidelines provided. Determine the total square footage of space available that could be used by Bible study groups such as Sunday School classes and departments.
- Determine the square footage needed by all the Sunday School departments and classes in all age groups.
- Based on community changes and age-group shifts, determine whether more space is needed or whether reallocation of space is an option.
- Determine whether multiple use of space is a possibility.
- Determine whether any additional space is available for church use (either by the purchase or lease of portable buildings or other nearby buildings).
- Evaluate whether a new building is a priority.
- Follow church policies in acquiring any new building space and equipment.

Note:

It is difficult to sustain attendance beyond 80 percent of the room's capacity in classrooms where members attend by choice. For example, 10 babies may be placed in an area with a capacity of 10, but adults generally will not attend a class that is regularly more than 80 percent filled.

Securing Equipment and Furnishings

Equipment is another factor that affects the climate or setting for Bible study. The type of equipment and furnishings needed will differ according to the age group being taught. Few churches are able to provide everything. Provide what you are able at the time. One annual goal may be to make improvements in providing equipment and furnishings for classrooms.

Meeting Space Specifications Chart

Age Group	Space/Person	Maximum Attendance	Room Size	Leader: Learner Ratio
Preschool				
Babies	35 sq. ft.	12	420 sq. ft.	1:2
Ones–Twos	35 sq. ft.	12	420 sq. ft.	1:3
Threes–Pre-K	35 sq. ft.	16	560 sq. ft.	1:4
Kindergarten	35 sq. ft.	20	700 sq. ft.	1:5
Children				
Grades 1-6	20-25 sq. ft.	24	480-600 sq. ft.	1:6
Youth				
Gr. 7-12 (class)	10-12 sq. ft.	12	120-144 sq. ft.	1:12
Gr. 7-12 (dept.)	8-10 sq. ft.	65	520-650 sq. ft.	1:12
Young Adults 18-24 yrs				
Department	10 sq. ft.			
Class	12 sq. ft.	25	300 sq. ft.	1:4
Dual Use	15-18 sq. ft.	25	375-450 sq. ft.	
Adults 25 yrs-up				
Department	10 sq. ft.			
Class	12 sq. ft.	25	300 sq. ft.	1:4
Dual Use	15-18 sq. ft.	25	375-450 sq. ft.	

Recommended Preschool Equipment

Symbols: **x** - recommended; **o** - optional; *all* - specialized equipment purchased in limited quantity for use by all ages.

General	B	1	2	3	4	K	All	B-2	3-K	B-K
Rest mats or towels		x	o					x		o
Cribs (hospital 27"x42")	x	o						x		x
Adult rocking chair (2)	x							x		x
Solid surface floor mat (42" x 42")	x									
Wall cabinet (50" above floor)	x	x	x	x	x	x		x	x	x
Trash receptacles with lid	x	x	x	x	x	x		x	x	x
Diaper bag cubbies or hooks	x	x	x							
Vinyl changing pad		x	x							
Open shelf/closed back for toys (26"x36"x12")		o						o		o
Child safety gate										o
Water source for disinfecting	x	x	x					x		x
Slow cookers	x							x		x
Folding screen for nursing area	x							x		x
Rocking boat with enclosed steps		o								
Small counter top refrigerator	o									
Homeliving/Dramatic Play										
Horizontal unbreakable mirror 24" x 48" attached to wall	x							o		
Vertical unbreakable mirror 24" x 48" attached to wall		x	x	x	x	x			o	o
Wooden doll bed (16" x 28" x 8")		o	x	x	x	x		x	x	x
Child size rocker		o	x	x	x	x			x	x
Table (24"x36"x22")			x	x						
Table (24"x36"x24")					x	x			x	x
2-4 chairs (10")			x	x						
2-4 chairs (12"-14")				x	x				x	x
Wooden sink			x	x	x	x			x	x
Wooden stove			x	x	x	x			x	x
Chest of drawers						x				
Child size ironing board and iron*							o			
Music										
Cassette tape/CD player	x	x	x	x	x	x		o	o	o
Autoharp							x			
Rhythm instruments							x			

Blocks	B	1	2	3	4	K	All	B-2	3-K	B-K
Cardboard or vinyl blocks		x	x					x		
Wooden unit blocks (various shapes and sizes)										
1. 29-70				x					x	x
2. 100-150					x	x				
Open shelf/closed back (26"x36"x12")			o	x	x	x			x	x
Art										
Table (30"x48"x22")			x	x					x	x
Table (30"x48"x24")					x	x				
2-4 chairs (10")			x	x						
2-4 chairs (12"-14")					x	x			o	o
Art Easel/ adjustable legs *		x	x	x	x	x			o	o
Drying rack		x	x	x	x					
Water source at child's height for clean up		x	x	x	x				x	x
Art shelf (36"x46"x16")						x				
Nature/Science										
Open shelf with closed back (26"x30"x12")			x	x	x				o	o
Water/table (1 per church)							o			
Table (24"x36"x24")					o					
2-4 chairs (12"-14")					o					
Manipulatives/Puzzles										
Puzzle rack			o	o	o				o	o
Table (24"x36"x24")					o					
2-4 chairs (12"-14")					o					

Maximum number of two tables per room in 2-4 year old rooms.

*One option for art easels would be to have one easel per every three rooms.

Recommended Equipment for Children, Youth, and Adult Departments

Equipment	Children	Youth	Adults
Chairs (age appropriate)	x^1	x^2	x^2
Coat rack	x	x	x
Resources cabinet	x	x	
Tables	x^3	x^5	o
Shelves	x^6	x	x
Book racks	x^7	x	o
Tackboard or bulletin boards	x^8	x	x
Wastebasket	x	x	x
Podium/table for teacher	o	o	o
Sink	o		
Autoharp	x		
Cassette player	x	x	x
TV/VCR combination	o	o	o
CD player	o	x	o
Piano	o	o	o
Chalk/marker board(s)	x	x^4	x^4
Tear sheets	x	x	x
Equipment	**Children**	**Youth**	**Adults**
Felt-tip markers	x	x	x
Other art/writing supplies	x	x	x
Picture rails	x^9		

[1] Recommended chair sizes for children:
    Grades 1&2: 12–13 inches
    Grades 3&4: 14–15 inches
    Grades 5&6: 16-17 inches
[2] Standard chairs 18 inches above the floor.
[3] Tabletops for children should be 10 inches above chair seats.
[4] 36x45 inches min. for hanging boards, freestanding and movable of comparable size or larger are preferred.
[5] Folding chairs for youth should be no more than 28 inches high.
[6] 14–19 inches deep, 42–46 inches high, and 3–4 feet long, with shelves 12–14 inches apart.
[7] Bookracks should be 42–46 inches high and 30–42 inches long.
[8] Tackboards should be 24–30 inches in height and 6–10 feet in length, with the bottom edge 24–30 inches above the floor.
[9] Picture rails should be about 30 inches above the floor on the front wall and 12 feet long.

Appendices

1999-2000 Sunday School Ministry Suggestions to the Churches: Approaches and Projects Overview

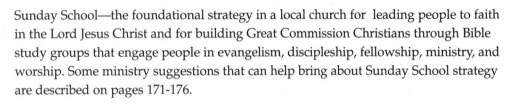

Sunday School—the foundational strategy in a local church for leading people to faith in the Lord Jesus Christ and for building Great Commission Christians through Bible study groups that engage people in evangelism, discipleship, fellowship, ministry, and worship. Some ministry suggestions that can help bring about Sunday School strategy are described on pages 171-176.

Sunday Morning Bible Study

Ongoing Sunday morning Bible study through classes and departments represents one of the church's best means of spiritual growth. Classes and departments can be structured intentionally to meet the needs of persons in the church and in the community. Bible study and caring relationships enable members to come to a better understanding of what it means to know and follow Christ. New units can help reach special target groups and facilitate more effective teaching and ministry.

Resources:

Dated Sunday School materials

EXTRA! (adult, youth, children's, and preschool sixes teaching supplements, available from LifeWay Web site at: http//www.lifeway.com

Sunday School for a New Century series

Articles in *The Sunday School Leader*

January Bible Study

January Bible Study (JBS) is an annual Bible study project for all ages. Adults and youth participate in an intensive, concentrated study of a Bible book or a portion of a Bible book. Adults and youth study the same Bible book, but with separate study materials for each age group. Separate groups are recommended for youth and adults. Appropriate Bible-learning experiences also are provided for preschoolers and children. The suggested dates for January Bible Study, 2000, are January 3-7.

First and Second Thessalonians are the Bible books to be studied during JBS 2000. This study is designed to help people understand Paul's message to the Thessalonian Christians and the significance of that message for our day.

Originally 1 and 2 Thessalonians were addressed to Christians who were troubled by some questions about the future. To comfort and encourage these believers, the letters offered a strong emphasis on Christian ethics.

For our day the imminent unveiling of the year 2000 and a new millennium has heightened interest in the future, especially in eschatology. This interest can motivate people to be receptive to the message of these important letters of Paul, including their emphasis on the ethical behavior of believers.

Through this study, 21st-century Christians can be challenged about the character of their own behavior and comforted and encouraged about the security of the future.

January Bible Study for children will be a study of *God in Charge* (grades 1-3) or *God's Plan: Now and Forever* (grades 4-6). Each updated book contains new artwork, learner activities, and a teaching guide. Unit 2 from *Baby Steps with the Bible, Set 1* is suggested when provisions are made for babies—twos. Unit 9, *Anytime-Anywhere Bible Study for Preschoolers*, is suggested for threes through kindergartners.

Resources:

Live for the Future Now: A Study of 1 and 2 Thessalonians (adult textbook)
Expository Notes for Live for the Future Now: A Study of 1 and 2 Thessalonians
Resource Kit for Live for the Future Now: A Study of 1 and 2 Thessalonians
The Last Word: 1 and 2 Thessalonians (youth)
January Bible Study Planning and Promotion Packet, 2000
God in Charge (children, grades 1-3)
God's Plan: Now and Forever (grades 4-6)
Baby Steps with the Bible, Set 1
Anytime-Anywhere Bible Study for Preschoolers

Read the Bible and Pray Daily

Plan for encouraging Sunday School members to grow in spiritual disciplines by reading the Bible and praying daily. Lead adults, youth, children, and preschoolers and their parents to engage in a systematic plan of daily Bible reading and prayer for others, using appropriate personal devotional guides. Class leaders in adult and youth classes can encourage their members to grow in intercessory prayer, pray for the Holy Spirit's guidance in sharing a personal witness, discover spiritual gifts and use them in service, and develop a prayer fellowship within the Sunday School.

Adult and youth class leaders can share information as appropriate in classes and departments about the work of missionaries around the world. Preschool and children's leaders emphasize praying for others through use of suggested prayer activities in curriculum materials.

Resources:

Leading Your Church to Read the Bible and Pray Daily (free brochure; contact your state
    Sunday School department); *The Sunday School Leader;* ministry development
    pages in adult and youth teacher books
Open Windows; Open Windows, Large Print Edition; Open Windows, Audiocassette;
    essential connection; Student DayMaker; Bible Express; More; Adventure;
    "Bible Impressions" (devotional resources for preschoolers incorporated into
    learner guide).

Sunday School Launch, 1999-2000

Sunday School Launch is an annual emphasis designed to help a church launch its new year. The Launch event will help prepare Sunday School leaders and members to be involved in carrying out the Sunday School strategy in 1999-2000.

This emphasis is flexible and may be conducted whenever it fits into a church's calendar and annual plan. The suggestions below assume a September beginning for the new church year and a September Annual Promotion Day. Churches observing Annual Promotion Day earlier or later than September can calendar and conduct the same emphasis using the sequential actions recommended in this plan. The primary event is the Launch Weekend. Some churches include a series of events over several weeks that help prepare leaders and members.

The following is an example of a launch event series built around promotion day for September 5. Substitute dates for your emphasis accordingly.

Not later than June, July, or August	Sunday School Annual Planning
August 30—September 4	Literature Visitation
September 5	Promotion Day
September 10-12	Launch Weekend
During September—October	Youth and Adult Class Leader Training
October 3	On Mission: To Share the Gospel Sunday
October 31	Sunday School High Attendance Day

Resources:
Sunday School for a New Century
Sunday School for a New Century Planning and Training Pack
Articles in *The Sunday School Leader*
Share Jesus Without Fear
On Mission: To Share the Gospel Sunday Packet from North American Mission Board

Strengthen the Family Through Sunday School

Strengthen families that participate in your Sunday School by planning and conducting an annual family emphasis that focuses on families attending Bible study together. This project provides a variety of avenues designed to enable Sunday School leaders and members to reach, evangelize, and strengthen families.

• Family Bible Study and Worship Emphasis—Families are encouraged to have a special time during the week to study the Bible and worship as a family.

• Family Visitation—Families are encouraged to make visits as families during Sunday School visitation.

• Festivals of Marriage and Covenant Marriage events—Adults who are not members of Bible study groups can be invited to attend these events.

• Distribution of family enrichment and leisure-devotional periodicals—Members can deliver enrichment reading resources to members and prospects to assist families in the development of healthy relationships.

• Special workshops with family emphases—Consider offering during this emphasis special parenting workshops; teen parenting workshops; and seminars on subjects such as dating, preparation for life after high school, and choosing the right mate.

• Family fellowships—Plan events for all family members, with various intergenerational activities.

• All-age Vacation Bible School—Every person has a place in VBS.

Resources:

The Sunday School Leader; Open Windows; essential connection; Bible Express; Adventure; More; Bible and Me (available 9/99), *Kindergarten Connection* (available 9/99) *"Bible Impressions"* (devotional resources for preschoolers incorporated into learner guides); *ParentLife, Home Life,* and *Living with Teenagers*; teacher book ministry development pages; annual Vacation Bible School materials

New Member Assimilation Event

A New Member Assimilation study/event can be the organized beginning point of assimilating new members into the life, vision, and ministry of a congregation. Primarily a small-group educational experience, the study/event undergirds the discipling process in order to (1) help people become connected to organized Bible study and discipleship opportunities; (2) link people to the fellowship of the congregation as an integral part of the Christian growth process; (3) keep people active and help them to grow; and (4) educate people in Christian stewardship, including the use of spiritual gifts.

Designed for all new church members, children through adults, a study/event is suggested for the Sunday morning time slot in a church. But it can be held at any time and any location. The study/event may be approached through short-term classes, large groupings with smaller breakout groups in a retreat setting, one-on-one personal contacts, or another approach developed to address specific individual needs. Plans for new member assimilation also should be considered to follow such events as Vacation Bible School, revivals, and youth retreats or camps.

Resources:

Taking the Next Step: A Guide for New Church Members
Taking the Next Step: A Guide for New Church Members Leader Guide
Basic Church Stuff: A Guide for Assimilating New Youth Church Members
Now That I'm a Christian
The Power to Change Lives series
Need a New Hook? A Guide to Bible Study Groups

Ongoing Ministry by Departments, Classes, Bible Study Groups

Classes, department, and Bible study groups are regular vehicles by which participants express care and concern for members and prospects. This ongoing ministry becomes an expression of God's love and models the self-giving aspect of the Christian lifestyle. Such expression and modeling can help people understand and experience God's love through Jesus Christ.

Ongoing ministry requires a planned approach for maintaining contact with members and prospects, disseminating information about needs, and determining appropriate responses. In adult and youth classes, class leaders have responsibility for providing care for members and prospects assigned to them. However, plans also are to include ways other members can demonstrate care and can minister to the needs of others.

Resources:

Follow Christ's Example series

On Mission: To Share the Gospel Sunday

The first Sunday in October is designated as a time to call on church members to make a commitment to share the gospel during the year. Actions include

- communicating the meaning of this day in Sunday School classes through On Mission: To Share the Gospel Sunday commitment forms, prayer/ witness lists, and evangelism application during Bible study;
- setting Sunday School goals for enrollment, attendance, and witness training;
- promoting Sunday morning Bible study attendance and special worship services culminating on High Attendance Day the last Sunday in October;
- commissioning Sunday School outreach-evangelism leaders (and Church Evangelism Council), among other workers, during a worship service in October.

Resources:

Ministry development pages in teacher books

Articles in *The Sunday School Leader*

On Mission: To Share the Gospel Packet, 1999 mailed to all SBC churches in Summer 1999 by the Personal Evangelism Department, North American Mission Board

Evangelism Day in Sunday School

Evangelism Day in Sunday School, suggested for Easter, April 23, 2000, spotlights a primary purpose of Sunday School: to lead people to faith in the Lord Jesus. Christ. On this day evangelistic lessons are taught in older children, youth, and adults classes. Evangelism Day in Sunday School can be scheduled anytime a church chooses.

Resources:

Bible study curriculum materials for older children, youth, and adults

First Contact

First Contact is an outreach plan and ministry to expectant parents and families with young preschoolers (birth to one year). The Sunday School director or a church staff member may be responsible for First Contact if a church does not have a Preschool Division director. A core group of visitors, who have a love for young families, is responsible for visiting prospect families.

Suggested actions include promoting the availability of First Contact, enlisting a core group of visitors, developing a prospect-discovery plan, making assignments, training visitors, and developing a calendar of activities. Coordination with adult departments helps ensure that reaching efforts include the entire family.

Resources:

First Contact leaflet

Preschool Sunday School for a New Century

Care4Kids

An overarching approach to Children's Sunday School ministry, **Care4Kids** offers activities to enhance outreach, evangelism, fellowship, and ministry to children and their families. Each member/prospect is assigned to a worker for ongoing relationship.

Resources:

Good News for Kids: The Power to Change Lives

contact 1•2•3

This plan creates a unified reaching approach for Preschool and Children's Sunday School; offers flexibility for maintaining regular contacts; and helps reach preschoolers, children, and their families. Each member and prospect is assigned to a worker, who maintains contact either by mail, telephone, or personal visit.

Resources:

Children's Sunday School for a New Century

Preschool Sunday School for a New Century

Ministry development pages in teacher books

Vacation Bible School

Vacation Bible School is an annual flagship event for churches, providing significant outreach and Bible-teaching opportunities. Age-appropriate materials are available for preschoolers through adults and persons with special needs. Workers are encouraged to participate in VBS according to their abilities, interests, and spiritual gifts, and to build relationships with pupils and with their family members. The 2000 theme will be announced in September 1999.

Resources:

Look for your copy of the 2000 VBS Resources Catalog to arrive by mail.

Special Emphasis/Recognition Days

Special emphasis days—Single Adult Day, Senior Adult Day, Student Sunday School—provide opportunities to highlight teaching and ministry. Leaders can be recognized and the increased outreach and ministry provided by these units can be highlighted for the entire church. Other special groups, such as homebound adults, may be the focus of a church's attention based on annual goals. Enter emphasis events and actions, suggested for December 1999, Student Day at Christmas; May 2000, Senior Adult Day, and September 2000, Single Adult Day.

Resources:

Articles in *The Sunday School Leader*

Discovering and Enlisting Leaders

Ongoing leader-discovery efforts can contribute to greater involvement in service as potential leaders are identified and placed in positions that match their gifts and interests. Effective enlistment contributes to greater effectiveness in Sunday School ministry and includes sharing clear expectations of the job, giving leaders helpful evaluation, and expressing appreciation for them and their work. Enter dates of emphasis events and actions planned from May 1999—August 2000.

Resources:

Sunday School for a New Century

Articles in *The Sunday School Leader*

Ministry development pages in teacher books

1999-2000 Leadership Development and Bible Study Curriculum Guide

LifeWay Christian Resources of the Southern Baptist Convention is a major publisher of leadership training and Bible study curriculum materials. The annual Church Materials Catalog is a primary source for identifying resources you need to train leaders and to study the Bible. The Planning Guide included in the quarterly order packet describes recent releases.

For your reference and convenience, a list of leadership training and Bible study resources is given on pages 178-202 of this guide .

Leadership Training Curriculum Resources - See pages 178-179..

Undated Bible Study Curriculum Resources- See page 180.

Dated Bible Study Curriculum Materials and Outlines- See pages 182-202.

How to Order

Several optional methods may be used to order material.

• By Mail. Most resources appear on the dated and undated order forms that come in the quarterly order packet. Mail the order to

Customer Service Center, MSN 113

LifeWay Christian Resources

127 Ninth Avenue, North

Nashville, TN 37234-0113.

If your church does not receive the quarterly order packet, write the Customer Service Center at the address above.

• By Internet. You may order Dated Church Literature by accessing the Dated Resources Order Form at: www.lifeway.com.

• By Fax. You may fax your quarterly order form or other LifeWay order form to 1-615-251-5933.

• By Email. You may send an email addressed to customer service@lifeway.com. When sending an order by email, please provide complete product and shipping information.

• By Telephone. Dated products may be ordered from any touch-tone phone via ACCESS, the Automated Customer Service System, at 800-376-1140. Have your account number and Dated Resources Order Form ready when calling.

Products also may be ordered by calling toll-free 1-800-458-2772, 8:00am-5:00pm (CT), Monday-Friday.

• At LifeWay Christian Stores. Most undated products are available at the store in your area.

Language Materials

LifeWay publishes leadership training resources and Bible study curriculum materials in several languages. Some items are described in the *Church Materials Catalog*. For additional information about language materials, write to

Language Materials, MSN 180

127 Ninth Avenue, North

Nashville, TN 37234.

Leadership Training Curriculum Resources

The Power to Change Live Series

The Complete Guide for Building a Great Commission Sunday School, 1998-99: The Power to Change Lives

The Power to Change Lives Power Pack

Good News for Adults: The Power to Change Lives

Good News for Youth: The Power to Change Lives

Good News for Kids: The Power to Change Lives

Good News for Preschoolers and Their Families: The Power to Change Lives

Teaching Series (This series will go out of print in March 2000. Look for a new series with a focus on transformational teaching to be released April 2000.)

21 Truths, Traditions, and Trends: Propelling the Sunday School Into the 21st Century

21 Truths, Traditions, and Trends Leader Training Pack

Vision, Vitality, and Variety: Teaching Today's Adult Generations

Vision, Vitality, and Variety Leader Training Pack)

Connected, Committed, and a Little Bit Crazy: Teaching Youth Today

Connected, Committed, and a Little Bit Crazy Leader Training Pack

Crayons, Computers, and Kids: Teaching Children Today

Crayons, Computers, and Kids Leader Training Pack

Love, Laughter, and Learning: Teaching Preschoolers Today

Love, Laughter, and Learning Leader Training Pack

Caring, Fellowship, Outreach, and Witnessing Series

Follow Christ's Example Leader Training Pack

Follow Christ's Example: Becoming Mentor, Friend, and Guide

The Jesus Touch, Follow Christ's Example: Adult

The Jesus Touch: Leader Edition

The J Files, Follow Christ's Example: Youth

The J Files: Leader Edition

Follow the Leader, Follow Christ's Example: Children

Follow the Leader: Leader Edition

Just Like Jesus, Follow Christ's Example: Preschool

Just Like Jesus: Leader Edition

Administration Series

Sunday School for a New Century

Sunday School for a New Century Planning and Training Pack

Adult Sunday School for a New Century

Youth Sunday School for a New Century

Children's Sunday School for a New Century

Preschool Sunday School for a New Century

Outreach and Evangelism

Need a New Hook? A Guide for Bible Study Groups
Going . . . One on One: A Complete Guide for Making Personal Visits (out of print 11/99)
Prospect Assignment Pocket & Card
Evangelism Through the Sunday School: A Journey of FAITH
Effective Evangelistic Churches
Share Jesus Without Fear

Sunday School General Leaders

The Sunday School Leader (monthly magazine)
Revitalizing the Sunday Morning Dinosaur: A Sunday School Growth Strategy
   for the 21st Century
Kingdom Principles for Church Growth
Kingdom Leadership: A Call to Christ-Centered Leadership

Special Education

A Place for Everyone: A Guide for Special Education Bible Teaching-Reaching Ministry
Special Education Today (quarterly magazine)

Training Videos

The ABC's of Teaching Preschoolers and Children
What Every Preschool Teacher Wants to Know
Teaching Bible Learners, 1st and 2nd Graders
Teaching Bible Discoverers, 3rd and 4th Graders
Teaching Bible Searchers, 5th and 6th Graders

New Member Assimilation

Taking the Next Step: A Guide for New Church members
Taking the Next Step: A Guide for New Church Members, Leaders Guide
Basic Church Stuff: A Guide for Assimilating New Youth Church members
Now That I'm a Christian, Revised Edition (children)

Devotional Magazines

Open Windows, Open Windows, Large Print Edition,
   Open Windows, Audiocassette Edition (quarterly, adults)
essential connection—"ec" (monthly, youth)
Bible Express (monthly, grades 5-6)
Adventure (monthly, grades 3-4)
More (monthly, grades 1-2)
Journey
Stand Firm

Other

Adult Class Leader Administration Kit

Undated Bible Study Curriculum Resources

For Adults

I Take Thee to Be My Spouse: Bible Study for Newlyweds
Special Delivery homebound member leaflets/teacher packet
TouchPOINTS: Sowing Seeds
TouchPOINTS: Sowing Seeds from the Gospels
TouchPOINTS: Sowing Seeds at Home and Work
TouchPOINTS: Encouraging New Growth
TouchPOINTS: Growth Basics
My Place in HIStory Media Pack

For Youth

StraighTrak: Teen Bible Studies on Current Issues
The Way It Was: Youth Explore the Old Testament
Coming and Going: Youth Explore the New Testament
The Crossroad: Youth Explore the Book of Matthew
Action!: Youth Explore James, 1 & 2 Thessalonians, and Galatians
Essentials for Life After High School
Roller Coaster: Youth Explore Judges and Ruth
Youth Explore Revelation

For Children

Anytime-Anywhere: Learning from the Bible
Anytime-Anywhere: The Bible and Me
Adventure Zone: Adventures of Jesus
Adventure Zone: Bible Heroes
Adventure Zone: Adventures of Paul
Everything You Need to Know to Be a Teenager (Vol. 1-4, grade 6; additional volumes becoming available between Fall 1999-Summer 2000)

For Preschoolers

Baby Steps with the Bible
Adventure Zone: Adventures of Jesus
Adventure Zone: Bible Heroes
Adventure Zone: Adventures of Paul, Preschool
Anytime-Anywhere Bible Study for Preschoolers

January Bible Study

Live for the Future Now: A Study of 1&2 Thessalonians (adults)
The Last Word: 1 and 2 Thessalonians (youth)
God Is in Charge (children, grades 1-3)
God's Plan: Now and Forever (children, grades 1-4)

Sunday School Curriculum Series Characteristics

	Life and Work Series	Explore the Bible Series	Family Bible Series
Bible Study Approach	Focuses on life issues affecting learners and their churches, and on doctrine, ethics, and missions.	Provides a systematic approach to all the books of the Bible in ways appropriate to the needs of youth or adults.	Focuses on the primary relationships of life through a systematic approach to major areas of the Bible in ways appropriate to the needs of learners.
Bible Translation	Based on the New International Version. Some adult periodicals also print the King James Version.	Based on the New American Standard Bible (1995 Update). Adult periodicals also print the King James Version.	Based on the King James Version.
Content Selection	Distinctive content is selected for each age division based on the life needs and/or issues affecting that age division.	Youth curriculum plan provides studies from all 66 Bible books over a six-year period. Adult curriculum plan covers all 66 Bible books in an open-ended approach (no set cycle).	Based on the International Sunday School Lessons. Generally all age divisions study the same Bible passages, but on occasion alternate Bible passages may be selected for the preschool and children's age divisions.
Target Audience	Designed for people primarily in churches who desire studies developed in light of life needs and/or issues of preschoolers, children, youth, and all generations of adults, who organize by more narrowly defined age groupings.	Designed for youth and adults in churches of all sizes who desire book studies covering all the books of the Bible using a curriculum plan driven by Bible structure.	Designed primarily for preschoolers, children, youth, and adults in churches that want common Bible study themes for all age groups and an intentional focus on families and relationships. Assumes class structure.
Content Development	Studies are developed in light of life needs and/or issues of preschoolers, children, youth, and all generations of adults and how the Bible speaks to these needs and issues.	Studies are based on the nature, structure, and content of the Bible as a whole and of Bible books in light of youth and adult needs.	Studies are based on the nature of the Bible passage in light of preschoolers', children's, youth, and adult needs and learning readiness for the content.
Resources	Resources are designed for workers who teach a closely graded grouping and who plan with other workers. Electronic teaching plan supplements are provided weekly for teachers of kindergartners, children, youth, and adults.	Resources are designed for workers who plan alone as well as by workers who plan together for a team approach to Bible study. Electronic teaching plan supplements are provided weekly for teachers.	Resources are designed for workers who teach a multi-age grouping and who often plan alone. Electronic teaching plan supplements are provided weekly for youth and adult teachers.

Dated Bible Study Curriculum Resources and Outlines, 1999–2000

Special Education Curriculum Overview
Special Education Bible Study, Special Education Teacher Packet, Special Education Cassette Recording, Bible Discoverers Teaching Pictures

September 1999—The Bible Is God's Message to All People
Bible Truth: The Bible is God's message to all people and is a guide for living.
Scripture: Jeremiah 36; 2 Kings 22:1—23:3; Acts 17; 2 Timothy 3:10–17

October 1999—God Is an Awesome God
Bible Truth: God demonstrates His care, power, nearness, concern, holiness, and righteousness.
Scripture: 1 Kings 17:1–16; 1 Kings 18:16–46; 1 Kings 19:1–18; 2 Kings 5:1–15; 2 Kings 6:8–23

November 1999—God Wants Us to Pray
Bible Truth: People can pray to God for themselves and others, thank Him for His goodness, and ask for His forgiveness.
Scripture: 1 Samuel 1; Genesis 18:16–33; 1 Kings 8:1–30; Nehemiah 1

December 1999—God Sent His Son
Bible Truth: God sent His Son, Jesus, to be the Savior.
Scripture: Isaiah 7:14; 9:6; 11:1–5; Micah 5:2; Luke 2:1–20; Matthew 2:1–12

January 2000—Obey the Ten Commandments
Bible Truth: We should obey the Ten Commandments that God gave.
Scripture: Exodus 20:1–11; Daniel 3:1–30; Exodus 20:12,14; Luke 2:41–52; Exodus 20:13; 1:15—2:10; Exodus 20:15,17; 1 Kings 21; Exodus 20:16; 2 Kings 5:15–27

February 2000—Make Wise Choices
Bible Truth: People can make choices that please God.
Scripture: 1 Samuel 17:1–50; 2 Samuel 9; Psalm 23: 105:1–4

March 2000—Jesus Worked Miracles
Bible Truth: Jesus has the power to do all things.
Scripture: John 6:1–15; Matthew 14:22–33; John 11:1–44; Mark 10:46–52

April 2000—Jesus Is Alive!
Bible Truth: Because Jesus died and rose again, people can choose to ask Jesus to be their Savior as they are led to do so by the Holy Spirit.
Scripture: Luke 19:28–40; Luke 22:7–23; Luke 23:13–56; John 21:1–17

May 2000—What Is a Believer?
Bible Truth: The Bible teaches how to become a Christian and what believers do.
Scripture: Acts 16:25–34; Matthew 3:13–17; Acts 16:13–15; Acts 2:41–47; Philippians 2:25–30; 4:14–19; Matthew 28:16–20; Acts 8:26–40

June 2000—What Is a Follower?
Bible Truth: The Bible teaches how to live as Jesus' follower.
Scripture: John 1:35–51; John 12:1–8; Acts 4:32–37; 9:26–30; 11:19–26; 15:36–41; Acts 9:36–43

July 2000—Honor God by Helping Others
Bible Truth: People can honor God by helping others.
Scripture: Mark 2:1–11; Acts 12:1–17; Acts 18:1–3,18–26; Romans 16:3–4; 1 Corinthians 16:19; Acts 16:1–5; Philippians 2:19–24; 1 Thessalonians 3:2–6; 2 Corinthians 8:1–15; 9:6–15

August 2000—Live in Ways That Please God
Bible Truth: The Bible teaches how to live in ways that please God.
Scripture: Genesis 37:12–36; 45:1–15; Ruth 2; Judges 7:1–21; Daniel 1:1–17

Preschool Curriculum Overview
Family Bible Series
Early Bible Steps, FBS: Preschool Bible Fun,
FBS: Preschool Teacher, FBS: Preschool Teaching Kit

September 1999—Following God
Bible Teaching Aim: Teachers will provide opportunities for the child to hear that God loves and cares for people.
Scripture: Exodus 3:1-12; Exodus 13:17-22; 14:10-31; Exodus 19:3-6; 20:1-17; Deuteronomy 9:9-18; 10:1-5; Exodus 35:1-21; 36:2-8; 39:32-43; 40:1-5

October 1999—People Help Others
Bible Teaching Aim: Teachers will show the children many ways people help them.
Scripture: Exodus 18:13-26; Numbers 13:25-31; 14:1-8; Exodus 16:14-30; Deuteronomy 6:1-9,20-24; Deuteronomy 24:17-21; 27:1-10

November 1999—Choosing to Obey God
Bible Teaching Aim: Teachers will give the child opportunities to hear that God knows what is best for people.
Scripture: Deuteronomy 31:1-8; 34:5-9; Joshua 3:15-17; 4:1-8; Joshua 6:1-5,15-16,20; Joshua 24:14-22

December 1999—Jesus Is Born
Bible Teaching Aim: The session can increase the children's awareness of Jesus' birth and the events surrounding His birth.
Scripture: Luke 1:26-35; Luke 1:39-56; Luke 2:1-20; Matthew 2:1-12

January 2000—Jesus Helped People
Bible Teaching Aim: Teachers will help the child understand that Jesus loved and cared for people.
Scripture: Matthew 4:18-22; 9:9-12; 10:1-4; Matthew 6:1-13; Matthew 9:18-19,23-26; Mark 5:21-24,35-43; Luke 8:41-42,49-56; Matthew 12:9-13; Matthew 15:29-39

February 2000—Doing What the Bible Says
Bible Teaching Aim: Teachers will guide the child to understand he can do many things that people in the Bible did.
Scripture: Matthew 26:6-13; Matthew 22:34-40; Mark 12:28-34; Matthew 16:13-16; Matthew 28:16-20

March 2000—My Family Teaches Me
Bible Teaching Aim: Teachers will lead the child to realize that she can learn many important lessons at home.
Scripture: Acts 18:1-4; John 1:35-42; 1 Samuel 17:12-15,17-21; Daniel 1:3-20

April 2000—Jesus Shows Love
Bible Teaching Aim: Session provides opportunities for the child to understand that Jesus showed His love in many ways.
Scripture: Luke 22:8-19; Luke 10:25-37; Matthew 21:1-11,14-17; John 20:1-18; John 21:1-13

May 2000—The Church Cares for Others
Bible Teaching Aim: Session provides opportunities for the child to hear about ways people at church serve God and others.
Scripture: Acts 6:1-7; Acts 8:26-39; Acts 11:27-30; Acts 2:41-47

June 2000—I Can Learn from the Bible
Bible Teaching Aim: Teachers will guide the child to realize he can help others.
Scripture: Acts 16:12-15; John 13:3-15; Acts 16:19-34; Ruth 1:22; 2:1-18

July 2000—God Made the World
Bible Teaching Aim: Teachers will help the child grow in her awareness that God made the world.
Scripture: Genesis 1:3-5,9-10,14-19; Genesis 1:11-12,29-30; Psalm 104:14; Genesis 1:20-25; 2:19-20a; Psalm 104:17-25; Genesis 1:26-28,31; 2:8-10,18-24; 3:20-21; Genesis 2:7-8,18-24; 3:20; 4:1-2

August 2000—Telling Others About God
Bible Teaching Aim: Session will help the child become aware that he can learn about God from many different people.
Scripture: Acts 17:22-27,33-34; Acts 16:1-3; 2 Timothy 1:1-5; 3:14-15; Acts 17:1-2,4-10; 1 Thessalonians 4:9-12; Philemon 1-25

Preschool Curriculum Overview, Life and Work Series:
Babies, Ones and Twos
Early Bible Steps, Bible Teaching for Babies Leader Pack; Bible Teaching for Ones and Twos;
Bible Teaching for Ones and Twos Leader Pack; Music for Babies, Ones, and Twos

September 1999—I Am Special
Bible Teaching Aim: Teachers will guide children to an awareness that God made them and they are important and special to God and others.
Scripture: Genesis 1:26-28; 2:18-24; 3:20-21; 4:1-2; 5:1-4; Psalm 139:14; Ruth 4:13-17; 1 Samuel 1:24-25; 2:11,18-21,26; 3:1-3,15,19-20; 1 Samuel 18:1-4

October 1999—My Church
Bible Teaching Aim: Teachers will help children develop feelings of love and security as they learn about church and the people who are there.
Scripture: Exodus 35:1-35; Exodus 36:1-38; 39:32-43; 2 Chronicles 5:11-14; 7:10; Colossians 3:16; Luke 4:14-22; Acts 16:11-15,40

November 1999—God's Love and Care
Bible Teaching Aim: Teachers will lead preschoolers to thank God for His love and care.
Scripture: Genesis 6:9-10,14-22; 7:1-2,7-10; 8:1-3,18-20; 2 Kings 4:8-13; Luke 17:11-19; Matthew 5:1-2; 6:25-34; 9:35

December 1999—The Baby Jesus
Bible Teaching Aim: Teachers will help children learn about the birth of Jesus.
Scripture: Luke 1:26-38; Luke 1:39-56; Luke 2:8-20; Luke 2:21-39

January 2000—Stories of Jesus
Bible Teaching Aim: Teachers will lead children to become familiar with some people in Jesus' life.
Scripture: Matthew 2:1-12; Matthew 2:13-23; Matthew 2:19-23; 13:55-56; Luke 2:4-7,40, 51-52; Luke 10:30-37; Luke 19:1-10

February 2000—The Bible
Bible Teaching Aim: Teachers will guide preschoolers to an awareness and appreciation of the Bible as a special Book that tells about God and Jesus.
Scripture: 2 Kings 22:1-20; 23:1-3; Mark 12:28-34; Acts 8:26-39; Acts 16:1-3; 2 Timothy 1:1-5; 3:14-15

March 2000—Discovering God's World
Bible Teaching Aim: Teachers will help preschoolers associate God's name with the natural world and to learn that everything God made was good.
Scripture: Genesis 1:3-5,11-19; Leviticus 26:4; Psalm 104:19-23; Genesis 1:1-12,29-30; Leviticus 26:4; Psalms. 104:14,27; 136:25; Genesis 1:24-25,30-31; Psalms 104;14,17-25,27; Genesis 1:26-28; 2:18-24; 3:20; Proverbs 20:12

April 2000—Jesus, Friend and Helper
Bible Teaching Aim: Teachers will guide preschoolers to an awareness of Jesus' love and kindness for people.
Scripture: Mark 3:13-19; Luke 6:12-16; John 1:35-51; Mark 10:46-52; Matthew 21:1-11,14-16; John 13:1-7,13-17; John 21:1-13

May 2000—My Family
Bible Teaching Aim: Teachers will help preschoolers know that God gave them families to love and care for them.
Scripture: Genesis 30:22-25; 35:24; 37:2-3,12-17;
Exodus 2:1-10; Ruth 2:1-23; Genesis 37:1-3

June 2000—See What I Can Do
Bible Teaching Aim: Teachers will lead preschoolers to know God planned for each person to grow and do many things.
Scripture: Luke 2:21-39; Luke 9:10-17; John 6:1-12; 1 Samuel 16:11-13,18-20; 17:15; Matthew 19:13-15; Mark 10:13-16; Luke 18:15-16

July 2000—I Learn About God
Bible Teaching Aim: Teachers will guide preschoolers to learn that God loves each person and cares about him.
Scripture: Genesis 1,2; Psalms 104; 136:1; 139:14; Genesis 12:1-9; Daniel 1:3-20; John 4:3-30,39-41; Acts 18:1-4

August 2000—Friends Love and Care
Bible Teaching Aim: Teachers will lead preschoolers to discover ways people show their love for others.
Scripture: 2 Kings 5:1-16; Mark 2:1-5,11-12; Luke 5:17-20,24-26; Luke 10:38-42; Luke 13:10-13

Preschool Curriculum Overview, Life and Work Series:
Threes—Pre-K
Bible and Me, Bible Teaching for Threes—Pre-K (teaching guide),
Bible Teaching for Threes—Pre-K Leader's Pack, Music for Threes—Pre K

September 1999—God Loves Me
Bible Teaching Aim: Teachers will guide preschoolers to learn that God shows His love for people in many ways.
Scripture: Genesis 1:26-28; 2:18-24; 3:20-21; 4:1-2; 5:1-4; Psalm 139:14; Ruth 1:1-18; Ruth 4:13-17; 1 Samuel 1:20-28; 2:11,18-21,26; 3:1-3,15,19-20; 1 Samuel 14:49; 18:1-4

October 1999—I Like To Go To Church
Bible Teaching Aim: Teachers will provide opportunities to learn about things people do at church.
Scripture: Exodus 35:1-35; Exodus 36:1-38; 39:32-43; 2 Chronicles 5:11-14; 7:10; Colossians 3:16; Luke 4:14-22; Acts 16:11-15,40

November 1999—I Can Talk To God
Bible Teaching Aim: Teachers will provide opportunities to talk to God in everyday experiences.
Scripture: Genesis 6:9-10,14-22; 7:1-2,7-19; 8:1-3,18-20; 1 Kings 17:1-17; 18:1-2,41-45; Luke 17:11-19; Matthew 5:1; 6:5-15

December 1999—Jesus Was Born
Bible Teaching Aim: Teachers will guide preschoolers to discover that God showed His love for us by sending Jesus.
Scripture: Isaiah 7:14; 9:6-7; Luke 1:26-38; Luke 1:39-56; Matthew 1:25; Luke 2:1-20; Luke 2:21-40

January 2000 —People Loved Jesus
Bible Teaching Aim: Teachers will provide opportunities for preschoolers to learn that people are important to Jesus.
Scripture: Matthew 2:1-12; Matthew 2:13-23; Matthew 1:8-25; 13:55-56; Luke 1:26-38; 2:7,21-52; Luke 10:30-37; Luke 19:1-10

February 2000—My Bible
Bible Teaching Aim: Teachers will give preschoolers opportunities to discover that learning what the Bible says can help them live happily.
Scripture: 2 Kings 22:1-20; 23:1-3; Mark 12:28-34; Acts 8:26-39; Acts 16:1-3; 2 Timothy 1:1-5; 3:14-15

March 2000—God Made the World For Me
Bible Teaching Aim: Teachers will develop the child's understanding that God made the world.
Scripture: Genesis 1:3-5,14-19; Psalm 104:19-23; Genesis 1:11-12,29-30; Leviticus 26:4; Psalms 104:14,27; 107:37; 136:25; Matthew 6:11; Genesis 1:20-25,30-31; Psalms 104:14,17-25,27; Genesis 1:26-28; 2:18-24; 3:20-21; 5:1-2; Proverbs 20:12

April 2000—Jesus Loves Me
Bible Teaching Aim: Teachers will help preschoolers become more aware that Jesus showed God's love for people.
Scripture: Mark 3:13-19; 6:7-11; Luke 6:12-16; 9:1-6,10; John 1:35-51; Mark 10:46-52; Matthew 21:1-11,14-16; John 13:1-7,13-17; John 21:1-13

May 2000—My Family
Bible Teaching Aim: Teachers will guide the preschoolers to know that God places people in families.
Scripture: Genesis 30:22-25; 35:24; 37:2-3,12-17; Exodus 2:1-10; Ruth 2:1-23; 2 Kings 4:8-13

June 2000—The Bible Helps Me

Bible Teaching Aim: Teachers will guide preschoolers to become aware that the Bible helps them know what God wants them to do.

Scripture: Luke 2:40-52; John 6:1-12; 1 Samuel 16:10-13,18-20; 17:12-22; Matthew 19:13-15; Mark 10:13-16; Luke 18:15-16

July 2000—God Loves and Cares for Me

Bible Teaching Aim: Teachers will provide opportunities for preschoolers to learn that God loves and cares for them.

Scripture: Genesis 1,2; Psalms 104; 136:1; 139:14; Genesis 12:1-12; 13:1-12; Exodus 19:1-6;20:1-17; John 4:3-30,39-41; Acts 18:1-4,24-26; Romans 16:3-4;1 Corinthians 16:19

August 2000—Friends Help One Another

Bible Teaching Aim: Teachers will guide preschoolers to discover that God wants friends to show their love by helping one another.

Scripture: 2 Kings 5:1-16; Mark 2:1-5,11-12; Luke 5:17-20,24-26; Luke 5:1-11; Luke 13:10-13

Preschool Curriculum Overview, Life and Work Series: Kindergarten
Kindergarten Connection, Bible Teaching for Kindergarten (teaching guide)
Bible Teaching for Kindergarten Leader Pack, Music for Kindergarten

September 1999—God Loves Me

Bible Teaching Aim: Teachers will guide children to learn that God loves and cares for them and that they are persons of worth.

Scripture: Genesis 1: 26-28; 2:18-24; 3:20-21; 4:1-2; 5:1-4; Psalm 139:14; Ruth 4:13-17; 1 Samuel 1:20-25; 2:11,18-21,26; 3:1-3,15,19-20; 1 Samuel 18:1-4; 20:4,17

October 1999—Learning About Church

Bible Teaching Aim: Teachers will lead children to become aware of what people do at church.

Scripture: Exodus 35:1-35; Exodus 36:1-38; 39:32-43; 2 Chronicles 5:11-14; 7:10; Colossians 3:16; Luke 4:14-22; Acts 16:11-15,40

November 1999—I Can Pray to God

Bible Teaching Aim: Teachers will lead children to become aware that they can pray (talk) to God at anytime and any-place about anything.

Scripture: 1 Samuel 1:1-23; 1 Kings 17:1-17; 18:1-2, 41-45; Luke 17:11-19; Matthew 5:1; 6:5-15

December 1999—God Sent Jesus

Bible Teaching Aim: Teachers will provide opportunities for children to learn that God showed His love for us by sending Baby Jesus.

Scripture: Isaiah 7:14; 9: 6-7; Luke 1:26-56; Luke 2:1-7; Matthew 1:25; Luke 2:8-20; Isaiah 7:14; 9:6-7; Luke 2:21-39

January 2000—People Loved Jesus

Bible Teaching Aim: Teachers will guide children to become aware that people loved and cared for Boy Jesus and that people help others because they love Jesus.

Scripture: Matthew 2:1-12; Matthew 2:13-14,19-23; Luke 2:6-7,21-52; Luke 10:30-37; Luke 19:1-10

February 2000—Learning About the Bible
Bible Teaching Aim: Teachers will guide children to discover that they can learn about God and Jesus from the Bible.
Scripture: 2 Kings 22:1-20; 23:1-3; Mark 12:28-34; Acts 8:4-6,26-38; Acts 16:1-3; 2 Timothy 1:1-5; 3:14-15

March 2000—Caring for God's World
Bible Teaching Aim: Teachers will provide opportunities for children to learn that they can help take care of God's world.
Scripture: Genesis 1:3-5,14-19; Psalm 104:19; Genesis 1:1-12,29-30; Leviticus 26:4; Psalms 104:14,27; 136:25; Matthew 6:11; Genesis 29:1-20; Daniel 1:1-20

April 2000—Jesus Showed God's Love
Bible Teaching Aim: Teachers will guide children to learn that Jesus showed God's love for people.
Scripture: Mark 3:13-19; Luke 6:12-16; John 1:35-51; Mark 10:46-52; Matthew 21:1-11,14-16; John 20:1-18; John 21:1-17

May 2000—Living In My Family
Bible Teaching Aim: Teachers will help children learn that God made people to live in families.
Scripture: Genesis 30:22-25; 37:2-11; Exodus 2:1-10; Ruth 2:1-23; 2 Kings 4:8-13

June 2000—I Can Make Choices
Bible Teaching Aim: Teachers will guide children to discover that the Bible teaches them how to make good choices.
Scripture: John 6:1-12; 1 Samuel 16:11-13,18-20; 17:15; Genesis 26:12-29

July 2000—God Loves and Cares for People
Bible Teaching Aim: Teachers will lead children to learn that God loves and cares for all people.
Scripture: Genesis 1-2; Psalms 104; 136:1; Genesis 12:1-9; Exodus 19:1-6; 20:1-17; John 4:3-30,39-41; Jeremiah 29:1,4-7,10-13

August 2000—Jesus Helped People
Bible Teaching Aim: Teachers will guide children to develop an awareness that Jesus did things people cannot do.
Scripture: Matthew 12:9-10; 13; Mark 3:1-5; Mark 2:1-5,11-12; Luke 5:17-20,24-26; Luke 5:1-11; Luke 13:10-13

Children's Curriculum Overview
Family Bible Series: Children
Children's Teacher, Power Pages (grades 1-3), Power Plus Pages (grades 4-6)

September 1999—God Calls and Gives Power

September 5: God Calls Moses (Ex. 3); *September 12:* God Uses His Power (Crossing the Red Sea) (Ex. 13:17–14:31); *September 19:* God Gives Rules (God's Commandments) (Ex. 19:1–20:21); *September 26:* Remembering and Worshiping God (Preparing the Tabernacle) (Ex. 35:20-29; 36:1-2; 40:1-33; Lev. 26)

October 1999—Learning to Obey God
(Wilderness Wanderings)

October 3: Follow Directions (The Cloud and Fire) (Ex. 40:34-38; Num. 9:15-23); *October 10:* Make Good Choices (The People Rebel) (Num. 12:1–14:25); *October 17:* Obey God (God Provides Manna) (Ex. 16:11-30); *October 24:* Love God (The Great Commandment) (Deut. 6); *October 31:* Remember God's Goodness (Deut. 8)

November 1999—Following God's Way

November 7: Following God's Leaders (Moses Turns Things Over to Joshua) (Deut. 31:1-8; 34); *November 14:* Trusting God's Leaders (Israel Crosses the Jordan) (Josh. 3); *November 21:* Working with God's Leaders (The Destruction of Jericho) (Josh. 6); *November 28:* Choosing to Follow God (Choosing to Serve the Lord) (Josh. 24)

December 1999—God Sent the Savior

December 5: An Angel Speaks to Mary (Luke 1:26-40); *December 12:* An Angel Speaks to Joseph (Matt. 1:18-25); *December 19:* Jesus Is Born (Salvation) (Luke 2:1-20); *December 26:* Wise Men Worship Jesus (Matt. 2:1-12)

January 2000—Jesus' Teachings and Ministry

January 2: Jesus Calls Twelve Disciples (Salvation) (Matt. 4:18-22; 9:9-12; 10:1-5,7); *January 9:* Jesus Teaches About Prayer (Matt. 6:1-15); *January 16:* Jesus Heals the Synagogue Ruler's Daughter (Matt. 9:18-26,36; Mark 5:42; Luke 8); *January 23:* Jesus Heals a Man's Hand (Matt. 12:9-15); *January 30:* Jesus Teaches About Forgiveness (Matt. 18:21-35)

February 2000—Honoring, Loving, Knowing, and Going

February 6: Honoring Jesus (Matt. 26:6-13); *February 13:* Loving Jesus (Matt. 22:34-40); *February 20:* Knowing Jesus (Matt. 22:34-40); *February 27:* About Jesus (Matt. 28:1-10,16-20)

March 2000—I Can Grow Spiritually

March 5: I Can Serve Others (Aquila and Priscilla Care for Paul); (Acts 18:1-4,18-28; 1 Cor. 1:1-17); *March 12:* I Can Build on the Solid Rock (Building on Sand or Rock); (Matt. 7:24-27, 1 Cor. 3:10-11); *March 19:* I Can Use My Gifts (The Buried Talents); (Matt. 25:14-29; 1 Cor. 4:1-2); *March 26:* I Can Make Good Choices (Daniel Makes a Wise Choice); (Dan. 1:3-17; 1 Cor. 6:19-20)

April 2000—Jesus: The Giver of Live

April 2: Jesus' Supper with His Friends (Luke 22:7-20); *April 9:* Jesus' Entry into Jerusalem (Matt. 21:1-17; Luke 19:28-40); *April 16:* Jesus' Crucifixion (Luke 23:13-53); April 23: Jesus' Resurrection (Salvation); (John 20:1-18; Mark 16:1-7) *April 30:* Breakfast with Jesus (John 21:1-17)

May 2000—Joy in Ministry

May 7: The Joy of Serving (Church Helpers); (Acts 6:1-8; 2 Cor. 1:21-24); *May 14:* The Joy of Telling Good News (Salvation); (Philip and the Ethiopian Eunuch) (Acts 8:26-40; 2 Cor. 4:5) *May 21:* The Joy of Giving (Agabus's Message and the Church Offering); (Acts 11:27-30; 2 Cor. 9:1-8); *May 28:* The Joy of Sharing (Early Believers Share); (Acts 2:41-47; 2 Cor. 13:11)

June 2000—Living to Please Jesus

June 4: Showing Hospitality to Others (Lydia); (Acts 16:11-15; Phil. 1:19-21); *June 11:* Following Jesus' Example (Jesus Washes the Disciples' Feet); (John 13:3-15; Phil. 2:1-18);
June 18: Responding to the Good News (Philippian Jailer); (Acts 16:19-34; Phil. 3:12-16); *June 26:* Rejoicing Together (Phil. 4:4-20)

July 2000—Living in God's Family

July 2: Asking About God's Family (Salvation) (The Rich Young Ruler) (Matt. 19:16-26; Eph. 1:1-14); *July 9:* Joining God's Family (Eph. 2:8-22); *July 16:* Growing in God's Family (Working Together); (Eph. 4:1-16); *July 23:* Loving in God's Family (Being Responsible); (Eph.5:1—6:4); *July 30:* Being Strong in God's Family (The Armor of God); (Eph. 6:10-20)

August 2000—Jesus Is Lord of All

August 6: Jesus: Creator of All (John 1:1-14; Col. 1:1-18); *August 13:* Jesus: Worthy of Our Faith (Timothy Is Reminded of His Heritage of Faith); (Col. 2:6-19; 2 Tim. 1:3-8,13-14; 3:14-15); *August 20:* Jesus: Alive in Me (Col. 3:1-17); *August 27:* Jesus: A Friend to All (The Woman at the Well); (John 4:1-26)

Children's Curriculum Overview
Life and Work Series
Bible Learners; Bible Learners: Teacher; Bible Discoverers; Bible Learners: Teacher; Bible Searchers; Bible Searchers: Teacher

September 1999—The Bible Is God's Message to All People

September 5: The Bible Is God's Message (Jer. 36:1-32); *September 12:* The Bible Is for All Times (2 Kings 22:1—23:3); *September 19:* The Bible Is for All People (Acts 17:1-34); *September 26:* The Bible Teaches (2 Tim. 3:10-17)

October 1999—God Is an Awesome God

October 3: God Cares (1 Kings 17:1-16); *October 10:* God Has Power (1 Kings 18:16-46); *October 17:* God Is Near (1 Kings 19:1-18); *October 24:* God Expects People to Obey (2 Kings 5:1-15); *October 31:* God Hears and Answers Prayers (2 Kings 6:8-23)

November 1999—God Wants Us to Pray

November 7: I Can Ask God for What I Need (1 Sam. 1:1-28); *November 14:* I Can Ask God to Help Others (Gen. 18:6-33); *November 21:* I Can Thank God for His Goodness (1 Kings 8:1-30); *November 28:* I Can Ask God to Forgive Me (Neh. 1:1-11)

December 1999—God Sent His Son

December 5: God Promised a Son (Isa. 7:14; 9:6; 11:1-5; Mic. 5:2); *December 12:* Angels Told About God's Son (Matt. 1:18-25; Luke 1:26-38); *December 19:* Shepherds Found God's Son (Luke 2:1-20); *December 26:* Wise Men Gave Gifts to God's Son (Matt. 2:1-12)

January 2000—Obey the Ten Commandments
January 2: Worship Only God (Ex. 20:1-11; Dan. 3:1-30); *January 9:* Honor Your Family (Ex. 20:12,14; Luke 2:41-52); *January 16:* Respect Life (Gen. 1:27; Ex. 1:15 (2:10; Ex. 20:13; Matt. 5:13-16, 21-22, 43-45); *January 23:* Respect the Property of Others (Ex. 20:15,17; 1 Kings 21:1-29); *January 30:* Tell the Truth (Ex. 20:16; 2 Kings 5:15-27)

February 2000—Make Wise Choices
February 6: David Chose to Do Right (1 Sam. 17:1-50); *February 13:* David Chose to Obey God (1 Sam. 26:1-25); *February 20:* David Chose to Be a Friend (2 Sam. 9:1-13); *February 27:* David Chose to Praise God (Ps. 23; 105:1-4)

March 2000—Jesus Worked Miracles
March 5: Jesus Fed the Five Thousand (John 6:1-15); *March 12:* Jesus Walked on Water (Matt. 14:22-33); *March 19:* Jesus Raised Lazarus from the Dead (John 11:1-44); *March 26:* Jesus Healed Blind Bartimaeus (Mark 10:46-52)

April 2000—Jesus Is Alive!
April 2: Jesus Rode into Jerusalem (Luke 19:28-40); *April 9:* Jesus Ate Supper with His Disciples (Luke 22:7-23); *April 16:* Jesus Died on the Cross (Luke 23:13-56); *April 23:* Jesus Arose from the Grave (John 20:1-18) *April 30:* Jesus Talked with His Disciples (John 21:1-17)

May 2000—Jesus Is the Savior
May 7: Believers Trust Jesus (John 1:12; 3:16-17; Acts 16:25-34; Rom. 3:23; 5:8-10; 6:23; 10:9-10; 1 John 1:8-10); *May 14:* Believers Want to Be Baptized (Matt. 3:13-17; Acts 2:38; 16:13-15; Rom. 6:3-4); *May 21:* Believers Are Church Members (Acts 2:41-47; 1 Cor. 12:13-20,26-27; Phil. 2:25-30; 4:14-19); *May 28:* Believers Tell About Jesus (Matt. 28:16-20; Acts 8:26-40

June 2000—Learn from Bible People
June 4: Bring People to Jesus (John 1:35-51); *June 11:* Honor Jesus (John 12:1-11); *June 18:* Encourage Others (Acts 4:32-37; 9:26-30; 11:19-26; 15:36-41); *June 25:* Do Good (Acts 9:36-43

July 2000—Honor God by Helping Others
July 2: Help by Caring (Matt. 25:31-46; Mark 2:1-12); *July 9:* Help by Praying (Acts 12:1-17); *July 16:* Help by Serving (Acts 18:1-3,18-26; Rom. 16:3-4; 1 Cor. 16:19); *July 23:* Help by Being a Friend (Acts 16:1-5; Phil. 2:19-24; 1 Thess. 3:2-6); *July 30:* Help by Giving (2 Cor. 8:1—9:15; Phil. 2:25-30; 4:14-20)

August 2000—Live in Ways That Please God
August 6: Control Your Anger (Prov. 4:20-27; 14:16-17; 15:1-7; 16:32; 25:18) (Story for Bible Learners and Bible Discoverers will come from Gen. 37:12-36; 45:1-15); *August 13:* Do Your Best (Prov. 6:6-11; 10:4-5; 13:4; 18:9; 20:4; 24:30-34; 28:19) (Story for Bible Learners and Bible Discoverers will come from Ruth 2:1-23); *August 20:* Choose Good Friends (Prov. 3:27-30; 11:12-13; 14:21; 25:17-18) (Story for Bible Learners and Bible Discoverers will come from Judges 7:1-21 and the title will be "Trust God"); *August 27:* Beware of Alcohol and Drugs (Prov. 20:1; 21:17; 23:20-21,29-35; 31:4-5; Daniel 1:1-17) (Story for Bible Learners and Bible Discoverers will come from Dan. 1:1-17 and the title will be "Take Care of Your Body)

Youth Curriculum Overview
Youth Explore the Bible Series
Youth Explore the Bible Student Journal; Youth Explore the Bible Teacher; Youth Explore the Bible Resource Kit

Fall 1999

Body Building: A Study of Ephesians, Philippians, Colossians, Philemon

The Abundant Life (Eph.); A Good Example (Phil.); Questions to Be Answered (Col. and Philem.)

Winter 1999–2000

A Tale of Two Kingdoms: A Study of 1 Kings 13–22, 2 Kings, 2 Chronicles 11–36, Joel, and Jonah

Double Troubles (1 Kings 13–22); The Eternal King (Christmas lesson from Luke); Making a Difference (2 Kings 1–12); The End? (2 Kings 13–25); Turn Around (Joel and Jonah)

Spring 2000

Close Encounter: A Study of the Book of Luke

Getting Ready (Luke 1:1–4:13; Making Contact (Luke 4:14–9:50); Important Questions (Luke 9:51–19:27); Paying the Bill (Luke 19:28–24:53)

Summer 2000

A Study of the Book of Acts

Preparation for the Trip (Acts 1:1–13:3); When the Going Gets Tough (Acts 13:4–20:38); He Keeps on Going (Acts 21:1–28:31)

Youth Curriculum Overview
Family Bible Series
FBS: Youth Student Book, FBS: Youth Teacher Book, FBS: Youth Teaching Kit

Fall 1999—From Slavery to Promised Land

Unit 1: Liberation and Covenant

Unit Description: This unit, "Liberation and Covenant," consists of four sessions that survey the exodus and the making of the covenant at Mount Sinai.

September 5: Who, Me? (Ex. 3:1-12); *September 12:* Hope Out of Despair (Ex. 13:17-22; 14:26-31); *September 19:* What Are the Limits? (Ex. 19:3-6; 20:2-4,7-8,12-17); *September 26:* A Point of Contact (Ex. 40:1-9; Lev. 26:2-6,11-13)

Unit 2: Wilderness Wanderings

Unit Description: This five-session unit focuses on God's leadership in the wilderness wanderings of the children of Israel, the rebellion of the people during that period of time, and God's charge to remember and love Him completely.

October 3: Following Faithfully (Ex. 40:34-38; Num. 9:15-19,22-23); *October 10:* Hitting the Panic Button (Num. 13:1-3,32; 14:4,20-24); *October 17:* Paying the Price (Deut. 1:41-44; 2:1-7,16-18); *October 24:* Link in the Chain (Deut. 6:1-9,20-24; *October 31:* Don't Forget (Deut. 8:7-20)

Unit 3: Entering the Land

Unit Description: This study consists of four sessions that cover the death of Moses, the passing of leadership to Joshua, the crossing of the Jordan River, and the battle at the city of Jericho.

November 7: Receiving the Torch (Deut. 31:1-8; 34:5-8); *November 14:* Trusting Promises (Josh. 3:7-17; *November 21:* Sticking to the Plan (Josh. 6:1-5,15-20); *November 28:* Making Life's Choices (Josh. 24:24:1-2,14-22,25)

Winter 1999–2000—Studies in Matthew
Unit 1: Beginnings: Birth and Ministry
Unit Description: This four-session unit introduces John the Baptist as the herald of Jesus' coming. In addition, the unit takes a look at Jesus' temptation. The birth of Jesus is the focus of the third session which is the Christmas lesson. The unit closes with the story of the coming of the wise men to see the child Jesus.
December 5: Fire and Water (Matt. 3:1-8,11-17); *December 12:* Temptation! (Matt. 4:1-14); *December 19:* A King is Born (Matt. 1:1-6,18-25; *December 26:* Search Until You Find (Matt. 2:1-12)

Unit 2: Jesus' Teachings and Ministry
Unit Description: This five-session unit continues the study of the Gospel of Matthew. Sessions include the calling of the twelve disciples, teachings on prayer, examples of Jesus' miracles of compassion, growing opposition to Jesus, and the parable of the laborers in the vineyard.
January 2: Follow Me (Matt. 4:18-22; 9:9-12; 10:1-4); *January 9:* Private Conversations (Matt. 6:1-15); *January 16:* Healing Touch (Matt. 9:18-31,35-36); *January 23:* Trouble! (Matt. 12:22-32,38-40); *January 30:* Turn It Around (Matt. 20:1-16)

Unit 3: Fulfillment of Jesus' Mission
Unit Description: This four-session unit focuses on the last days of Jesus' ministry here on earth. Sessions include the triumphal entry of Jesus, preparation for Christ's return, the crucifixion and resurrection of Jesus, and the commissioning of His followers.
February 6: Greatness Through Humility (Matt. 21:1-13); *February 13:* Be Ready! (Matt. 24:45—25:13); *February 20:* Darkness Before Dawn (Matt. 27:38-54); *February 27:* Being a Winner (Matt. 28:1-10,16-20)

Spring 2000 —Continuing Jesus' Work
Unit 1: Christ the Basis of Unity
Unit Description: This four-session unit is taken from the book of 1 Corinthians. Sessions will look at the call for unity among Christians, the role of the Holy Spirit as teacher, the leaders of the church as servants of Christ, and the need for discipline in the church.
March 5: What Unites? (1 Cor. 1:2-17); *March 12:* In the Know (1 Cor. 2:1-2,4-16); *March 19:* Lead, but Serve (1 Cor. 4:1-13); *March 26:* Who Enforces? (1 Cor. 5:1-13)

Unit 2: Unity in Human Relationships
Unit Description: This five-session unit continues the study of 1 Corinthians. Sessions deal with relationships: marriage, singleness, and family; how to let love and knowledge work together; spiritual gifts; the resurrection (Easter session); and the way to live by love.
April 2: Sex and Marriage (1 Cor. 7:1-5,8-16); *April 9:* You Can, But Don't (1 Cor. 8); *April 16:* Many Parts, One Body (1 Cor. 12:4-20,26); *April 23:* What's the Last Word? (1 Cor. 15:20-27,35-44); *April 30:* What's Real Love? (1 Cor. 12:31—13:13)

Unit 3: The Power of Christian Ministry
Unit Description: This four-session unit is taken from 2 Corinthians. Sessions will deal with the victory that Christians can have through Jesus Christ in spite of trials and difficulties, directions concerning Christian giving, and an appeal to live by the faith that is professed.
May 7: Discipline from Love (2 Cor. 2:4-17); *May 14:* Power from Weakness (2 Cor. 4:5-18); *May 21:* Joy from Giving (2 Corinthians 9:1-13); *May 28:* Growth from Confrontation (2 Cor. 13:1-13)

Summer 2000—New Life in Christ
Unit 1: Living in Christ
Unit Description: This four-session unit focuses on Paul's letter to the church at Philippi. Themes for the study include living in Christ, having the mind of Christ, pressing on in Christ, and rejoicing in Christ.
June 4: Hope Under Pressure (Phil. 1:12-26); *June 11:* Setting Aside Privileges (Phil. 2:1-13); *June 18:* Press Ahead! (Phil. 3:7-21); *June 25:* Rejoicing in Christ (Phil. 4:4-18)

Unit 2: Called to Be a New Humanity
Unit Description: This five-session unit is based on Ephesians wherein Christians are called to spiritual blessings, oneness in Christ, the use of spiritual gifts, responsible living, and to stand firm as participants in the new community.
July 2: That's the Spirit! (Eph. 1:1-14); *July 9:* All for One! (Eph. 2:8-22); *July 16:* Use Your Gifts! (Eph. 4:1-16); *July 23:* A Place for Me! (Eph. 5:1-5,21-29; 6:1-4); *July 30:* Stand Firm! (Eph. 6:10-20)

Unit 3: Christ Above All
Unit Description: This four-session unit centers on Paul's Letter to the church at Colosse with emphasis on the supremacy, completeness, and righteousness of Christ. Paul's personal letter to Philemon concerning his new relationship with Onesimus concludes the study for the quarter.
August 6: The Image of God (Col. 1:15-28); *August 13:* A Full Life in Christ (Col. 2:6-19); *August 20:* Life on a Higher Level (Col. 3:1-3,5-17); *August 27:* A Plea for Acceptance (Philem. 4-21)

Youth Curriculum Overview
Youth Life and Work Series
Youth in Discovery; Youth in Discovery: Teacher; Youth in Action; Youth in Action: Teacher

*These are *Youth in Discovery* titles. *Youth in Action* titles may vary.

Fall 1999
Unit 1: Don't Underestimate What God Can Do Through You
Unit Description: This four-session unit will examine how God used Esther and her unique abilities to provide deliverance for the Jewish people. Youth will be challenged to examine their abilities and opportunities to determine how and where God desires to use them. This book study is entirely from the Book of Esther.
September 5: Me? Why Me? (Esth. 2:5-9,17-18,21-23); *September 12:* Take a Stand (Esth. 3:1-4; 4:1-3,12-17); *September 19:* A Humble Heart (Esth. 5:1-4,12-14; 6:6-10); *September 26:* God Is Good (Esth. 7:1-6; 8:15-17; 9:29-32)

Unit 2: Showing Real Faith . . .
Unit Description: This five-session unit, based on selected passages from the Old and New Testaments, describes how to experience an everyday, vibrant, firsthand faith.
October 3: . . . in Commitment (Josh. 24:14-15,31; Judg. 1:1,28; 2:10-13; 1 Cor. 2:14–3:3); *October 10:* . . . in Love (Matt. 19:3-12; Mal. 2:13-14; 1 Cor. 7:2-4); *October 17:* . . . in Families (Mal. 2:15; Eph. 6:1-4; Titus 2:1-8; Gen. 18:19); *October 24:* . . . in Repentance (Evangelistic lesson) (Ps. 51); *October 31:* . . . in Service (Isa. 6:1-8; Matt. 6:33; Eph. 2:8-10; 4:11-13)

Unit 3: Where Will You Be?
Unit Description: This four-session unit, based on selected passages from the Old and New Testaments, considers questions that youth ask about Christ's second coming and life after death.
November 7: Watching for Jesus' Return (Mark 13:32-37; Luke 12:35-40; 2 Pet. 3:3-4,8-9); *November 14:* Approaching the End of the World (Dan. 12:1-3; Mark 13:26-27; 1 Cor. 15:20-26,51-57); *November 21:* Staying Away from Hell (Luke 13:22-30; Rev. 20:10-15); *November 28:* Heading to Heaven (Rev. 21:1-5,22–22:5)

Winter 1999-2000

Unit 1: Family Matters

Unit Description: This two-session unit, based on passages from Proverbs, John, Acts, Ephesians, and Colossians, will demonstrate to youth the need to witness to their families by exposing their families to the gospel message and by living a consistent Christian lifestyle.

December 5: Did I Say That? (John 1:35-42; Acts 16:13-15,31-34); *December 12:* Did I Do That? (Prov. 23:15-19,22-25; Col. 3:8-14)

Unit 2: And Now, a Word for Our Sponsor

Unit Description: This two-session unit, based on selected Scripture passages from Matthew, Luke, and 1 Peter, encourages youth to glorify God with their words and actions, and to live so that their lives cause other people to glorify God.

December 19: The Sky Tells (Luke 1:46-49; 2:8-20); *December 26:* Got Salt? (Matt. 5:13-16; 1 Peter 2:1-12)

Unit 3: Y2W

Unit Description: This two-session unit, based on passages from 1 Chronicles, Psalms, Colossians, Hebrews, and Revelation, will encourage youth to practice expressions of true worship with other Christians.

January 2: Connected (1 Chron. 16:23-36; Ps. 95:1-7a); *January 9:* Networking (Col. 3:15-17; Heb. 10:19-25; Rev. 7:9-12)

Unit 4: Who Cares?

Unit Description: This three-session unit, based on passages from Jeremiah, Psalms, Daniel, and Luke will help youth realize the value of life. Includes the Sanctity of Human Life and the Alcohol and Drug lessons.

January 16: I Care (Sanctity of Human Life lesson) (Ps. 82; Jer. 7:2b-7); *January 23:* We Care (Alcohol and Other Drugs lesson); (Dan. 1:5-17); *January 30:* God Cares (Evangelistic lesson); (Luke 15:11-24,31-32)

Unit 5: Worth the Wait

Unit Description: This two-session unit, based on Romans 8, challenges our human desire for personal, instant gratification by showing how we are given new life in Christ, freed from the selfish desires of our sin natures and have a future, greater glory waiting for us.

February 6: I Want It Now! (Rom. 8:1-2,5-17); *February 13:* Something Better Is on the Way (Rom 8:18-30)

Spring 2000

Unit 1: Banded Together

Unit Description: This two-session unit, based on passages from 1 Corinthians and 1 Timothy, reveals how everyone can contribute to the unity and work of the church by valuing the diverse gifts that build up the church body and by living lives of high personal and moral standards.

March 5: All for One (1 Cor. 12:12-24a,27-31a); *March 12:* One for All (1 Tim. 3:1-13; 4:12-16)

Unit 2: Getting Ready for Missions

Unit Description: This two-session unit, based on selected passages from 2 Corinthians, Isaiah, and Psalms, will help youth understand why and how they should participate in missions.

March 19: Get Ready! (2 Cor. 5:9-21); *March 26:* Get Set, Go! (Isa. 61:1-3; Ps. 145:4-12)

Unit 3: Ouch! That Hurts!

Unit Description: This two session unit, based on passages from Romans, 1 Thessalonians, and 1 Peter, will help youth to understand that they can expect to suffer for their faith but that their faith will become stronger as a result.

April 2: Don't Be Surprised (1 Pet. 4:12-19; 1 Thess. 3:2-8); *April 9:* Good Will Come Out of It (Rom. 5:1-5; 1 Pet. 1:6-9; 2:19-23)

Unit 4: Jesus' Cross, My Cross

Unit Description: This three-session unit examines the historical account of Jesus' death and resurrection and helps youth understand the implications of the cross for their daily living.

April 16: Friday (Luke 23:33-47; Rom. 5:8); *April 23:* Sunday (Evangelistic lesson) (John 20:1-9,19-23; Rom. 8:11); *April 30:* Today (Col. 2:13–3:4)

Unit 5: You Don't Say!

Unit Description: This two-session unit will help youth realize the words that flow from their mouths do matter. Words should be a reflection of their relationship with Christ and be uplifting—to others and to God.

May 7: Say What? (Jas. 3:2-12; Ex. 20:7,16; Prov. 12:18-19,22; Eph. 4:25); *May 14:* Fightin' Words! (Prov. 10:11-14; 2 Tim. 2:14-16,20-26)

Unit 6: Of Death and Life

Unit Description: This two-session unit, based on passages from Job, Psalms, John, and 1 Thessalonians, will help youth discuss and deal with the deaths of family members and friends with the understanding that there is hope for Christians.

May 21: Dead Certain (Ps. 89:47-48; Job 14:1-12,14-15); *May 28:* Life Assurance (John 11:21-27; 1 Thess. 4:13-18)

Summer 2000

Unit 1: Faith in Christ

Unit Description: This five session unit is a study of the Book of Galatians. This unit will help youth understand what it means to be justified by faith in Christ as well as the freedom Christians enjoy because of their relationship with Christ. This unit will also challenge youth to demonstrate the fruit of the Spirit through Christian love and service.

June 4: A Living Faith (Gal. 1:1-10; 2:17-21); *June 11:* A Justified Faith (Evangelistic lesson) (Gal. 3:1-5,10-14,23-29); *June 18:* A Free Faith (Gal. 4:1-11; 5:1-6); *June 25:* A Fruitful Faith (Gal. 5:7-9,13-26); *July 2:* A Demonstrated Faith (Gal. 6:1-15)

Unit 2: Which Way?

Unit Description: This two-session unit, using passages from Leviticus, Romans, 1 Corinthians, and Ephesians, confronts popular beliefs about homosexuality with biblical truth by showing that homosexuality is sin and that there is hope for freedom from homosexuality.

July 9: The Wrong Way (Lev. 18:22; Rom. 1:18-28); *July 16:* The Way of Hope (Eph. 4:17-24; 1 Cor. 6:9-11; 10:13)

Unit 3: No Hocus Pocus

Unit Description: This two-session unit, based on selected Old Testament passages, will lead youth to trust in God for guidance rather than horoscopes, psychics, tarot cards, and palm readers.

July 23: The Maker of the Stars (Gen. 1:14-19; Deut. 4:19; 2 Kings 23:4-5,26-27); *July 30:* Who Holds Your Future? (Lev. 19:26b-28,31; Deut. 18:9-15; Isa. 47:12-15; Eccl. 7:13-14)

Unit 4: What Does God Want Me to Do?

Unit Description: This two-session unit, based on passages from the Books of Psalms, John, and 1 Thessalonians, will help youth understand the importance of knowing Scripture and heeding the direction of the Holy Spirit to understand God's will in their lives.

August 6: Read the Directions! (Ps. 119:1-16,33-40); *August 13:* Follow the Call (John 14:23-27; 16:13-15; 1 Thess. 5:16-24)

Unit 5: Pilgrim's Progress

Unit Description: This two-session unit, based on various passages, examines the process of spiritual transformation by looking at the life of Paul. By seeing how Christ changed Paul and how He continued to transform Paul through his life, youth will see that their spiritual transformation is a lifelong process that is possible only through the work of the Holy Spirit.

August 20: The Trip Begins (Acts 22:1-16); *August 27:* The Adventure Continues (1 Tim. 1:12-17; Phil. 3:12-14; 1 Cor. 10:31–11:1)

Adult Curriculum Overview
Explore the Bible Series
Explore the Bible: Adults, Explore the Bible: Adults–Large Print; Explore the Bible: Adult Study Guide, Explore the Bible: Teacher

Fall 1999—Leviticus, Numbers: Building Blocks of a Nation
Unit 1: Relating to God in Worship
September 5: Appropriate Worship (Lev. 1:1–7:38); *September 12:* Serious Worship (Lev. 8:1–10:20); *September 19:* Atoning Worship (Lev. 11:1–16:34)

Unit 2: Relating to God in Holy Living
September 26: Holiness in Relationships (Lev. 17:1–21:24) *October 3:* Holiness in Worship Practices (Lev. 22:1–25:55); *October 10:* Holiness in Choices (Lev. 26:1–27:34)

Unit 3: Following God's Leadership
October 17: Needing God's Leadership (Num. 1:1–10:10); *October 24:* Rebelling Against God (Num. 10:11–14:45); *October 31:* Relating to God's Appointed Leaders (15:1–18:32) *November 7:* Triumphing over Obstacles (19:1–21:35)

Unit 4: Moving Toward God's New Beginning
November 14: Renewed Blessing (Num. 22:1–25:18); *November 21:* New Leader (Num. 26:1–30:16); *November 28:* New Venture (Num. 31:1–36:13)

Winter 1999–2000—1,2,3 John; Jude: A Call To Action
Unit 1: Life In Christ
December 5: Live in Light (1 John 1:1–2:2); *December 12:* Live in Love (1 John 2:3-17); *December 19:* Welcome the Light (John 1:1-18); *December 26:* Live in Truth (1 John 2:18-27)

Unit 2: Christian Distinctives
January 2: Pursuing Righteousness (1 John 2:28-3:10); *January 9:* Practicing Love (1 John 3:11-24); *January 16:* Protecting Life (Gen. 1:26-28; Ps. 139:1-18; Matt. 18:10,14; 19:13-15); *January 23:* Perfecting Love (1 John 4:1-21); *January 30:* Strengthening Faith (1 John 5:1-12); *February 6:* Developing Confidence (1 John 5:13-21)

Unit 3: Commitment To The Faith
February 13: Be Alert (2 John); *February 20:* Be Hospitable (3 John); *February 27:* Be on Guard (Jude)

Spring 2000—Joshua, Judges: New Beginnings
Unit 1: The Lord Gives His People Victory
March 5: Promise of Victory (Josh. 1:1-2:24); *March 12:* Preparing for Victory (Josh. 3:1-5:15) (Mar. 12); *March 19:* Experiencing Victory (Josh. 6:1-9:27); *March 26:* Obeying the Lord Fully (Josh. 10:1-12:24)

Unit 2: The Lord Keeps His Promises
April 2: Claiming an Inheritance (Josh. 13:1-21:45); *April 9:* Remembering the Lord's Faithfulness (Josh. 22:1-23:16); *April 16:* Committing to Faithful Service (Josh. 24:1-33); *April 23:* Easter: Making Disciples (Matt. 28:1-20) (Apr. 23, Easter)

Unit 3: The Lord Works With His Unfaithful People

April 30: Repeatedly Forsaking the Lord (Judg. 1:1-3:31); *May 7:* Depending on the Lord (Judg. 4:1-9:57); *May 14:* Bargaining with God (Judg. 10:1-12:15); *May 21:* Living Irresponsibly (Judg. 13:1-16:31); *May 28:* Doing Your Own Thing (Judg. 17:1-21:25)

Summer 2000—Revelation: A Vision Of Triumph
Unit 1: Christ's Messages To His Churches

June 4: The Glorified Christ (Rev. 1:1-20); *June 11:* Christ Speaks to His Churches (Rev. 2:1-3:22); *June 18:* Worship the Redeemer (Rev. 4:1-5:14)

Unit 2: Christ's Call To Faithfulness

June 25: Assurance for the Saved (Rev. 6:1-7:17); *July 2:* Judgment on the Unrepentant (Rev. 8:1-9:21); *July 9:* Encouragement to Faithful Witnesses (Rev. 10:1-11:19)

Unit 3: Cosmic Conflict

July 16: Satan vs. Christ (Rev. 12:1-13:18); *July 23:* Salvation vs. Judgment (Rev. 14:1-20); *July 30:* Wrath vs. Blessing (Rev. 15:1-16:21)

Unit 4: Ultimate Triumph

August 6: Doom for False Religion (Rev. 17:1—18:24) *August 13:* The Triumphant Christ (Rev. 19:1-21); August 20: Total Triumph (20:1-15); *August 27:* The Great Invitation (Rev. 21:1-22:21)

Adult Curriculum Overview
Family Bible Series
Family Bible Series: Adult, FBS: Adult Large Print, FBS: Adult Teacher,
Family Bible Series: Adult Teaching Kit

Fall 1999—Our Spiritual Pilgrimage
Unit 1: Commitment

September 5: Called to Involvement (Ex. 3:1-22); *September 12:* Called to Deliverance (Ex. 13:17-14:31); *September 19:* Called to Covenant (Ex. 19:1-20:21); *September 26:* Called to Obedience (Ex. 40:1-33; Lev. 26:1-46)

Unit 2: Struggle

October 3: Needed Guidance (Ex. 40:34-38; Num. 9:15-23); *October 10:* Missed Opportunity (Num. 12:1-14:25); *October 17:* Renewed Purpose (Deut. 1:41-2:25); *October 24:* Shared Faith (Deut. 6:1-25); *October 31:* Required Perspective (Deut. 8:1-20)

Unit 3: Advance

November 7: Coping with Transition (Deut. 31:1-8; 34); *November 14:* Continuing with Conviction (Josh. 3:1-17); *November 21:* Conquering with Instruction (Josh. 6:1-27); *November 28:* Choosing with Deliberation (Josh. 24)

Winter 1999-2000—Christ: Our Example
Unit 1: Commencing

December 5: Time of Preparing (Matt. 3:1-17); *December 12:* Time of Testing (Matt. 4:1-17); *December 19:* Time of Rejoicing (Matt. 1:1-25); *December 26:* Time of Worshiping (Matt. 2:1-23)

Unit 2: Continuing

January 2: Focus on Commitment (Matt. 4:18-22; 9:9-12; 10:1-4); *January 9:* Focus on Prayer (Matt. 6:1-15); *January 16:* Focus on Compassion (Matt. 9:18-38); *January 23:* Focus on Jesus' Power (Matt. 12:22-45); *January 30:* Focus on Rewards (Matt. 19:16-20:16)

Unit 3: Completing

February 6: Guidance of the Word (Matt. 21:1-17); *February 13:* Joy of Being Prepared (Matt. 24:1-25:13); *February 20:* Death on Our Behalf (Matt. 27:32-61); *February 27:* Basis of Our Authority (Matt. 27:62-28:20)

Spring 2000—Solving Church Problems
Unit 1: Problems with Church Harmony

March 5: Basis of Harmony (1 Cor. 1:1-17); *March 12:* Heart of Harmony (1 Cor. 2:1-3:3); *March 19:* Threat to Harmony (1 Cor. 3:4-4:13); *March 26:* Appearance of Harmony (1 Cor. 5:1-6:11)

Unit 2: Problems in Personal Relationships

April 2: Different Marital Standings (1 Cor. 6:12-7:16); *April 9:* Different Convictions (1 Cor. 8:1-13); *April 16:* Different Gifts (1 Cor. 12:4-20,26); *April 23:* Confident Hope (1 Cor. 15:1-58); *April 30:* Ultimate Solution (1 Cor. 12:31-13:13)

Unit 3: Problems in Ministry

May 7: From Sorrow to Joy (2 Cor. 1:1-2:17); *May 14:* From Suffering to Glory (2 Cor. 4:1-18); *May 21:* From Reluctance to Joyful Giving (2 Cor. 9:1-15); *May 28:* From Confrontation to Growth (2 Cor. 13:1-13)

Summer 2000—Life in Christ
Unit 1: Characteristics of Believers

June 4: Confidence (Phil. 1:12-30); *June 11:* Humility ; (Phil. 2:1-18); *June 18:* Persistence (Phil. 3:1-21); *June 25:* Joy (Phil. 4:4-20)

Unit 2: Provisions for Believers

July 2: Salvation (Eph. 1:1-23); *July 9:* New Relationships (Eph. 2:1-22); *July 16:* Ministry (Eph. 4:1-16); *July 23:* Responsibilities (Eph. 5:1-6:4); *July 30:* Armor (Eph. 6:10-24)

Unit 3: Instructions for Believers

August 6: Source of Life (Col. 1:1-29); *August 13:* Fullness of Life (Col. 2:6-19); *August 20:* Way of Life (Col. 3:1-17); *August 27:* Grace of Life (Philemon 1-25)

Adult Curriculum Overview
Adult Life and Work Series

Collegiate
Adult Life and Work Collegiate, Adult Life and Work Collegiate Teacher

Adults 18-34 years
Directions: Bible Studies for Early Adulthood, Directions: Bible Studies for Young Adults; Directions: Teacher Edition

Adults 35–54 years
Pursuits: Bible Studies for Adults, A Single Pursuit; Pursuits: Teacher Edition, Pursuits: Resource Kit

Adults 55 years–up
Ventures, Pathways; Ventures and Pathways: Teacher, Ventures and Pathways Resource Kit

Fall 1999—Angels: God's Special Helpers
September 5: What Angels Are (Pss. 34:7; 91:11; 148:2-5; Matt. 18:10; 26:53-54; Luke 20:34-36; Heb. 1:14; 2 Pet. 2:10b-11); *September 12:* What Angels Do (Ps. 103:20-21; Matt. 13:39b-42; Mark 13:26-27; Acts 12:7-9,11; 27:23-24); *September 19:* Keeping Angels in Their Place (Deut. 32:15-18; Ps. 106:35-37; 1 Cor. 10:19-20; Gal. 1:6-9; Col. 2:18-19); *September 26:* Jesus Is Superior to Angels (Heb. 1:3-9,13; 2:2-3,9-10,14-16).

Experiencing Spiritual Breakthroughs
October 3: Experiencing Spiritual Breakthrough in Your Faith (Josh. 24:14-15,31; Judg. 1:1,28; 2:10-13; 1 Cor. 2:14–3:3); *October 10:* Experiencing Spiritual Breakthrough in Marriage (Gen. 2:18,20b-22; Matt. 19:3-9; Eph. 5:22-25,28,33); *October 17:* Experiencing Spiritual Breakthrough in the Family (Gen. 18:18-19; Deut. 6:5-7; Ps. 78:4-8; Eph. 6:4; Titus 2:4-5); *October 24:* Experiencing Spiritual Breakthrough by Repentance [Evangelism Lesson] (Ps. 51:1-12,15-17); *October 31:* After Spiritual Breakthrough: Work for the Kingdom (Isa. 6:1-8; Matt. 6:33; Eph. 2:8-10; 1 Pet. 4:10-11)

Jonah: Responses to God's Missionary Call
November 7: Running From God (Jonah 1:1-16); *November 14:* Turning to God (Jonah 1:17–2:10); *November 21:* Obeying God (Jonah 3:1-10); *November 28:* Playing God (Jonah 4:1-11)

Winter 1999–2000—Playing Supporting Roles in the Drama of Redemption
December 5: Zechariah: Persistent Faithfulness (Luke 1:5-7,11-16,18-20,68-69,76); *December 12:* Mary: Submissive Servanthood (Luke 1:30-35,38,42-45; 2:33-35,39); *December 19:* Joseph: Exemplary Character (Matt. 1:18-21,24-25; 2:13-15,19-23); *December 26:* The Wise Men: Determined Worshippers (Matt. 2:1-12)

Managing God's Assets
January 2: A World to Manage (Gen. 2:15; 2 Chron. 7:13-14; Pss. 8:6-8; 24:1; 115:16; Hos. 4:1-3); *January 9:* Time to Value (Pss. 90:12; 103:15-16; Eccl. 3:1,17; Eph. 5:8-17); *January 16:* Life to Treasure [Sanctity of Human Life Sunday/Evangelism Lesson] (Ps. 139:13-16; Jer. 7:3-7; John 3:15-16; 10:10; 1 Tim. 4:7-8); *January 23:* Gifts to Use (Rom. 12:6-8; 1 Cor. 12:1,4-11); *January 30:* Money to Manage (2 Cor. 8:1-15)

Victory in Jesus Now and Forever
Unit 1: The Lord's Call to Faithfulness
February 6: Reasons to Be Faithful (Rev. 1:1-8,12-18); *February 13:* Expectations of Faithfulness (Rev. 2:1-5,12-16,18-22); *February 20:* Evidences of Faithfulness (Rev. 2:8-11; 3:7-13); *February 27:* Restoration to Faithfulness (Rev. 3:1-5,14-21)

Spring 2000—Victory in Jesus Now and Forever (cont'd.)
Unit 2: The World's Destiny and the Lord's Victory
March 5: What About Persecuted Believers? (Rev. 4:2-3; 6:9-11,15-17; 7:9,13-17); *March 12:* What About Satan? (Rev. 12:1-5,7-12,17); *March 19:* What About the Antichrist? (Rev. 13:1-10,16-17); *March 26:* What About Christ's Return? (Rev. 19:6-9,11-16,19-21); *April 2:* What About the Judgment? (Rev. 20:1-15); *April 9:* What About Heaven? (Rev. 21:1-4,9-11,18-19,21; 22:1-5); *April 16:* What About Now? (Rev. 22:7-17,20-21); *April 23:* Great Day in the Morning! [Easter: Coordinated Evangelism Lesson] (John 20:1-8,11-19,21)

Seeking God's Heart: Lessons from David's Life
April 30: Willing to Serve (1 Sam. 16:1,6-13); *May 7:* Courage to Stand (1 Sam. 17:8-11,32-33,37,45-47,50); *May 14:* Honest About Sin (2 Sam. 12:1-14); *May 21:* Driven by Devotion (1 Chron. 22:1,5-13,17-19); *May 28:* Faithful to the End (2 Sam. 23:1-7; 1 Kings 2:1-4)

Summer 2000—Adopting a Biblical Worldview
Unit 1: Worldview? Everybody Has One
June 4: Worldview? Everybody Has One (Isa. 55:8-9; Ps. 1:1-6; Prov. 14:12; Matt. 7:24-27)

Unit 2: Contours of a Biblical Worldview
June 11: How We Know What We Know (Eccl. 8:16-17; Rom. 8:5-8; Eph. 4:17-18,22-24; Heb. 11:1-2); *June 18:* Here Is Your God (Isa. 40:10-11,18-31); *June 25:* God's Good Creation (Gen. 1:3,11-12,14-15,20-22,24-25,29-31);
July 2: God's Highest Creation (Gen. 1:27; 2:7; Ps. 145:8-9,17; Eccl. 12:13; Matt. 22:34-40; Rom. 5:8-10); *July 9:* Humanity's Greatest Failure (Gen. 3:1-6,16-19; Rom. 5:12-14,18-19); *July 16:* Who Is in Control? (Gen. 1:16-18; 8:22; Ps. 33:10-11; Jer. 33:25-26; John 5:17; Rom. 8:28; 13:1-5); *July 23:* God Reveals Truth (John 14:9-11; 16:13-15; Rom. 1:18-20; 2 Tim. 3:15-17);
July 30: What's Right and What's Wrong? (Pss. 9:7-8; 19:7-11; Ezek. 18:1-4,19-20; Rom. 2:14-15;
August 6: The Way to Spiritual Freedom [Evangelism Lesson] (Gal. 3:15-25; 4:4-7); *August 13:* A Place to Belong (Eph. 4:1-7,11-13,14-16); *August 20:* The Key to Fulfillment (Phil. 1:3-6,9-11,27-30; 2:14-16); *August 27:* When Time Will Be No More (2 Pet. 3:3-15a)

June 1999

SUNDAY	MONDAY	TUESDAY	WEDNESDAY	THURSDAY	FRIDAY	SATURDAY
		1	2	3	4	5
6	7	8	9	10	11	12
13	14	15	16	17	18	19
20 Father's Day	21	22	23	24	25	26
27 Christian Citizenship Sunday	28	29	30			

Southern Baptist Convention, Atlanta 15-17

EMPHASES AND EVENTS

Weekly Leadership Team Meetings
Weekly Visitation
Vacation Bible School
Sunday School Leadership Event, Glorieta™
Sunday School Leadership Event, Green Lake,
   Wisconsin

NOTES

_____   _____
_____   _____
_____   _____
_____   _____
_____   _____

July 1999

SUNDAY	MONDAY	TUESDAY	WEDNESDAY	THURSDAY	FRIDAY	SATURDAY
				1	2	3
4 INDEPENDENCE DAY	5	6	7	8	9	10
11	12	13	14	15	16	17
18	19	20	21	22	23	24
25	26	27	28	29	30	31

EMPHASES AND EVENTS

Weekly Leadership Team Meetings

Weekly Visitation

Sunday School Leadership Event, Green Lake, Wisconsin

Sunday School Leadership Event, Ridgecrest™

Vacation Bible School

NOTES

August 1999

SUNDAY	MONDAY	TUESDAY	WEDNESDAY	THURSDAY	FRIDAY	SATURDAY
1 Day of Prayer for World Peace	2	3	4	5	6	7
8	9	10	11	12	13	14
15 Day of Prayer for Students	16	17	18	19	20	21
22	23	24	25	26	27	28
29	30	31				

EMPHASES AND EVENTS
Weekly Leadership Team Meetings
Weekly Visitation

NOTES

_____ _____
_____ _____
_____ _____
_____ _____
_____ _____

September 1999

SUNDAY	MONDAY	TUESDAY	WEDNESDAY	THURSDAY	FRIDAY	SATURDAY
			1	2	3	4
5 Promotion Day	6 LABOR DAY	7	8	9	10	11
12 Single Adult Day	13	14	15	16	17	18
19 Anti-Gambling Emphasis Sunday	20	21	22	23	24	25
26	27	28	29	30		

EMPHASES AND EVENTS

Weekly Leadership Team Meetings
Weekly Visitation
State Missions Season of Prayer
State Missions Day in the Sunday School

NOTES

_____ _____

_____ _____

_____ _____

_____ _____

_____ _____

October 1999

SUNDAY	MONDAY	TUESDAY	WEDNESDAY	THURSDAY	FRIDAY	SATURDAY
					1	2
3 On Mission: To Share the Gospel Sunday	4	5	6	7	8	9
10 World Hunger Sunday	11	12	13	14	15	16
17	18	19	20	21	22	23
24 31 Sunday School High Attendance Day	25	26	27	28	29	30

EMPHASES AND EVENTS
Weekly Leadership Team Meetings
Weekly Visitation

NOTES
_____ _____
_____ _____
_____ _____
_____ _____

November 1999

SUNDAY	MONDAY	TUESDAY	WEDNESDAY	THURSDAY	FRIDAY	SATURDAY
	1	2	3	4	5	6
7 On Mission: The Next Generation Sunday	8	9	10	11	12	13
14	15	16	17	18	19	20
International Missions Study 14-20						
21	22	23	24	25 THANKSGIVING	26	27
28	29	30				
Week of Prayer for International Missions Nov. 28–Dec. 5						

EMPHASES AND EVENTS
Weekly Leadership Team Meetings
Weekly Visitation
Stewardship and Budget Promotion

NOTES
_____   _____
_____   _____
_____   _____
_____   _____

December 1999

SUNDAY	MONDAY	TUESDAY	WEDNESDAY	THURSDAY	FRIDAY	SATURDAY
			1	2	3	4
			Week of Prayer for International Missions and Lottie Moon Christmas Offering			
5	6	7	8	9	10	11
Nov. 28–Dec. 5						
12	13	14	15	16	17	18
19	20	21	22	23	24	25
						CHRISTMAS
26	27	28	29	30	31	
Student Day at Christmas						

EMPHASES AND EVENTS

Weekly Leadership Team Meetings
Weekly Visitation
Student Day at Christmas

NOTES

_____   _____
_____   _____
_____   _____
_____   _____
_____   _____

January 2000

SUNDAY	MONDAY	TUESDAY	WEDNESDAY	THURSDAY	FRIDAY	SATURDAY
						1 NEW YEAR'S DAY
2	3	4	5	6	7	8
			January Bible Study 3-7			
9	10	11	12	13	14	15
16 Sanctity of Human Life Sunday	17	18	19	20	21	22
23	24	25	26	27	28	29
30	31					

EMPHASES AND EVENTS
Weekly Leadership Team Meetings
Weekly Visitation

NOTES

February 2000

SUNDAY	MONDAY	TUESDAY	WEDNESDAY	THURSDAY	FRIDAY	SATURDAY
		1	2	3	4	5
6 Baptist World Alliance Day	7	8	9	10	11	12
13 Racial Reconciliation Sunday	14	15	16 Focus on WMU 14-20	17	18	19
20	21	22	23	24	25	26
27	28	29				

EMPHASES AND EVENTS	NOTES
Weekly Leadership Team Meetings Weekly Visitation True Love Waits Emphasis VBS Planning	_____ _____ _____ _____ _____ _____ _____ _____

March 2000

SUNDAY	MONDAY	TUESDAY	WEDNESDAY	THURSDAY	FRIDAY	SATURDAY
			1	2	3	4
5	6	7	8 Day of Prayer for Spiritual Awakening in North America	9	10	11

On Mission in North America: Week of Prayer and Mission Study and Annie Armstrong Easter Offering 5-12

SUNDAY	MONDAY	TUESDAY	WEDNESDAY	THURSDAY	FRIDAY	SATURDAY
12	13	14	15	16	17	18

Youth Week 13-19

SUNDAY	MONDAY	TUESDAY	WEDNESDAY	THURSDAY	FRIDAY	SATURDAY
19 Substance Abuse Sunday	20	21	22	23	24	25
26 On Mission: Planting New Congregations Sunday	27	28	29	30	31	

EMPHASES AND EVENTS

Weekly Leadership Team Meetings
Weekly Visitation
VBS Planning

NOTES

_____   _____
_____   _____
_____   _____
_____   _____

April 2000

SUNDAY	MONDAY	TUESDAY	WEDNESDAY	THURSDAY	FRIDAY	SATURDAY
						1
2 SBC Seminaries Sunday	3	4	5	6	7	8
9 Cooperative Program Sunday	10	11	12	13	14	15
16	17	18	19	20	21 GOOD FRIDAY	22
23 Easter/ Evangelism Day in the Sunday School 30 Life Commitment Sunday	24	25	26	27	28	29

Baptist Doctrine Study 17-21

EMPHASES AND EVENTS
Weekly Leadership Team Meetings
Weekly Visitation
VBS Planning

NOTES

_____   _____
_____   _____
_____   _____
_____   _____
_____   _____

May 2000

SUNDAY	MONDAY	TUESDAY	WEDNESDAY	THURSDAY	FRIDAY	SATURDAY
	1	2	3	4	5	6
7 Senior Adult Day	8	9	10	11	12	13
Christian Home Week 7-14						
14 MOTHER'S DAY	15	16	17	18	19	20
21	22	23	24	25	26	27
	Associational Missions Week 22-28					
28	29 MEMORIAL DAY	30	31			

EMPHASES AND EVENTS

Weekly Leadership Team Meetings

Weekly Visitation

Annual Planning Event

Ordering decisions made/SON 2000
order placed for new *Family Bible Study: Building the Family of Faith to Live by God's Truth* curriculum

NOTES

_____ _____

_____ _____

_____ _____

_____ _____

_____ _____

June 2000

SUNDAY	MONDAY	TUESDAY	WEDNESDAY	THURSDAY	FRIDAY	SATURDAY
				1	2	3
4 RELIGIOUS LIBERTY SUNDAY	5	6	7	8	9	10
11	12	13	14 Southern Baptist Convention, Orlando 13-14	15	16	17
18 FATHER'S DAY	19	20	21	22	23	24
25 CHRISTIAN CITIZENSHIP SUNDAY	26	27	28	29	30	

EMPHASES AND EVENTS

Christian Home Emphasis, May 7-June 18
Weekly Leadership Team Meetings
Weekly Visitation
Vacation Bible School
Sunday School Leadership Event, Glorieta™
Sunday School Leadership Event,
   Green Lake, Wisconsin

NOTES

_____   _____
_____   _____
_____   _____
_____   _____
_____   _____

July 2000

SUNDAY	MONDAY	TUESDAY	WEDNESDAY	THURSDAY	FRIDAY	SATURDAY
						1
2 Citizenship and Religious Liberty Sunday	3	4 INDEPENDENCE DAY	5	6	7	8
9	10	11	12	13	14	15
16	17	18	19	20	21	22
23	24	25	26	27	28	29
30	31					

EMPHASES AND EVENTS
Weekly Leadership Team Meetings
Weekly Visitation
Sunday School Leadership Event, Green Lake, Wisconsin
Sunday School Leadership Event, Ridgecrest™
Vacation Bible School

NOTES

_____   _____
_____   _____
_____   _____
_____   _____

August 2000

SUNDAY	MONDAY	TUESDAY	WEDNESDAY	THURSDAY	FRIDAY	SATURDAY
		1	2	3	4	5
6 Social Issues Sunday: Religious Persecution	7	8	9	10	11	12
13 Day of Prayer for Students	14	15	16	17	18	19
20	21	22	23	24	25	26
27	28	29	30	31		

EMPHASES AND EVENTS

Weekly Leadership Team Meetings

Weekly Visitation

NOTES

_____   _____

_____   _____

_____   _____

_____   _____

_____   _____

September 2000

SUNDAY	MONDAY	TUESDAY	WEDNESDAY	THURSDAY	FRIDAY	SATURDAY
					1	2
3 Promotion Day	4 LABOR DAY	5	6	7	8	9
10 Single Adult Day	11	12	13	14	15	16
17 Anti-Gambling Sunday	18	19	20	21	22	23
24	25 Discipleship Rally	26	27	28	29	30

EMPHASES AND EVENTS
Weekly Leadership Team Meetings
Weekly Visitation

NOTES
_____ _____
_____ _____
_____ _____
_____ _____
_____ _____

Group Study Plan

In preparation for this study, become familiar with the contents of this book and the contents of the *Sunday School for a New Century Planning and Training Pack*. View the videotape and make decisions about its use. Provide a copy of *Sunday School for a New Century* for each participant.

Preparation for the Session

1. Create a learning environment that makes good use of the space you have been provided for this session. Provide extra pencils or pens and paper.

2. Cut a large circle from yellow poster board. Make the circle as large as possible, as it will become part of the focal wall for the training. From navy or dark blue poster board, cut a placard on which you print the words *Sunday School for a New Century*. Extend the blue placard out from the center of the yellow circle so that it overlaps beyond the circle.

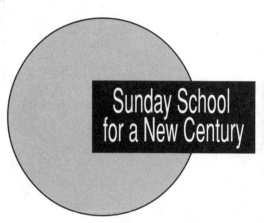

3. From the Training Pack select several items, mounting each one on remaining navy poster board. Use the yellow circle and the navy placards to form your focal wall. Allow room between the circle and the other items to view either PowerPoint® or cels or to use a chalkboard/markerboard.

4. Obtain yellow or blue sheets of construction paper to make different clock-motif assignment sheets, for overviewing each section of the book.

5. To present "Section 1: Laying the Foundation" information—
• prepare the five "Sunday School Strategy and (function)" worksheets; write "Nine Critical Questions" on a chalkboard/markerboard or use PowerPoint® or overhead transparencies; familiarize yourself with "Your Time Is Now" activities; prepare clock-face worksheets.

6. To present "Section 2: Knowing the People" information—
• preview the content and overview "Your Time Is Now" activities.

7. To present "Section 3: Planning and Organizing the Strategy"—
• prepare "The Clock Is Ticking" worksheets; familiarize yourself with "Your Time Is Now" activities and section content; vertically print each letter in *ORGANIZATION* to form a visual; review organization and budget information and ways your Sunday School approaches each area;

8. To present "Section 4: Developing Leaders Who Can Lead"—
• prepare leadership placards (or use the Training Pack item); familiarize yourself with "Your Time Is Now" activities and section content.

9. To present "Section 5: Implementing the Strategy" information—
• for every person, prepare a worksheet illustrated with a clock face; familiarize yourself with "Your Time Is Now" activities and content.

10. To present "Section 6: Teaching That Transforms" information—
• familiarize yourself with "Your Time Is Now" activities and section content; review curriculum used by your church and changes in Fall 1999 resources (note: preschool materials).

Teaching the Session

Section 1: Laying the Foundation

1. As people arrive, give them yellow or dark blue sheets of construction paper on which one or more clock faces have been printed. Ask conferees to design on the page what they think Sunday School of the future will look

Written by Jerri Herring, consultant, Sunday School/FAITH Ministry Department, LifeWay Christian Resources of the Southern Baptist Convention.

like. Allow them several minutes to work.

Take a few moments to allow for sharing of ideas. Then begin the study of this book by presenting a minilecture on "Section 1: Laying the Foundation."

2. Provide conferees a sheet of paper. Ask them to write their definition of Sunday School. Give them several minutes to work; then provide an overview of the definition of Sunday School for the 21st century.

3. Divide the group into five smaller groups. If you only have five people, give each person an assignment. Provide the following worksheets: *Sunday School Strategy and Evangelism, Sunday School Strategy and Discipleship, Sunday School Strategy and Fellowship, Sunday School Strategy and Ministry,* and *Sunday School Strategy and Worship.* Ask each group to offer a two-minute overview of its material based on pages 14-18 in the book.

4. Provide time for the group to do the "Your Time Is Now" activity (p. 24). Review the five Strategic Principles on pages 20-21. Present the "best practices" summarized on page 23, and remind conferees that these will be topics for the rest of this study.

5. Point out these "Nine Critical Questions" to ask and answer in relation to our Sunday School:

Nine Critical Questions

- What needs to be our strategy for reaching people?
- Do we have the right people in place?
- Do we have the right organization in place to reach them?
- Do we have the right organization in place to keep them?
- Do we have options in place? (for example, different times and places for Bible study)
- What are our options?
- If we could only do one thing in the next 6, 9, or 12 months, what would be the most significant thing for us to do?

Section 2: Knowing the People

6. Give a brief overview of the importance of knowing about each age or people group in this section. Use the "Your Time Is Now" activities to stimulate discussion.

Section 3: Planning and Organizing the Strategy

7. Distribute the worksheet with faces of several clocks imprinted and the title "The Clock Is Ticking." Ask conferees to begin thinking about the future. On the worksheet, ask them to list factors they believe will influence what takes place in the 21st century.

Allow time for discussion. Then review the items listed on page 49, adding them to the list already developed by conferees.

8. Remind the group that fewer than 4 percent of Americans write specific goals for themselves. Ask, Why do you think this is the case? Begin a discussion of the need for planning, being certain to include the "Your Time Is Now" activities and the 6-step annual planning process. Call attention to the checkup sheets that can be duplicated for use in your church (pp. 57-61).

9. Review budget planning as an important part of strategic annual planning. Remind leaders that, for many churches, the budget drives the ministry. Suggest ways Sunday School as strategy can change this mindset.

10. On a chalkboard/markerboard, overhead cel, or PowerPoint® frame, print vertically the letters of the word *ORGANIZATION*. As you talk about each letter, add the appropriate descriptive statement:

O pen to change

R ecruitment with integrity

G rowth orientation

A ccountability

N ew units

I nstill kingdom-building

Z ealous in attention to details

A ction strategy in place

T raining

I ntentional

O ptions

N urturing

11. Review the organization chart for each age group. Highlight the new organizational suggestions for preschool ministry and adult ministry. Lead conferees through the "Your Time is Now" activity on page 79.

Section 4: Developing Leaders Who Can Lead

12. Display and discuss the following statements about leadership. Ask, Do you agree or disagree? Why? How do we measure up?

Leadership is not about being famous.
Leadership is about making a difference.

People rarely rise above the know expectations of the leaders.
Everything rises and falls on leadership

13. Review the information on pages 89-96. Allow time for conferees to explore the need for this type of organization. Remind them that they have the responsibility to raise up leaders. Give time for participants to do and to discuss the "Your Time Is Now" activity on page 96.

14. Share the information on spiritual gifts and Sunday School leadership. Ask conferees to discuss how spiritual gifts sometimes are misused. Ask, How can we uplift the proper use of spiritual gifts? Provide time for the group to do and to discuss the "Your Time is Now" activity on page 105.

15. On a sheet of paper, ask conferees to list all the ways training can be done in the church. Ask them to develop a Sunday School Leader Needs Assessment Sheet using information in this section of the book (pp. 107-108). Instruct participants to include such areas of need as Bible knowledge, understanding/use of resources, teaching skills, knowledge of age groups, ministry action possibilities, assimilation, outreach, and so forth.

16. Call special attention to the Volunteer Leader Screening Form found on page 113. Indicate how your church uses it and any special guidelines all workers need to know.

Section 5: Implementing the Strategy

17. Ask each conferee to list on a sheet of paper the things they most fear in being able to launch the planning that has been done in their church. Allow time for discussion.

18. Preview the information on pages 117-121. Ask, How beneficial would it be for every church to have a commissioning service for the Sunday School leadership team? Who has the responsibility for seeing that this gets done in our church? Assign responsibilities as needed.

19. Provide each conferee the assignment sheet on which the face of a clock has been printed. Ask the group to design a weekly Sunday School leadership team meeting and to mark the minutes that would be designated to each item on the agenda. Call for feedback.

Discuss how these planning times can be the most valuable use of time a church can make. Provide information on how these meetings can be done and who needs to participate. Indicate the schedule (or plans to begin) for your church.

20. Ask conferees to go back to the nine critical questions first discussed with "Section 1: Laying the Foundation." Ask, How did you answer those questions? Provide a minilecture on the "Identifying Prospects for Your Church," and overview the process as shown on page 134.

21. Divide the group into smaller groups. Instruct each group to answer these questions:
- Why is a good record system valuable to Sunday School leaders?
- How would you begin a process of keeping records?

Provide the Sunday School records used by your church to help leaders know what information is being obtained and how more information might be helpful.

22. Present information on assimilating people into the class and ask each conferee to list some entry-level jobs that make non-Christians or non-class members feel welcome. (The list may include such items as greeting, making coffee, and so forth.) Allow time for this discussion to take place.

Section 6: Teaching That Transforms

23. Present a minilecture based on pages 151-161. Using the "Your Time Is Now" activity, allow small groups to discuss ways these important issues can be addressed in their class/department.

Finish this training session by asking individuals to give testimony to how Sunday School has been meaningful in their lives. What part, if any, did dated curriculum play in this experience? How did a prepared, transformed teacher contribute?

Close in prayer, asking God to bless the efforts in planning, training, organizing, and reaching as the new year begins.

CHRISTIAN GROWTH STUDY PLAN

Preparing Christians to Serve

In the **Christian Growth Study Plan (formerly Church Study Course),** this book, *Sunday School for a New Century,* is a resource for course credit in **three** Leadership and Skill Development diploma plans. To receive credit, read the book, complete the learning activities, show your work to your pastor, a staff member or church leader, then complete the following information. This page may be duplicated. Send the completed page to:

Christian Growth Study Plan
127 Ninth Avenue, North, MSN 117
Nashville, TN 37234-0117
FAX: (615)251-5067

For information about the Christian Growth Study Plan, refer to the current Christian Growth Study Plan Catalog. Your church office may have a copy. If not, request a free copy from the Christian Growth Study Plan office (615/251-2525).

COURSE CREDIT INFORMATION

Please check the appropriate box indicating the diploma you want to apply this credit. You may check more than one.

❑ **Developing the Administrative Skills of the General Church Leader (LS-0048, Sunday School)**

❑ **Planning and Administering Associational Ministry (LS-0066, Sunday School)**

❑ **The Special Education Leader's Role in Ministry, Witnessing, and Reaching People with Special Needs (LS-0107, Sunday School)**

PARTICIPANT INFORMATION

Social Security Number (USA Only) | Personal CGSP Number* | Date of Birth (Mo., Day, Yr.)

| | | – | | | – | | | | | | | | | – | | | | – | | | | | | | | | | – | | | – | | |

Name (First, MI, Last)
❑Mr. ❑Miss
❑Mrs. ❑

Home Phone
| | | – | | | | – | | | | |

Address (Street, Route, or P.O. Box) | City, State, or Province | Zip/Postal Code

CHURCH INFORMATION

Church Name

Address (Street, Route, or P.O. Box) | City, State, or Province | Zip/Postal Code

CHANGE REQUEST ONLY

❑Former Name

❑Former Address | City, State, or Province | Zip/Postal Code

❑Former Church | City, State, or Province | Zip/Postal Code

Signature of Pastor, Conference Leader, or Other Church Leader | Date

*New participants are requested but not required to give SS# and date of birth. Existing participants, please give CGSP# when using SS# for the first time.
Thereafter, only one ID# is required. *Mail To:* Christian Growth Study Plan, 127 Ninth Ave., North, MSN 117, Nashville, TN 37234-0117. Fax: (615)251-5067